INSIDE POETRY

Dedication

For our parents

INSIDE POETRY

Glen Kirkland / Richard Davies

HARCOURT
BRACE
CANADA

Harcourt Brace & Company, Canada
Toronto • Orlando • San Diego • London • Sydney

Canadian Cataloguing in Publication Data

Kirkland, Glen
Inside Poetry

For secondary school students.
Includes index.
ISBN 0-7747-1224-4

1. Poetry—History and criticism. 2. Canadian poetry—History and criticism. 3. Poetry—Collections.
4. Canadian Poetry. I. Davies, Richard. II. Title.

PN1111.K57 1984 808.1 C84-098837-0

ISBN 0-7747-1224-4

94 95 96 97 11 10 9 8

Cover photograph: Ellie Forrest

Printed and bound in Canada

Authors' Preface

Inside Poetry has been organized to enable different readers to use it in different ways. It can, of course, be used working from the beginning to the end,or it can be used according to the following four sections:

1. Chapter One, a collection of twenty-one poems without commentary or exercises. This chapter is an introductory immersion, a place to browse and get used to the demands of the form before the guided tour begins in Chapter Two.
2. Chapters Two to Seven, an introduction to the study and appreciation of poetry containing, as well as critical prose, sample poems and exercises.
3. Chapter Eight, an anthology of over one hundred poems, grouped according to theme and each followed by specific questions, projects and activities.
4. Appendices, containing advice on how to write about poetry, short essays by and about poets and their art, a glossary, and two indexes (author and title).

These sections refer to each other, but may be used individually and in any order. Just as there is always more than one way to read a poem, there is also more than one way to approach the study of poetry. We hope this book will accommodate the preferences of every interested reader.

Contents

Chapter 1 – The Voices of Poetry

Chapter 2 – Poetry is All Around Us

Chapter 3 - What is Poetry?

Chapter 4 – How Poetry Works

Chapter 5 – Poetry: You Can Do It

Chapter 7 - Becoming a Critical Reader

CHAPTER 1

THE VOICES OF POETRY

If you listen to the way you and the people around you talk, you will soon discover something surprising: we do not talk in prose. How we speak is usually very different from the way we write. Spoken language is irregular - we often use sentences that are intricately tangled or so brief as to be incomplete; we pause in unusual spots; we repeat ourselves; and we sometimes make odd leaps in logic. We choose and arrange our words to suit the situation - which means that how we speak is affected by our reasons for speaking at a given moment, our listeners, and the message we want to communicate. Our open, more informal talk is not like written prose, then; it is more like poetry. And since we speak poetically, reading poetry is important: it keeps us in touch with our natural voice and helps us to think and feel with greater understanding.

To properly study poetry we must first get inside it - we must listen to its voices. This chapter is a collection of twenty-one poems to read and enjoy before we go on to talk about the art of poetry in a more organized way in Chapter 2.

Birdsong

He doesn't know the world at all

Who stays in his nest and doesn't go out.
He doesn't know what birds know best
Nor what I want to sing about,
That the world is full of loveliness.

When dewdrops sparkle in the grass
And earth's aflood with morning light,

A blackbird sings upon a bush
To greet the dawning after night.
Then I know how fine it is to live.

Hey, try to open up your heart
To beauty; go to the woods someday
And weave a wreath of memory there.
Then if the tears obscure your way
You'll know how wonderful it is

To be alive.

H. VOLAVKOVÁ

Saturday Matinee

Twenty-five cents
bought oh henrys
and the privilege
of seeing Roy Rogers
kiss his horses ears
and the nasal
desert moon
that shone noisily
over Texas
where trios
of cactus bushes
sang off-key
or the second feature
where grade B
detectives
in striped cars
shot robbers
through their oversized hats
and the glamour girls
opened revlon lips
with difficulty
and the heroes
said their one important
word
or the dubious pleasure
of those awful moments
when the two huge

cinema mouths
collided
and the quick smell
of embarrassment
rose from the noisy
audience
as we searched the
seats and wooden floors
for hidden jawbreakers
or any popcorn
leavings.

FLORENCE MCNEIL

A Tough Life

I figure you've got it easy
Slop the pigs   milk a few cows
Huh   You shoulda seen the ol days
The first barn we had
was just a hole dug in the hill
with a roof slung across it
Hell that first winter
Maw and Paw took the shack
us boys had to sleep in the barn
Good thing we was bushed
from all the work we did
cause holy ol Nellie it was cold
the barn roof snappin overhead like ice
We'd roll in grey woollen blankets
kind of burrow into a bed of hay
sweet smellin hay   I remember
We'd drift to sleep on a steady rhythm
the horses munchin on their feed
Sometimes after a snowstorm
we'd just lay for hours in the hay
tellin jokes makin up yarns
Wasn't no use gettin up
till Paw had dug us out

What dya mean   it sounds like fun?

ROBERT CURRIE

Terry

The children running
                    running home
to be the first to tell:
  "The tractor rolled over,
  yesterday, yes, after school,
  on the way to the field,
  crushed him, yes."
Eager with the disaster,
watching their parents greedily,
knowing that only such news
will make them pause—
  hands for once still
  on the unfinished fences,
  on the axe incomplete over wood—
knowing that only such news
will make them look deeply
              at their children,
see the fields and the farms
make their premature claim,
see their own children
dead under the overturned machines.

LEONA GOM

The Piano

I sit on the edge
of the dining room, almost
in the living room where my parents,
my grandmother, & the visitors
sit knee to knee along the chesterfield & in
the easy chairs. The room is full, & my feet
do not touch the floor, barely
reach the rail across the front
of my seat. 'Of course
you will want Bobby to play,'—words
that jump out from the clatter
of teacups & illnesses. The piano
is huge, unforgettable.
It takes up the whole end wall
of the living room, faces me down
a short corridor of plump
knees, balanced saucers, hitched
trousers. 'Well when is

Bob going to play?'
one of them asks. My dad says,
'Come on, boy, they'd like you
to play for them,' & clears
a plate of cake
from the piano bench. I walk between
the knees & sit down
where the cake was, switch on
the fluorescent light
above the music. Right at the first notes
the conversation returns to long tales
of weddings, relatives bombed out again
in England, someone's mongoloid
baby, & there I am at the piano,
with no one listening or even
going to listen
unless I hit sour notes, or stumble
to a false ending.
I finish.
Instantly they are back to me. 'What a nice
touch he has,' someone interrupts
herself to say.
'It's the hands,' says another,
'It's always the hands, you can tell
by the hands,' & so I get up
& hide my fists
in my hands.

FRANK DAVEY

The Man Who Finds That His Son Has Become a Thief

Coming into the store at first angry
At the accusation, believing in
The word of his boy who has told him:
I didn't steal anything, honest.

Then becoming calmer, seeing that anger
Will not help in the business, listening painfully
As the other's evidence unfolds, so painfully slow.

Then seeing gradually that evidence
Almost as if tightened slowly around the neck

Of his son, at first vaguely circumstantial, then
gathering damage.
Until there is present the unmistakable odour of guilt
Which now seeps into the mind and lays its poison.

Suddenly feeling sick and alone and afraid,
As if an unseen hand had slapped him in the face
For no reason whatsoever: wanting to get out
Into the street, the night, the darkness, anywhere to hide
The pain that must show in the face to these strangers,
the fear.

It must be like this.
It could hardly be otherwise.

RAYMOND SOUSTER

Then

poverty teaches no one
it's just dark and small
like a revolver
always ready to be
the final judge.

i remember dirty walls
macaroni, television and
dumping the slop pail.
there was no beauty
you just survived
between paydays.

my father
drank every friday
and saturday nights.
he lived between the
borders of the day shift
and the night shift.
that was the only
structure i knew.

i know now
that he sold
what little of himself
he had so that i could eat.
what kind of change is that?

where one generation sacrifices
itself so that the next one
can walk on its bones
with a new pair of shoes.

ROBERT HILLES

Graduation Evening

I remember the night of high-school graduation:
the nervous, sixth-time combing of hair before a mirror
in the classroom turned dressing-room; girls refastening
belts and collars, telling each other how skirts hung.
Someone restlessly played with chalk, and dropped a boxfull.
In the hallway leading to the auditorium
the music teacher beat ta-tum tum-ta:
Can't you keep time, for once, to the beat of the music?
The pointer tapped on the floor, the head nodded.

Then we marched through the rows of waiting parents,
heads up, military in this year of war.
We sat on the platform, rigid, remembering not to cross our knees.
They played *God Save the King* and *Rule Britannia.*
Somebody made a speech about the war,
and all life being a war, and carrying torches.
Prizes were handed out, diplomas rustled.
They made us sing—what was it? *Alouette*?

I remember that night, going to bed, tired,
wetting my pillow with a flood of tears.
For what? I can't remember. Maybe not winning
a prize I wanted, maybe winning one
I didn't care for.
                    Maybe suddenly,
I was frightened, knowing that the classroom
with chalk, globes, books, and blackboard, maps and desks
was floating out to sea, ungraspable;
and I was left, as the man had said,
with life as a war
and the world
          an exploding time bomb
                              in my hands.

ELIZABETH BREWSTER

Child's Song

Goodbye, Mama. Goodbye to you too, Pa.
Little sister, you'll have to wait awhile to come along.
Goodbye to this house and all its memories.
We all just got too old to say we're wrong.

I've got to make one last trip to my bedroom.
Guess I'll have to leave some stuff behind.
Funny how the same old crooked pictures
Just don't look the same to me tonight.

There ain't no use in shedding no more tears, Ma.
There ain't no use in shouting at me, Pa.
I can't live no longer with your fears, Ma.
I love you, but that hasn't helped at all.

All of us have got to do what matters.
And each of us must see the things that we can see.
Though it was long ago, you must remember
That you were once as young and scared as me.

Mama, I don't know how hard it is yet
When you realize that you're growing old.
I know how hard it is now to be younger.
And I know you tried to keep me from the cold.

Well, thanks for all you've done—it may sound hollow.
Thank you for the good times that we've known.
But I must have my own road now to follow.
You will all be welcome in my home.

So I have my suitcase and I must go now.
I don't mind about the things you said.
Sorry, Mama, I don't know where I'm going.
Remember, little sister, look ahead.

Tomorrow I'll be in some other sunrise.
Maybe I'll have someone by my side.
Mama, give your love back to your husband.
Father, you've taught me well. Goodbye.

Goodbye, Mama. Goodbye to you too, Pa.

MURRAY MCLAUCHLAN

King of Pain

There's a little black spot on the sun today
        That's my soul up there
It's the same old thing as yesterday
There's a black hat caught in a high tree top
There's a flag pole rag and the wind won't stop

I have stood here before inside the pouring rain
With the world turning circles running 'round my brain
I guess I'm always hoping that you'll end this reign
But it's my destiny to be the king of pain

There's a fossil that's trapped in a high cliff wall
There's a dead salmon frozen in a waterfall
There's a blue whale beached by a springtide's ebb
There's a butterfly trapped in a spider's web

There's a king on a throne with his eyes torn out
There's a blind man looking for a shadow of doubt
There's a rich man sleeping on a golden bed
There's a skeleton choking on a crust of bread

There's a red fox torn by a huntsman's pack
There's a black winged gull with a broken back
There's a little black spot on the sun today
It's the same old thing as yesterday
That's my soul up there.....

I have stood here before inside the pouring rain
With the world turning circles running 'round my brain
I guess I'm always hoping that you'll end this reign
But it's my destiny to be the king of pain.......

I'll always be the king of pain.........

STING

Song

You're wondering if I'm lonely:
OK then, yes, I'm lonely
as a plane rides lonely and level
on its radio beam, aiming
across the Rockies

for the blue-strung aisles
of an airfield on the ocean

You want to ask, am I lonely?
Well, of course, lonely
as a woman driving across country
day after day, leaving behind
mile after mile
little towns she might have stopped
and lived and died in, lonely

If I'm lonely
it must be the loneliness
of waking first, of breathing
dawn's first cold breath on the city
of being the one awake
in a house wrapped in sleep

If I'm lonely
it's with the rowboat ice-fast on the shore
in the last red light of the year
that knows what it is, that knows it's neither
ice nor mud nor winter light
but wood, with a gift for burning

ADRIENNE RICH

On Mona's Smile

I know what brought
that expression to her face.
During one of her sittings
Leo said to her, "You know, Mona
you're very intelligent
for a woman."

WINONA BAKER

To Kate, Skating Better Than Her Date

Wait, Kate! You skate at such a rate
You leave behind your skating mate.
Your splendid speed won't you abate?
He's lagging far behind you, Kate.

He brought you on this skating date
His shy affection thus to state,
But you on skating concentrate
And leave him with a woeful weight
Pressed on his heart. Oh, what a state
A man gets into, how irate
He's bound to be with life and fate
If, when he tries to promulgate
His love, the loved one turns to skate
Far, far ahead to demonstrate
Superior speed and skill. Oh, hate
Is sure to come of love, dear Kate,
If you so treat your skating mate.
Turn again, Kate, or simply wait
Until he comes, then him berate
(Coyly) for catching up so late.
For, Kate, he *knows* your skating's great.
He's *seen* your splendid figure eight,
He is not here to contemplate
Your supersonic skating rate—
That is not why he made the date.
He's anxious to expatiate
On how he wants you for his mate.
And don't you want to hear him, Kate?

DAVID DAICHES

You Take My Hand

You take my hand and
I'm suddenly in a bad movie,
it goes on and on and
why am I fascinated

We waltz in slow motion
through an air stale with aphorisms
we meet behind endless potted palms
you climb through the wrong windows

Other people are leaving
but I always stay till the end
I paid my money, I
want to see what happens

In chance bathtubs I have to
peel you off me
in the form of smoke and melted
celluloid

Have to face it I'm
finally an addict,
the smell of popcorn and worn plush
lingers for weeks

MARGARET ATWOOD

Wonderful Tonight

It's late in the evening
She's wondering what clothes to wear
She puts on her makeup
And brushes her long blonde hair
And then she asks me,
"Do I look all right?"
And I say, "Yes,
You look wonderful tonight."

We go to a party
Everyone turns to see
This beautiful lady
Who's walking around with me
And then she asks me,
"Do you feel all right?"
And I say, "Yes,
I feel wonderful tonight."

I feel wonderful because I see
The love light in your eyes
And the wonder of it all
Is that you just don't realize
How much I love you.

It's time to go home now
And I've got an aching head
So I give her the car keys
She helps me to bed
And then I tell her
As I turn out the light
I say, "My darling,
You are wonderful tonight.
Oh, my darling,
You are wonderful tonight."

ERIC CLAPTON

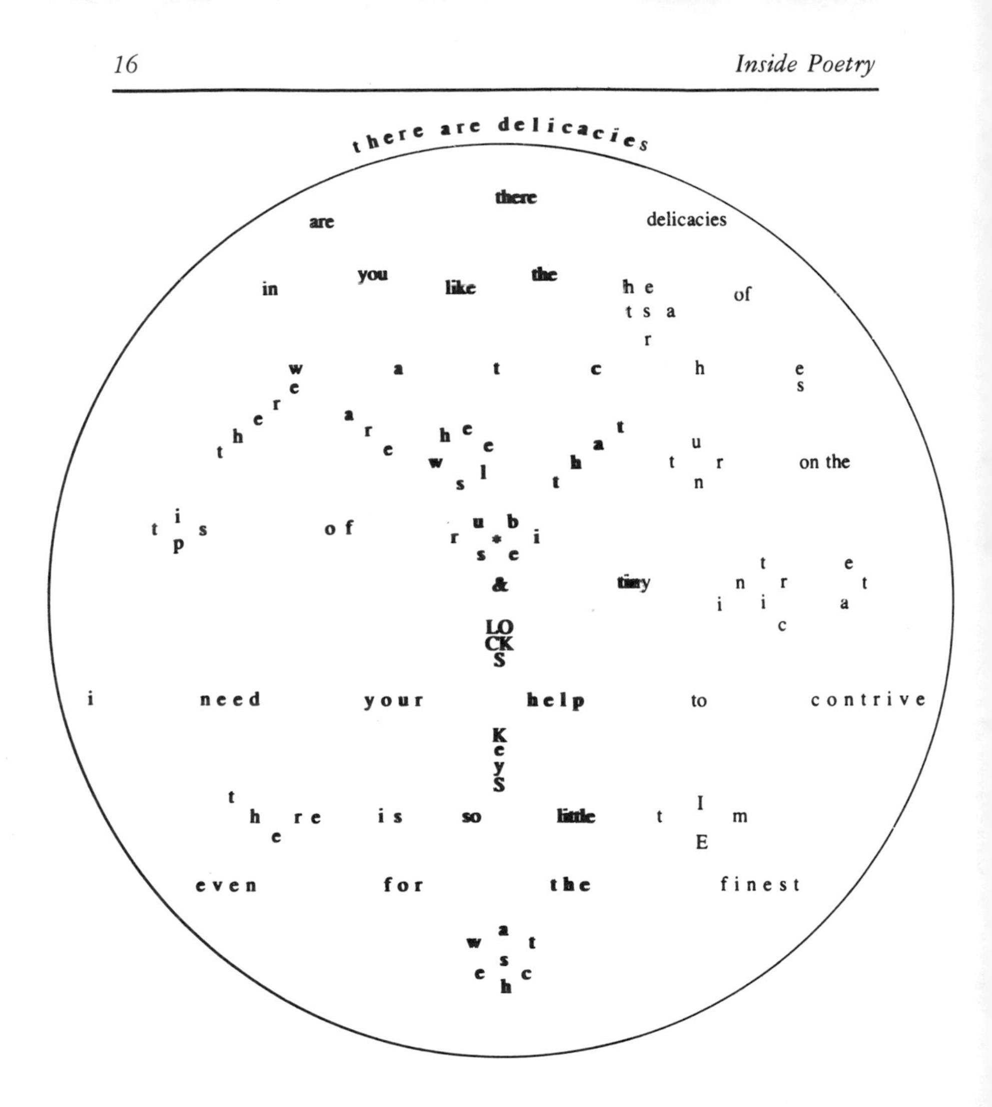

EARLE BIRNEY

Cross

He has leaned for hours against the veranda railing
gazing the darkened garden out of mind
while she with battened hatches rides out the wind
that will blow for a year or a day, there is no telling.

As to why they are cross she barely remembers now.
That they *are* cross, she is certain. They hardly speak.

Feel cold and hurt and stoney. For a week
have without understanding behaved so.

And will continue so to behave for neither
can come to that undemanded act of love—
kiss the sleeping princess or sleep with the frog—
and break the spell which holds them each from the other.

Or if one ventures towards it, the other, shy
dissembles, regrets too late the dissimulation
and sits hands slack, heart tiny, the hard solution
having again passed by.

Silly the pair of them. Yet they make me weep.
Two on a desert island, back to back
who, while the alien world howls round them black
go their own ways, fall emptily off to sleep.

P.K. PAGE

War on the Periphery

Around the battlements go by
Soldier men against the sky,
Violent lovers, husbands, sons,
Guarding my peaceful life with guns.

My pleasures, how discreet they are!
A little booze, a little car,
Two little children and a wife
Living a small suburban life.

My little children eat my heart;
At seven o'clock we kiss and part.
At seven o'clock we meet again:
They eat my heart and grow to men.

I watch their tenderness with fear
While on the battlements I hear
The violent, obedient ones
Guarding my family with guns.

GEORGE JOHNSTON

The Road Not Taken

Two roads diverged in a yellow wood,
And sorry I could not travel both
And be one traveler, long I stood
And looked down one as far as I could
To where it bent in the undergrowth;

Then took the other, as just as fair,
And having perhaps the better claim,
Because it was grassy and wanted wear;
Though as for that the passing there
Had worn them really about the same,

And both that morning equally lay
In leaves no step had trodden black.
Oh, I kept the first for another day!
Yet knowing how way leads on to way,
I doubted if I should ever come back.

I shall be telling this with a sigh
Somewhere ages and ages hence:
Two roads diverged in a wood, and I—
I took the one less traveled by,
And that has made all the difference.

ROBERT FROST

With Age Wisdom

At twenty, stooping round about,
I thought the world a miserable place,
Truth a trick, faith in doubt,
Little beauty, less grace.

Now at sixty what I see,
Although the world is worse by far,
Stops my heart in ecstasy.
God, the wonders that there are!

ARCHIBALD MACLEISH

The World is a Beautiful Place To Be Born Into

if you don't mind happiness
not always being
so very much fun
if you don't mind a touch of hell
now and then
just when everything is fine
because even in heaven
they don't sing
all the time

The world is a beautiful place
to be born into
if you don't mind some people dying
all the time
or maybe only starving
some of the time
which isn't half so bad
if it isn't you

Oh the world is a beautiful place
to be born into
If you don't much mind
a few dead minds
in the higher places
or a bomb or two
now and then
in your upturned faces
or such other improprieties
as our Name Brand society
is prey to
with its men of distinction
and its men of extinction
and its priests
and other patrolmen
and its various segregations
and congressional investigations
and other constipations
that our fool flesh
is heir to

yes the world is the best place of all
for a lot of such things as
making the fun scene
and making the love scene
and making the sad scene
and singing low songs and having inspirations
and walking around
looking at everything
and smelling flowers
and goosing statues
and even thinking
and kissing people and
making babies and wearing pants
and waving hats and
dancing
and going swimming in rivers
on picnics
in the middle of the summer
and just generally
'living it up'

Yes
but then right in the middle of it
comes the smiling

mortician

LAWRENCE FERLINGHETTI

CHAPTER 2

POETRY IS ALL AROUND US

I. Poetry in Daily Life

Poetry is much more than the poems that are studied in English class. If we take a look around us, we see that poetry, poetic language, rhymes and rhythms touch our lives nearly every day.

Remember the last time a classmate or friend asked you to sign a yearbook or autograph book? If you do, the chances are relatively high that you either read or wrote some variation of the famous "Roses are Red" poem. Often when we are called upon to be inspired or to reveal our true feelings about someone we know, we turn to verse forms for our writing models.

In an age of ever increasing paper and postage costs, the multi-million dollar greeting card industry continues to thrive because of people's reliance on verses in cards to announce or acknowledge the special occasions of their friends' or loved ones' lives.

You may also have read birth, birthday, engagement, wedding, or memoriam notices in your daily newspaper's classified section which have been composed in rhyme and stanza form. Clearly, when people have something important to say to others, they frequently "say it in verse."

In addition to greeting cards, song lyrics often speak for us on important occasions. Shortly, you yourself will be involved in one of the more significant events of your life - graduation. Your graduation committee, if it is like most of its kind, will choose an appropriate grad theme song, like the one below, which embodies some of the basic elements of poetry:

We May Never Pass This Way Again

Life—so they say
Is but a game and they let it slip away

WISH
YOU
WERE
HERE

Love—like the Autumn sun
Should be dying but it's only just begun
Like the twilight in the road up ahead
They don't see just where we're goin'
And all the secrets in the universe
Whisper in our ears and all the years will come and go
And take us up, always up

We may never pass this way again
We may never pass this way again
We may never pass this way again

Dreams—so they say
Are for the fools and they let them drift away
Peace—like the silent dove
Should be flying but it's only just begun
Like Columbus in the olden days
We must gather all our courage
Sail our ship out on the open sea
Cast away our fears and all the years will come and go
And take us up, always up

We may never pass this way again
We may never pass this way again
We may never pass this way again

So I want to laugh while the laughing is easy
I want to cry if it makes it worthwhile
I may never pass this way again
That's why I want it with you
'Cause you make me feel like I'm more than a friend
Like I'm the journey and you're the journey's end
I may never pass this way again
That's why I want it with you, baby

We may never pass this way again
We may never pass this way again
We may never pass this way again

JAMES SEALS AND DASH CROFTS

Some of the basic elements of poetry found in this selection are metaphors (e.g. "Life . . . Is but a game") and similes ("Love . . . like the autumn sun"), as well as end-line rhymes ("sun" and "begun") and repeated lines (the choruses). We will be coming back to popular songs in a few moments because they, of course, are one of the principal sources of poetry in the world around us.

EXERCISES

1. Using as models old or recent greeting cards you have on hand, design your own personalized greeting card (with illustration and verse) for an upcoming event in the life of a friend or a family member.
2. As fillers, your local newspaper publishes short poems that are humorous or thoughtful. Compose a short poem as a submission.
3. Many students graduate and soon forget some of the classmates with whom they shared many fine moments – especially in English. Take one sheet of blank paper and on it put a short poem and an illustration that will help the class remember you. Collate all these sheets into a class booklet.

As we have already said, when people have something important to say, they often say it in verse. During the 1982 Grey Cup week, as the Edmonton Eskimos prepared to play the Toronto Argonauts, Edmonton mayor Cec Purves made a bet with Toronto mayor Art Eggleton, and sent him the following selection:

Edmonton Esks, we love 'em lots.

Gonna tie your team in Argo knots.

Gonna pass and run, gonna prove we're best.

Gonna bring the Cup back to the West.

So sorry, Art, when the game is done,

You'll be sending your dough to Edmonton.

As your Double Blue is about to fold,

Think of your friend Cec and his Green and Gold.

EXERCISES

1. Why do you think Purves' chose to express his message in a poetic form?
2. Imagine and write an answer on behalf of the mayor and the Argonauts.

3. Write a poem celebrating the accomplishments of your favorite sports team or individual.

We never know where a poem may turn up. As you can see in the following two selections, many people from cartoon characters to normally reserved professional people, such as judges, have tried writing poetry:

A decree by any other name . . .

LANSING, Mich. (AP) – Three judges on a state appeals court offered rhyme and reason Tuesday when they upheld the dismissal of a lawsuit seeking damages for injuries to a tree hit by a car.

William Fisher claimed damages beyond the expense of having a tree surgeon repair his "beautiful oak" because it was "a living thing" with "aesthetic quality such as beauty, majesty and loveliness."

The suit, against the owner of the car and the woman driving it at the time of the accident, was dismissed in county circuit court. Fisher appealed.

In a unanimous decision written by Judge John Gillis, a three-member appeals court panel declared:

"We thought that we would never see
A suit to compensate a tree.
A suit whose claim in tort is prest
Upon a mangled tree's behest.
A tree whose battered trunk was prest
Against a Chevy's crumpled chest.
A tree that faces each new day
With bark and limb in disarray.
A tree that may forever bear
A lasting need for tender care.
Flora lovers though we three
We must uphold the court's decree."

Funky Winkerbean by Tom Batiuk © News Group Chicago, Inc. Courtesy of News America Syndicate.

EXERCISES

1. Which famous poem are these two adaptations based on? Can you recite any of it? (See page 258 if you need help)
2. Define any unknown words in the first poem. Then explain what the appeals court panel's poem is saying.
3. To what famous quotation does the news story's headline refer?
4. Does Crazy Harry's poem make sense to you? Explain.
5. Who are some other famous cartoon characters who write poetry? (See pages 32, 96)

Poetry can be found in many walks of life, and we are going to consider three of these: advertising, politics, and popular songs. The first area we are going to examine is advertising.

II. Poetry in Advertising

The advertisements we hear, see, and read often depend upon imagery or sound to grab our attention. If the advertiser can get us to sense, imagine, or feel what it would be like to bite into that hamburger, to ride in that new car, or to smell the aroma of that vacuum-packed coffee, then we might get "hooked by the pitch."

Using words and pictures, or sometimes words alone, advertisers try to make real or imagined features of their products come alive for us as experiences. In that way, we might want to run out to buy the real thing.

Let's look now at two examples of typical advertisements. Read them and ask yourself which hotel you would rather stay in:

1. "Warm, rich leather, cool marble and lovingly polished wood decor. Our beautifully renovated landmark hotel offers comfort and elegance at an affordable price."
2. "Quiet, friendly, bright, our hotel offers comfortable accommodations at reasonable rates."

Most people would choose the first hotel. Why? The advertisement uses imagery to make us form a mental picture of the hotel and feel its atmosphere. The words "warm," "rich," "cool," "lovingly," "beautifully" and "elegance" are especially appealing because they suggest a sense of comfort, luxury, and overall well-being.

The second advertisement, though informational, fails to create as clear and as powerful an impression of the hotel as the first ad did. Taken individually, the words "quiet," "friendly," "bright," "comfortable," and "reasonable" are all positive words, but they do not blend in well enough together to form a specific, concrete mood or experience for the reader.

Sounds, rhymes, and rhythms are as common and important as imagery in advertising. McDonald's well-known slogan, "We do it all for you," not only uses broadly connotative words (words suggesting additional meanings) such as "it" and "all," but also uses an effective combination of equally-weighted single syllable words that are easy for consumers to remember. Coca Cola's "Coke adds life" and "Coke is it" slogans work in much the same way.

As a final illustration of poetic advertising, consider this successful lyric promoting Alka Seltzer. It uses onomatopoeia as well as clever end-line rhyme:

Plop! Plop!
Fizz! Fizz!
Oh, what a relief
It is!

EXERCISES

1. Find two advertisements by different companies for the same type of product and copy down the words they use to describe their brand or service. In a paragraph or two, compare the two ads for effectiveness. (You may wish to comment on the sound quality of the words in the ads as well as on the imagery or word choice.)
2. Choose a television or magazine advertisement that really bothers you. Study the ad carefully and decide how it might be improved or invent a new and better ad for the product or service. Write a letter to the company presenting your criticisms and suggestions.
3. Assume for a moment that your school will be run like a business next year and that it will need advertising to attract students as clients. Prepare a television advertisement that

makes your school sound very appealing to potential new students.

4. Write a poetic-sounding ad for a product or service of your choice. Concentrate on using words that will attract the listeners' attention and make them want to buy or use the service. If you have access to a tape recorder, you may wish to record a reading of the ad with background music and sound effects.
5. Assume for a moment that big stores are now selling individual poems on their shelves—in much the same way as they sell novels. Create a radio or television ad that is designed to sell one of the poems in Chapter 1 of this text.

III. Poetry and Politics

Another sphere of life which, like advertising, makes use of the persuasive qualities of poetry is politics.

An American, Dr. Walker Trotter, heads a public relations consulting firm in Chicago called Preference Meters. P.M., as it is known in short, advises political candidates about how they can use "politic prosody," especially meter and rhyme to their advantage at election time. For example, Dr. Trotter predicted that Jimmy Carter would win the 1976 presidential election over Gerald Ford because the former candidate's names had desirable double trochaic meter (i.e. a stressed-unstressed pattern twice: Jím-my̆ Cár-tĕr), which Dr. Trotter feels has a more favorable effect on the ear of the American electorate.

According to Dr. Trotter, double trochee names have a predictable, regular pattern (i.e. the sound of the first name is echoed and continued in the second) which fosters trust in the ear and mind of the hearer. Names like James Carter and Gerald Ford disappoint or trick the listener's ear because of their metrical irregularities. In support of this, Dr. Trotter points to the interesting fact that ten past presidents' names bear the same meter as Jimmy Carter while only two men having the same meter as Gerald Ford have ever won.

The ideas of Dr. Trotter suggest that the rhythms of poetry may be playing a more far-reaching role in politics than the more obvious slogans and campaign songs promoting political candidates which we are barraged with at election time:

> Diefenbay-ker, Diefenbay-ker,
> Diefenbay-ker, Yea!
> He will lead us
> On to victory
> On Election day.
> John's the man
> Who'll get 'em swingin'
> Swinging back our way.
> It's Diefenbay-ker, Diefenbay-ker,
> Diefenbay-ker, Yea!
>
> ALISTAIR GROSART

EXERCISES

1. What poetic devices were used in the above campaign song which helped John Diefenbaker win the position of Conservative Party leader in 1957?
2. Dr. Trotter says that other poetic devices such as alliteration, assonance, and internal rhyme might also affect the outcome of an election. What might Dr. Trotter have had to say about the fact that Ronald Reagan defeated Jimmy Carter in the 1980 presidential election?
3. Consider candidates in recent Canadian municipal, provincial, or federal elections from the viewpoint of Dr. Trotter and Preference Meters. What advice about their names might have been given to some of the above-mentioned candidates?
4. Are there other meters which you feel are as strong or stronger than the double trochee pattern favored by Dr. Trotter?

IV. Poetry in Sports

Sports is another area of human activity which uses colorful poetic language. Football players "toss the pigskin," hockey goaltenders "tend the twine," and golfers "smoke the ball" off the tee.

Baseball commentators are probably among the most poetic of

all sports announcers; here are some of their vivid expressions:

"Rogers tosses a lollipop to Speier"
(Rogers flipped the ball underhand to Speier for the force-out on second base)

"The fireballin' southpaw threw that one right down the middle of the dish"
(the left-handed pitcher threw a strike)

"There are runners at the corners and one on the sandwich sack as well"
(there are runners on all three bases)

"There's some chin music"
(the pitcher nearly hit the batter's face with the pitch)

"What a Hoover he is!"
(the defending player catches the ball extremely well)

"Brett takes it downtown"
(the batter has just hit a home run)

"He's got an ice cream cone out there"
(the defending player barely made a catch; most of the ball was outside his glove)

B. C.

EXERCISES

1. Quote five examples of colorful poetic language from a sport of your choice.
2. Find or write a poem on a favorite sport and read it to the class. Tell what you like about it.
3. Paraphrase the following baseball expressions:

> "He toed the rubber and threw smoke."
> "The sacks are drunk; there's ducks on the pond."
> "He threw a faceball with that duster."
> "He hit a tater, a round-tripper, a circuit shot, a dinger."

4. Read the poem that follows. How does Robert Francis manage to capture the excitement of baseball?

The Base Stealer

Poised between going on and back, pulled
Both ways taut like a tightrope-walker,
Fingertips pointing the opposites,
Now bouncing tiptoe like a dropped ball
Or a kid skipping rope, come on, come on,
Running a scattering of steps sidewise,
How he teeters, skitters, tingles, teases,
Taunts them, hovers like an ecstatic bird,
He's only flirting, crowd him, crowd him,
Delicate, delicate, delicate, delicate—now!

ROBERT FRANCIS

V. Poetry in Popular Songs

Lastly, we return to a well-known form of poetry we mentioned earlier in this chapter—popular songs. Many pop song lyrics share the same features of poetry we have already mentioned: they make use of rhyme, rhythm, and imagery to communicate thoughts and feelings.

Consider for a few moments the following song lyric:

The Logical Song

When I was young, it seemed that life was so wonderful,
a miracle, oh it was beautiful, magical.
And all the birds in the trees, well they'd be singing so happily,
joyfully, playfully watching me.
But then they sent me away to teach me how to be sensible,
logical, responsible, practical.
And then they showed me a world where I could be so
dependable, clinical, intellectual, cynical.

There are times when all the world's asleep,
the questions run too deep
for such a simple man.
Won't you please, please tell me what we've learned?
I know it sounds absurd
but please tell me who I am.

Now watch what you say or they'll be calling you a radical,
liberal, fanatical, criminal.

Won't you sign up your name, we'd like to feel you're
acceptable, respectable, presentable, a vegetable!

But at night, when all the world's asleep,
the questions run so deep
for such a simple man.
Won't you please, please tell me what we've learned?
I know it sounds absurd
but please tell me who I am.

ROGER HODGSON AND RICK DAVIES

If you have heard the Supertramp recording of this selection, you were probably affected by the melody and pulsing rhythms created by the singers, guitars, keyboards, saxophone, and drums. When people listen to popular songs today, they often hum along with the tune, harmonize, keep time with the beat, or dance. Many people, however, also listen to the language and poetry of songs: their lyrics. The effectiveness of "The Logical Song" is related, certainly, to its rhyming words (e.g. "acceptable, respectable, presentable, a vegetable"), its imagery ("At night, when all the world's asleep,/the questions run so deep/for such a simple man"), and its poignant personal point of view ("I know it sounds absurd/but please tell me who I am").

If you were to strip away the music of other strong popular songs, you would make a similar find: that there are many delightful poems embedded in them.

If we stop now to consider the number of popular songs, advertisements, sports expressions, political slogans, and greeting card verses we encounter on a day-to-day basis, we gradually begin to realize just how influential poetry really is. Because poetry is so much a part of our daily lives, it seems reasonable to assume that we should spend some time in trying to understand what it is, which is what we will be discussing in the third chapter.

FOLLOW-UP

1. Copy down the lyrics to your current favorite song, and write a 1-2 page explanation of why you like it, isolating the figures of speech or examples of imagery that you think are especially successful.
2. It is your job to sell your favorite sport to non- sports fans. Write a) a magazine advertisement, b) a radio spot, and c) a

script for a television commercial aimed at interesting the public in your sport.

3. Write a one page handout designed to be part of your campaign for election as class president. Split up into groups of five or six and select the best one. Defend the handout you choose against those selected by the other groups.
4. Select from chapter one a poem which could be used as part of an advertisement, and design a magazine ad around it.

RELATED POEMS IN CHAPTER 8:

W.L.M.K., (F.R. Scott), p. 203
The Stickhandler, (David Solway), p. 224
Jump Shot, (Richard Peck), p. 225
400-Metre Free Style, (Maxine W. Kumin), p. 226
Don Quixote, (Gordon Lightfoot), p. 238
Saturday, August 27, (Carl Fernbach-Flarsheim), p. 243
Wired for Sound, (Alan Tarney, B.A. Robertson), p. 244
The Gambler, (Don Schlitz), p. 255

CHAPTER 3

WHAT IS POETRY?

I. The Nature of Poetry

We saw in the last chapter how poetry can be found in many forms in the world around us. Before we go any further, it might be helpful at this point to clarify what a poem is.

Most dictionaries and glossaries of literary terms define *poem* along the following lines: a condensed, rhythmical composition with specially arranged lines, figurative language, and sometimes rhyme.

Now although this definition is fairly concise, it is a rather simplistic statement of what this genre, poetry, is all about. So let's leave the issue of what poetry *is* temporarily open and move on to read what three high school students had to say about poetry:

> Poetry is the expression of the inner part of a human being.
>
> Neither prose nor the spoken language can match the intimacy that poetry holds.
>
> Poetry is words that express thoughts or feelings in a way that is very different from everyday language. Poetry affects the heart as well as the mind.

If we consider each opinion carefully, we can see that two qualities of poetry are being identified. First, poetry, as a type of writing, is especially effective for expressing emotions. Where ordinary social conversation or prose writing might fall short in capturing an emotion, poetry can be direct, precise, and vivid in its communications. Second, poetry is more personal than other forms of writing. Each reader is alone with the experience or thought described by a poem so that each poem, in turn, comes to life in a unique, personal way for each reader. Together, these two qualities make poetry a special form of writing that is enjoyable and challenging to talk about.

Two examples may serve to better illustrate this personal, emotional quality of poetry. Consider first the following account of a motorcycle accident, written as it might appear in your daily newspaper:

Man, 19, Dies in Cycle Accident

Yesterday afternoon a 19-year-old Calgary man died from injuries sustained when a semi-trailer collided with his motorcycle.

City police say Brian Smith was riding west along 107 Avenue near 101 Street when his vehicle was struck from behind by a truck operated by Carl Phillips of Edmonton. Mr. Smith died from neck injuries after he was thrown from his bike about 5 p.m.

Patrolmen had a difficult time controlling rush-hour traffic in the area. This delayed the arrival of an ambulance dispatched to the accident scene.

Police are continuing their investigation of the incident.

Now read another account of the same accident, this time from the viewpoint of a passing motorist:

5 p.m./july/the city

red-blue lights
blink on
and off

the mangled motorbike
sputters in defeat
its twisted metal
a cruel sacrifice
to the invincible semi

some young male
(caucasian, no previous record)
writhes in the dirt
and jagged glass

his black jacket
ridiculous with blood

onlookers and hangers-on
gape
await their turns
to babble with
tired police
who record the moment
for computer posterity

the inevitable vultures
cruise by slowly
eager for glimpses
of death and
gore

in my mirror
i see an urgent ambulance
approach the milling crowd
and wonder if
i'm late for
supper

RICHARD DAVIES

How do these two accounts compare with one another? The newspaper story is told in a factual, impersonal, objective manner. The data of the event are catalogued in a relatively straightforward way. There is no sense of how the experience was felt by anyone who witnessed it. The poem, however, uses selected images and descriptive words to draw the reader into the event. It speaks directly to the reader, shares a revealing insight, and creates a subjective experience. The poem moves outward from the specific event (described in the news story) to its larger significance - its effect on other lives - and this gives it an imaginative dimension which the news story, by its nature, lacks.

There is even more to poetry, though, than all of the above qualities. We have already mentioned two others: poetry as sound or music, and poetry as image. It is these qualities we would like to examine more closely.

II. Poetry as Sound

That poetry is sound or music simply means that poetry pays considerable attention to the sounds of words (e.g. rhymes, alliteration, assonance), rhythms of word-groupings, and arrangements of sounds or rhythms in interesting patterns (e.g. stanzas, concrete poems).

All this careful attention to sound and rhythm is for a purpose: the poet wants to achieve an effect such as humor or beauty, or wants the sounds of the poem to enhance or add impact to its meaning or message. If the poet can get the sound of the poem to match its sense, then he or she is guaranteed success in communicating his or her vision, and the poem will work.

You may be surprised to learn that poetry was originally intended to be recited in public or sung for an attentive audience. For many early civilizations, at a time when nothing could be written down, the poet was also the historian, story-teller, and priest. Poetry is also related to dance, and its rhythmical physical movements can still be glimpsed when the modern reader of a poem or singer of a song moves his or her head, body, hands or feet in time to the regular, repeated beats or stresses of words.

Either by yourself or with your classmates, try reading the next poem aloud without any physical movement or gesture:

Sea Fever

I must go down to the seas again, to the lonely sea and the
 sky,
And all I ask is a tall ship and a star to steer her by,
And the wheel's kick and the wind's song and the white
 sail's shaking,
And a gray mist on the sea's face and a gray dawn
 breaking.

I must go down to the seas again, for the call of the
 running tide
Is a wild call and a clear call that may not be denied;
And all I ask is a windy day with the white clouds flying,
And the flung spray and the blown spume, and the sea
 gulls crying.

I must go down to the seas again, to the vagrant gypsy life,
To the gull's way and the whale's way where the wind's like a whetted knife;
And all I ask is a merry yarn from a laughing fellow rover,
And quiet sleep and a sweet dream when the long trick's over.

JOHN MASEFIELD

As you can see, some poems (especially traditional ballads) contain strong, infectious rhythms that are difficult for the reader to keep entirely in check.

Actually, it is not all that surprising that rhythm plays such a major role in speech and writing, since rhythm is a common principle in all life, particularly in the related worlds of human culture (e.g. our divisions of day and year by watch and calendar) and nature (e.g. the changing of seasons, life cycles of various organisms). We may take rhythm for granted, so much so that we are not aware of how much it influences our choices.

Take our choice of favorite poetry, for instance. We do not have to understand a poem in order to enjoy it. We might like it simply for the pleasure of hearing or speaking its sounds or rhythms.

Each of us has been exposed to nursery rhymes, skipping songs, and children's poems at a very young age. When we first heard rhymes such as "Humpty Dumpty," "Jack and Jill," and "London Bridge," we might not have fully understood them, but we probably asked to hear them recited over and over again until we had them completely memorized. Even as we get older, we find that the earliest literature we were exposed to in childhood still delights us. Some of you may know Dennis Lee's "Alligator Pie," which is a good illustration of what we have just been talking about:

Alligator Pie

Alligator pie, alligator pie,
If I don't get some
    I think I'm gonna die.
Give away the green grass,
    give away the sky,

But don't give away
    my alligator pie.

Alligator stew, alligator stew,
If I don't get some
    I don't know what I'll do.
Give away my furry hat,
    give away my shoe,
But don't give away
    My alligator stew.

Alligator soup, alligator soup,
If I don't get some
    I think I'm gonna droop.
Give away my hockey stick,
    give away my hoop,
But don't give away
    my alligator soup.

DENNIS LEE

Our fascination with sound and rhythm is also evident in our speech as young children. We begin speech by toying with sounds, by repeating sounds or words over several times, by creating rhymes through nonsense words, and by speaking aloud as we play.

This demonstrates several important facts. Human beings are poetic creatures from the outset. Poetry is our natural language. It is also, incidentally, the source or centre of all literature: the first works of Western literature were Homer's epic poems *The Iliad* and *The Odyssey*.

Poetry, therefore, is not only the earliest language we use in life; it is also the first literary genre that developed in the Western world (or that develops first in any culture, for that matter). We are familiar with poetry long before we become acquainted with the language of practical sense and social conversation: prose. The reading, writing, and study of poetry are three ways in which we can regain our authentic identities as poetic creatures.

EXERCISES

1. To illustrate that we are poetic creatures, recite four lines of poetry from memory, followed by four lines of prose.

by Johnny hart

By permission of Johnny Hart and News Group Chicago, Inc.

2. Read or recite your favorite nursery rhyme to the class. Tell what you liked about it when you were a child, and try to explain why you were probably first attracted to it.
3. Make a tape recording of the speech of a baby or young child at play. Play it for the class and make some observations on the role played by sounds and rhythms of words in early human language development.
4. Some children's rhyming songs are designed to help children keep in rhythm for a game such as skipping rope. Compose a rhythmic, rhyming chant that you might use to help keep in rhythm while you jog, play ping-pong, dribble a basketball, or sharpen a pencil.

III. Poetry as Image

Though the main feature that distinguishes poetry from prose is its sound and music, its essence is surely imagery .

Here's how poet William Carlos Williams, in describing the importance of imagery, worded this point:

The Red Wheelbarrow

So much depends
upon

a red wheel
barrow

glazed with rain
water

beside the white
chickens.

WILLIAM CARLOS WILLIAMS

And the more you think about what this poem says, the more its statement rings true: so much *does* depend upon an awareness of our immediate surroundings; everything, in fact. Our conscious minds perceive the world primarily through the experience of images presented to our senses. Williams' poem, like all poetry, depends upon the naming and describing of images, objects, and sensations that can be read, felt, and understood by the reader of his poem.

Before we look further at the idea of poetry as image, we should try to clarify what imagery is. Imagery refers to the use of words that bring alive the thoughts, feelings, or experiences being described in a poem. Imagery helps to make clear and concrete what is abstract and difficult to understand.

The process that leads to the presence of imagery in a poem is relatively easy to describe: as a poet you perceive the world, an event, or an experience in a certain way, through its images. You feel moved to describe or re-create the experience and to share your insights with others. You do this primarily through the images you select: if the images are appropriate and they work well together, then the reader will experience some of what the poet wanted to share or reveal, and communication will take place. As we can see, much does depend upon the processes of image-sensing, image-making, and image-receiving.

How many senses do most people have? If you said "five," you are somewhat right. Poets, when they write, use images that appeal to more than five senses. The five senses familiar to us and their image-types are:

sight	(visual images)
hearing	(aural images)
smell	(olfactory images)
taste	(gustatory images)
touch	(tactile images).

Two other "senses" used by poets to describe their surroundings are:

heat	(thermal images)
motion	(kinesthetic images).

Because of the specialized physical characteristics of our species, it should be fairly obvious that we generally experience our world with our eyes and ears - through visual and aural images, so it is not unexpected that most images in poetry fall into these two categories. However, many individual poems, even relatively brief ones such as the one which follows, use all image-types to advantage:

Sound

At dawn I squat on the garage
with snuff under a lip
to sweeten the roofing nails—
my shoes and pant cuffs
are wet with dew.
In the orchard the peach trees
sway with the loud
weight of birds, green fruit, yellow haze.
And my hammer—the cold head taps,
then swings its first full arc;
the sound echoes against the barn,
muffled in the loft,

and out the other side, then lost
in the noise of the birds
as they burst from the trees.

JIM HARRISON

Through all seven types of images, the poet conveys strong, effective sense impressions of what it might be like to work on a garage roof at dawn. Harrison's poem is a free verse image poem that has its own internal rhythms and logical line structure.

A. Haiku

Another kind of image poem, but a more structured one, is a form already familiar to some of you perhaps: the Japanese haiku. The haiku is a three line poem with a total of seventeen syllables: five in the first line, seven in the second, and five in the third. It usually describes a moment in or an experience of nature and may also contain a little philosophizing by the poet. Haiku are like miniature paintings or snapshots, visual images being the main means of creating life-like exposures:

The day dark with rain.
Young leaves struggling to open,
you too have your tears.

ANN ATWOOD

Autumn morning wind
and the wild geese calling out . . .
knife edge of the sky.

C.M. BUCKAWAY

B. Concrete Poems

Yet another kind of image poem, more experimental and less traditional than haiku, is the concrete poem. Concrete poems represent an attempt by modern poets to combine poetry with the aural (e.g. music) and visual arts (e.g. painting, architecture). They use sounds, letters, or words arranged so they create a picture or an interesting sound pattern:

crickets
crickess
cricksss
cricssss
crisssss
crssssss
csssssss
ssssssss
ssssssts
sssssets
ssssskets
ssscke ts
ssickets
srickets
crickets

ARAM SAROYAN

Bear

bear. fat. cave. winter. sleep SLEEP SLEEP SLEEP SLEEP
sleep. trickle trickle. yawn. skinny bear.

KEITH GUNDERSON

like an eddy

EARLE BIRNEY

EXERCISES

1. Write a *parody* (humorous imitation of a serious work) of Williams' "The Red Wheelbarrow." You will find that your parody will work better if you make the images very trivial or commercialized, e.g.:

   so much depends
   upon

   a brown beef
   patty

smothered with red
sauce

beside the hot
french fries.

2. Write a paragraph in which you describe a moment in your day. Try to capture the moment so vividly and precisely that any reader could easily picture it.
3. If you have a video recorder at home, record three commercials which make clever use of imagery to sell their products (e.g. beer, soft drink, fast food commercials).
   Script a commentary on the role played by imagery in the ads, intended to be read after showing each ad to the class.
4. Write a haiku about some aspect of your yard or a field near your home. Remember, when picking a subject for haiku-writing, smaller is better. (Hint: your haiku will come easier if you record the images in an image list of nouns, adjectives, and forceful verbs first, before structuring them according to lines and syllables.)
5. Write two concrete poems on topics of your choice (e.g. nature, animals, pop music, sports).

All of the preceding image poems rely on imagery for their effects. Some students might ask why these examples should even be considered significant or worthwhile if all they do is describe commonplace things or experiences. Some may argue that these poems do not seem to present universal truths or insights into the human condition.

While the objects and experiences described by these poems may not be of great consequence, these poems are still worthwhile and valuable because they set forth in vivid imagery moments that are "hidden" in everyday things.

IV. Sound and Image Make a Poem

We have just examined the fundamental roles played by sound and imagery in poetry. Let us now see the two work together as related elements within an individual poem:

Annabel Lee

It was many and many a year ago,
  In a kingdom by the sea,
That a maiden there lived whom you may know
  By the name of Annabel Lee;
And this maiden she lived with no other thought
  Than to love and be loved by me.

I was a child and *she* was a child
  In this kingdom by the sea,
But we loved with a love that was more than love—
  I and my Annabel Lee;
With a love that the wingéd seraphs of Heaven
  Coveted her and me.

And this was the reason that, long ago,
  In this kingdom by the sea,
A wind blew out of a cloud, chilling
  My beautiful Annabel Lee;
So that her highborn kinsman came
  And bore her away from me,
To shut her up in a sepulchre
  In this kingdom by the sea.

The angels, not half so happy in Heaven,
  Went envying her and me—
Yes! that was the reason (as all men know,
  In this kingdom by the sea)
That the wind came out of the cloud by night,
  Chilling and killing my Annabel Lee.

But our love it was stronger by far than the love
  Of those who were older than we—
  Of many far wiser than we—
And neither the angels in Heaven above,

Nor the demons down under the sea,
Can ever dissever my soul from the soul
Of the beautiful Annabel Lee.

For the moon never beams, without bringing me dreams
Of the beautiful Annabel Lee;
And the stars never rise, but I feel the bright eyes
Of the beautiful Annabel Lee;
And so, all the night-tide, I lie down by the side
Of my darling—my darling—my life and my bride,
In the sepulchre there by the sea,
In her tomb by the sounding sea.

EDGAR ALLAN POE

Through a combination of simple and intriguing images (e.g. "A wind blew out of a cloud," "the demons down under the sea," "In her tomb by the sounding sea"), the poet assists us in imagining clearly the poem's places and characters. He also uses a variety of image-types to help us feel what the speaker feels: aural images ("the sounding sea"), visual images ("the moon never beams"), tactile images ("I lie down by the side"), and kinesthetic images ("bore her away from me/To shut her up in a sepulchre").

Through repetitions of words, names, and lines (e.g. "me," "Annabel Lee," "In this kingdom by the sea"), internal as well as end-line rhyme ("Chilling and killing my Annabel Lee"), parallel constructions ("Of those who were older than we –/Of many far wiser than we –"), assonance (note the number of e and i vowel sounds used by Poe), consonance (note how many times the m, l, and s sounds are repeated), Poe emphasizes the fairy tale flavor of his subject, and the lingering, obsessive effects the young girl's death have had on the speaker's mind.

In this manner, the images and sounds mesh together to communicate the feelings the poet wished to share with his audience, and to create the other-worldly sense of place and atmosphere, all for a single purpose: to make his point that love is an emotion that does not always end with the death of one of the lovers.

EXERCISE

Using one of the poems from Chapter 1, discuss how its images and sounds work together to produce an effective communication of thoughts and feelings.

In this chapter, we have seen that poetry is a personal form of writing which effectively expresses feelings, thoughts, and experiences. We have gained some insight, also, into the essential make-up of poetry as sound and as image. In Chapter 4, "How Poetry Works," we will take a closer look at how poetry uses figurative language and how a poet's purpose determines the type of poem he or she writes.

FOLLOW-UP

1. Write a poem based on a short, interesting item in your local newspaper. Include only enough specific detail to outline the event; try to evoke the mood or atmosphere rather than just describing what happened.
2. Write a short poem (a haiku or concrete poem, if you like) designed to describe one of our senses to someone who does not possess it.
3. Pick the poem in the *Visions* section of Chapter 8 which you feel best describes the way one of our senses works, and write one or two paragraphs explaining why the poem is particularly effective.
4. Write a children's poem modeled on Dennis Lee's "Alligator Pie." Concentrate on establishing a simple, musical rhythm, and try out the finished product on a child and an adult.

RELATED POEMS IN CHAPTER 8:

Catalogue, (Rosalie Moore), p. 169
The Beautiful Tiger, (Keith Gunderson), p. 170
View of a Pig, (Ted Hughes), p. 178
Leader of the Band, (Dan Fogelberg), p. 197
The freshly cut grass, (Dorothy Cameron Smith), p. 220
Klaxon, (James Reaney), p. 246
The Chimney Sweeper, (William Blake), p. 251
Do not go gentle into that good night, (Dylan Thomas), p. 281

CHAPTER 4

HOW POETRY WORKS

Poetry is an art form, the core of which is made, chiefly, of sound and image. In showing how poetry works in this chapter, we are going to discuss the following ideas:

1) how poetry extends language, especially through figures of speech such as similes, metaphors, and personification.
2) how most poetry can be divided into five major categories of poem-types.

I. Poetry Extends Language

Let's start with a look at the notion that poetry extends language. What this means is that poetry's chief devices – the figures of speech – extend language beyond its ordinary, everyday, denotative levels of usage. As the French writer Voltaire once said: "One merit of poetry few persons will deny: it says more and in fewer words than prose."

We have already mentioned in Chapter 3, the effects of poetry's ability to extend language. Poetry is a multi-dimensional response to the world which, in turn, creates multi-dimensional responses in its readers. The reader of a poem can be affected physically (through the senses), emotionally, intellectually, and spiritually.

Because the rewards of reading poetry depend so much upon language extension, it might be worth our while to examine the role played by two "extenders" or, as they are better known, figures of speech: similes and metaphors.

A. Similes and Metaphors

Earlier on, we said that poetry is our natural language. To go one step further, it might be said that similes and metaphors provide us with many of our daily expressions or sayings. How often have we heard the following figures of speech?

similes
I'm as fit as a fiddle
he swears like a trooper
she's as mad as a hatter
he's as proud as a peacock
she's like a fish out of water
it's as plain as the nose on his face
he's crazy as a loon
you can read him like a book

metaphors
he's an old goat
she's a pain in the neck
he's a son of a gun
the routine is old hat
this place is his old stomping grounds
the university is an ivory tower
the candidate is a dark horse
the issue was a tempest in a teapot

The fact that these well-known expressions have become clichés suggests that similes and metaphors play a major part in our everyday language as well as literature.

Why are these two figures of speech so common? Consider two possible explanations.

First of all, when we describe our world, we often make associations or draw comparisons. These comparisons occur naturally to us when we speak to others (e.g. "the U.F.O. was like a giant dinner plate covered with bright lights"). These comparisons are usually based on previous experience or what we already know: in other words, the familiar. We do this sort of thing all the time as we are growing up, gaining in life experience.

One illustration will show what we're getting at. How does a child who for the first time encounters a picture of a zebra describe it? He or she might say, "It's like a horse" or, more imaginatively, "a horse in striped pyjamas." Similes and metaphors, then, are logical, useful ways for us to relate or make sense of the many people, animals, objects, and experiences that make up our world.

And this brings us to a second explanation of why these comparative devices are so common. They stem from our fundamental desire to connect with or relate to the world around us.

As we grow older, some of us begin to feel separate from others and their surroundings. How many times have you heard the inner voice in you say, "Hey, that's not part of me," "He's not like me," or "This has nothing to do with me"? These feelings of separation are part and parcel of human consciousness.

Likewise, how many times have you caught yourself wanting to be like someone else or part of some happening or event? If you are like most people, you try to achieve this feeling of identity or identification with others or your surroundings.

One way to achieve this identification with the world around us is through our language, literature, and imagination. Read the following poem by Canadian poet P.K. Page, and you will see an example of what we mean:

Adolescence

In love they wore themselves in a green embrace.
A silken rain fell through the spring upon them.
In the park she fed the swans and he
whittled nervously with his strange hands.
And white was mixed with all their colours
as if they drew it from the flowering trees.

At night his two-finger whistle brought her down
the waterfall stairs to his shy smile
which, like an eddy, turned her round and round
lazily and slowly so her will
was nowhere—as in dreams things are and aren't.

Walking along the avenues in the dark
street lamps sang like sopranos in their heads
with a violence they never understood
and all their movements when they were together
had no conclusion.

Only leaning into the question had they motion;
after they parted were savage and swift as gulls.

Asking and asking the hostile emptiness
they were as sharp as partly sculptured stone
and all who watched, forgetting, were amazed
to see them form and fade before their eyes.

P.K. PAGE

This poem describes the merging of two teenagers in love, and the relationship between the lovers and their surroundings. These unions or identifications are vividly portrayed by similes ("street lamps sang like sopranos") and metaphors ("they wore themselves in a green embrace") to the extent that we, the readers, are moved by the feelings and experiences they represent.

The result is that, through the experience of reading the poem, we, too, feel a union of sorts with the characters of the poem, with the feelings described by the poet, with the poet herself, and with the countless others who have read or will one day read this poem and who may share the same feelings.

EXERCISES

1. Survey your classmates and other people your own age to find out what similes and metaphors they use in everyday conversation. For each simile or metaphor you identify, offer an explanation as to the appropriateness of the comparison it makes.
2. If you have younger brothers or sisters who are just learning to talk, listen to their descriptions of the environment. Indicate some of the metaphors they use and discuss possible reasons (e.g. connections, associations) for each comparison.
3. Write a brief poem containing several similes or one containing several metaphors. You might wish to use one of the following opening lines:
   A. For a simile poem:
      i) "My love has gone; I feel like a ________"
      ii) "I sat alone like a ________"
      iii) "I was as tired as a ________"
   B. For a metaphor poem:
      i) Start with "I used to be a ________," and later change to "Now I'm a ________"
      ii) Begin with "At night, the mountain is a ________"

PEANUTS
PSYCHIATRI HELP 5¢
THE DOCTOR IS IN
LIFE IS LIKE A GAME, CHARLIE BROWN...
Tm. Reg. U.S. Pat. Off.—All rights reserved
© 1971 by United Feature Syndicate, Inc.
SOMETIMES YOU WIN...
THE DOCTOR
SOMETIMES YOU LOSE
THE DOCTOR
I'LL BE HAPPY IF I JUST MAKE THE PLAYOFFS
THE DOCTOR IS IN
SCHULZ
1-19

iii) You might want to write a poem on tiredness, as in A, iii). For a metaphor poem, it could start with, "After working eight hours I was a ________."

Hints: In constructing similes and metaphors, comparisons are often made to something concrete or specific using nouns. These poems do not have to rhyme, if you like.

B. Personification

Another popular kind of comparison is personification, a figure of speech in which a lifeless thing or quality is described in human terms or given human characteristics. Like the simile and metaphor, personification is a type of comparison, and is most often used to describe an emotion or an abstract idea. Here is an example:

Time

Time
is a kindly father
tickling his loving child
into giggling senselessness
before carrying him off
to his eternal bed.

GLEN KIRKLAND

EXERCISE

Write a poem based on a personification, such as the poem on "Time." You might want to write on fear, boredom, love, or victory.

II. Five Types of Poetry

As well as extending language, poetry generally does at least one of the following:

1. it reveals deep personal feelings
2. it tells a story
3. it may present a drama or reveal character
4. it may make a serious social comment
5. it uses intrigue or humour to entertain us.

A. Lyric Poetry

The first type of poetry covers most poems that express deep, personal feelings of a speaker or poet in song-like form. Lyric poetry deals primarily with basic human needs, thoughts, feelings, common human experiences and well-known things, and helps us to view these in a new way.

The following selection by Joni Mitchell is a good illustration of a typical lyric poem:

Both Sides Now

Rows and flows of angel hair
And ice cream castles in the air
And feather canyons everywhere
I've looked at clouds that way

But now they only block the sun
They rain and snow on everyone
So many things I would have done
But clouds got in my way

I've looked at clouds from both sides now
From up and down, and still somehow
It's cloud illusions I recall
I really don't know clouds at all

Moons and Junes and ferris wheels
The dizzy dancing way you feel
As every fairy tale comes real
I've looked at love that way

But now it's just another show
You leave 'em laughing when you go
And if you care, don't let them know
Don't give yourself away

I've looked at love from both sides now
From give and take, and still somehow
It's love's illusions I recall
I really don't know love at all

Tears and fears and feeling proud
To say "I love you" right out loud
Dreams and schemes and circus crowds
I've looked at life that way

But now old friends are acting strange
They shake their heads, they say I've changed
But something's lost, but something's gained
In living every day

I've looked at life from both sides now
From win and lose and still somehow
It's life's illusions I recall
I really don't know life at all

I've looked at life from both sides now
From up and down, and still somehow
It's life's illusions I recall
I really don't know life at all

JONI MITCHELL

"Both Sides Now," like most lyric poems, describes scenes of nature (e.g. the clouds "only block the sun/They rain and snow on everyone") and presents a highly personal response to the scenes and experiences in question (i.e. the poet feels that she does not understand the ways of love and life in much the same way she does not understand clouds).

The poem also reveals deep personal feelings ("Tears and fears and feeling proud/To say 'I love you' right out loud") and fleeting states of mind ("So many things I would have done/But clouds got in my way"), as well as revealing to us new ways of viewing ordinary, familiar aspects of nature (in this poem, clouds).

The most common types of lyric poems include idylls, haiku, odes, sonnets, elegies, hymns, most free verse and popular song lyrics.

B. Narrative Poetry

A second type of poetry tells a story in simple, direct, rhythmical language with a strong emphasis on plot or physical action. Narrative poetry often deals with history, geography, or myth. The most common narrative poems are epics or ballads. A good example of this poetry type is Alfred Tennyson's "The Charge of the Light Brigade", which celebrates the death of 600 British soldiers at Balaclava in the Crimea on October 25, 1854:

The Charge of the Light Brigade

I

Half a league, half a league,
Half a league onward,
All in the valley of Death
Rode the six hundred
'Forward, the Light Brigade!
Charge for the guns!' he said:
Into the valley of Death
Rode the six hundred.

II

'Forward, the Light Brigade!'
Was there a man dismay'd?
Not tho' the soldiers knew
Some one had blunder'd:
Their's not to make reply,
Their's not to reason why,
Their's but to do and die:
Into the valley of Death
Rode the six hundred.

III

Cannon to right of them,
Cannon to left of them,
Cannon in front of them
Volley'd and thunder'd;
Storm'd at with shot and shell,
Boldly they rode and well,
Into the jaws of Death,
Into the mouth of Hell
Rode the six hundred.

IV

Flash'd all their sabres bare,
Flash'd as they turn'd in air
Sabring the gunners there,
Charging an army, while
All the world wonder'd:
Plunged in the battery-smoke
Right thro' the line they broke;
Cossack and Russian
Reel'd from the sabre-stroke
Shatter'd and sunder'd.
Then they rode back, but not,
Not the six hundred.

V

Cannon to right of them,
Cannon to left of them,
Cannon behind them
Volley'd and thunder'd;
Storm'd at with shot and shell,
While horse and hero fell,
They that had fought so well
Came thro' the jaws of Death,
Back from the mouth of Hell,
All that was left of them,
Left of six hundred.

VI

When can their glory fade?
O the wild charge they made!
All the world wonder'd.
Honour the charge they made!
Honour the Light Brigade,
Noble six hundred!

ALFRED, LORD TENNYSON

Despite the suggestion that the military command blundered (see second stanza, lines 3-4), Tennyson's concern is not with military strategy or an analysis of the causes of the British defeat. Instead, he wishes to tell a rousing tale of foolhardy heroism in a style which approximates the sound of the horsemen galloping to their deaths.

C. Dramatic Poetry

Although there is some drama in narrative poetry, it is not highlighted to the same degree as it is in dramatic poetry. Dramatic poetry is intended to be read aloud or performed in front of an audience. Dramatic monologues and Shakespeare's plays are two examples of this poetry type.

As we can see from reading the following selection, situation, characterization and conflict, as revealed through monologue or dialogue, all figure prominently in dramatic poetry:

She'd Say

'I'll never reach 40,' my mother would say,
'I have a short life-line,' she'd say,
holding out her palm solemnly
& pointing, 'I went to a fortune-teller
before the war,' she'd say, 'at the Exhibition,
& she took one look at my hand & she gasped
& said "Oh my dear, I'm so sorry,
you shouldn't have come in here," & I said
"What is it, can't you tell me?" & she said
"No, I can't bear to tell you.
oh you poor dear," she said.
& she threw her arms around me
& she hugged me just like that,' she'd say.
'& it was only later,' she'd say,
'that Genevieve told me about my life-line.'
'It was the same thing,' she'd say.

'with Dr. McCready, he'd be listening to my heart
& a sad look would come over his face,
& he'd put his arms around me & hold me tight
just for a minute, & afterward
he'd smile as if nothing had happened
& say I was okay, but I always knew
what he'd been thinking,' she'd say.
'I always knew,' she'd say.

'What will you do when I'm gone,' she'd say
when I brought a sock to be darned
or a book to be mended. Or to my dad
as she bustled around the kitchen.
'You're going to have to learn to cook

when I'm gone,' she'd say.
& when he growled 'Don't talk rubbish, honey,'
she'd say cheerily 'I know what you're thinking,
you're going to get yourself
a cute young floozie after I'm gone.'

'I nearly died when I had you,' she said.
'Dr. McCready didn't think I'd make it,' she said.
'He never said so but I could tell
by the way he looked at me,' she said.
'Look at my pot belly,' she said.
'That's what you did to me but it was worth it,'
she said. 'You were wanted,' she said.
'When I told Dr. McCready I was expecting
he put his arms around me & said
"Oh no, Jeannie, you're not."
& he looked sadly out the window & then said

"Well, we'll do the best we can,
but you're not to have another, you hear,
you be a good girl now, & don't have another."'
& my father would sit silently
when she talked like this,
but sometimes she'd keep going & ask
why he had not yet bought their burial plot.
'You can put me wherever you want,' she'd say.
'You'll have someone else to go in your double plot,'
she'd say. 'She won't want me,' she'd say.
'She'll sure make you toe the line,' she'd say.

& when they argued, or when she & I argued,
'You can count on one thing,' she'd say.
'You won't have me around much longer,' she'd say.
'You'll be able to have your own way soon,' she'd say.
She'd hold out her palm & say 'It's right here,
you can look at it,' she'd say. 'The fortune teller
was really upset,' she'd say.
'She took me in her arms & said "You poor thing,"
& sobbed on my shoulder,' 'I'll never make 50,'
she'd say.

FRANK DAVEY

The character of the mother is vividly presented through a series of episodes and conversations recollected by her child. Each episode or snippet of talk reveals an aspect of the mother's personality. For instance, the fortune teller incident in the first stanza suggests that the mother is a person who puts her faith in irrational systems such as palmistry.

Like most of its kind, this dramatic poem contains subtle conflicts: between the mother's curiosity about fate and her fears of death, between what the doctor actually says in the second stanza and how the mother interprets his behavior, and between the members of this family. Inevitably, we come away from the poem overwhelmed by the contradictory nature of this over-emotional, hypochrondriacal person.

If, as the child and father do, we assume the mother's morbid remarks are intended in jest, we may find some of them amusing. But at the same time, we find ourselves vaguely irritated, embarrassed, and confused by the old, familiar, double-edged anecdotes that are repeatedly dredged up by the mother.

D. Social Commentary

A fourth thing that poetry does is to comment on society. Social commentary poems criticize social habits, customs, attitudes, and problems in order to promote much-needed changes in the individual or in society.

The following poem, by World War I poet Wilfred Owen, makes a powerful anti-war statement against the old Latin saying that it is sweet and honorable to die for one's country:

Dulce et Decorum Est

Bent double, like old beggars under sacks,
Knock-kneed, coughing like hags, we cursed through sludge,
Till on the haunting flares we turned our backs,
And towards our distant rest began to trudge.
Men marched asleep. Many had lost their boots,
But limped on, blood-shod. All went lame, all blind;
Drunk with fatigue; deaf even to the hoots
Of gas-shells dropping softly behind.

Gas! GAS! Quick, boys! An ecstasy of fumbling,
Fitting the clumsy helmets just in time,
But someone still was yelling out and stumbling

And flound'ring like a man in fire or lime.—
Dim through the misty panes and thick green light,
As under a green sea, I saw him drowning.

In all my dreams before my helpless sight
He plunges at me, guttering, choking, drowning.

If in some smothering dreams, you too could pace
Behind the wagon that we flung him in,
And watch the white eyes writhing in his face,
His hanging face, like a devil's sick of sin,
If you could hear, at every jolt, the blood
Come gargling from the froth-corrupted lungs
Bitten as the cud
Of vile, incurable sores on innocent tongues,—
My friend, you would not tell with such high zest
To children ardent for some desperate glory,
The old Lie: *Dulce et decorum est*
Pro patria mori.[1]

WILFRED OWEN

Owen's intent is clearly to set the record straight on the nature of warfare and to change the minds of readers who hold pro-war opinions. He wants to take the reader beyond the smooth-sounding slogans of war and propaganda to the grim realities of the battlefield. Like all sociological-minded poets, he presents a case or an argument with evidence and a conclusion. The case presented in by this poem is overwhelmingly convincing, largely because of its catalogue of unnecessary human suffering through the horrors of war.

E. Light Verse

Another type of poetry is light verse, which includes such well-known forms as limericks, parodies, epigrams, occasional verse, and satire. The main purpose of light verse is to entertain, amuse, or intrigue, although it sometimes has a serious purpose behind its humor.

The following poem by Robert Frost is a good example of satire, a form of light verse which mocks a person, idea, or social institution.

[1]Dulce et decorum est pro patria mori: It is sweet and fitting to die for one's country (from the Roman poet Juvenal).

Departmental

An ant on the tablecloth
Ran into a dormant moth
Of many times his size.
He showed not the least surprise.
His business wasn't with such.
He gave it scarcely a touch.
And was off on his duty run.
Yet if he encountered one
Of the hive's enquiry squad
Whose work is to find out God
And the nature of time and space,
He would put him onto the case.
Ants are a curious race;
One crossing with hurried tread
The body of one of their dead
Isn't given a moment's arrest—
Seems not even impressed.
But he no doubt reports to any
With whom he crosses antennae,
And they no doubt report
To the higher up at court.
Then word goes forth in Formic:
"Death's come to Jerry McCormic,
Our selfless forager Jerry.
Will the special Janizary
Whose office it is to bury
The dead of the commissary
Go bring him home to his people.
Lay him in state on a sepal.
Wrap him for shroud in a petal.
Embalm him with ichor of nettle.
This is the word of your Queen."
And presently on the scene
Appears a solemn mortician;
And taking formal position
With feelers calmly atwiddle,
Seizes the dead by the middle,
And heaving him high in air,
Carries him out of there.
No one stands round to stare.
It is nobody else's affair.

It couldn't be called ungentle.
But how thoroughly departmental.

ROBERT FROST

Frost's poem is clever and entertaining, but, by describing ant society in terms of human society, it also comments on a serious matter: how bureaucracy can lead to insensitivity and institutional coldness. We have all seen situations in which people have avoided taking responsibility or acting because it "wasn't their job." Many examples of light verse contain, as "Departmental" does, a serious message mixed in with the fun.

F. Exceptions to the Rule

When poets write, they, like most writers, have a general purpose in mind. Depending on their purpose, they usually gravitate toward one type of poetry as opposed to another. For instance, a poet wanting to tell a story is likely to write a narrative poem, possibly a ballad or an epic. A poem expressing feelings about a recently deceased friend would probably be a lyric, an elegy being the logical lyric form to use.

Now, although the five general categories of poetry we have just discussed are useful in identifying many individual poems, they obviously can not and do not neatly or accurately describe every single poem ever written.

The reasons for this are many. For instance, some poets may have more than one purpose in mind. A poet may wish to express feelings, let's say, about a visit to his or her birthplace or home in the country. But, as he or she writes the poem, anger at the way the city has taken over and ruined rural areas may surface. Hence, the poem may begin as a lyric, perhaps an *idyll* (a descriptive poem about simple, charming rural settings), but may end by making serious points about how urban sprawl corrupts once-beautiful landscapes.

Another, very important thing to remember about poets is that some of them do not think consciously in terms of purpose or categories of poem types; they prefer to let inspiration shape the forms that their writing takes.

Having said all this, we point out that you will find poems like the following selection which may be difficult to classify:

Is My Team Ploughing?

"Is my team ploughing,
    That I was used to drive

And hear the harness jingle
  When I was man alive?"

Aye, the horses trample,
  The harness jingles now;
No change though you lie under
  The land you used to plough.

"Is football playing
  Along the river shore,
With lads to chase the leather,
  Now I stand up no more?"

Aye, the ball is flying,
  The lads play heart and soul;
The goal stands up, the keeper
  Stands up to keep the goal.

"Is my girl happy,
  That I thought hard to leave,
And has she tired of weeping
  As she lies down at eve?"

Aye, she lies down lightly,
  She lies not down to weep:
Your girl is well contented.
  Be still, my lad, and sleep.

"Is my friend hearty,
  Now I am thin and pine,
And has he found to sleep in
  A better bed than mine?"

Yes, lad, I lie easy,
  I lie as lads would choose;
I cheer a dead man's sweetheart,
  Never ask me whose.

A.E. HOUSMAN

Superficially, one might say this poem is a ballad because of its four-line rhyming stanzas. There also seems to be a storyline or plot that we can piece together suggesting that the selection is a narrative poem (i.e. the speaker has died and since his death his friend and sweetheart have become lovers).

On the other hand, though, the poem reveals dramatic tension; we can feel it growing as we near the conclusion in our first reading. We sense a conflict between the anxious speaker who asks earnest questions and the not-so-loyal friend who reluctantly supplies increasingly ambiguous answers. We also learn information about the speaker's and the friend's characters, something which is more likely to occur in a dramatic poem than in a narrative.

It would be inaccurate, therefore, to say the poem is solely dramatic or narrative. Rather, we might conclude that "Is My Team Ploughing?" has elements of both poetry types.

EXERCISE

Read the following poem and attempt to describe its content and form according to the five categories of poetry used in this chapter. Justify your opinion with references to characteristics of the five poem types and their forms (e.g. sonnet, free verse).

The World Is Too Much with Us

The world is too much with us; late and soon,
Getting and spending, we lay waste our powers:
Little we see in Nature that is ours;
We have given our hearts away, a sordid boon!
The Sea that bares her bosom to the moon;
The winds that will be howling at all hours,
And are up-gathered now like sleeping flowers;
For this, for everything, we are out of tune;
It moves us not.—Great God! I'd rather be
A Pagan suckled in a creed outworn;
So might I, standing on this pleasant lea,
Have glimpses that would make me less forlorn;
Have sight of Proteus[1] rising from the sea;
Or hear old Triton[2] blow his wreathèd horn.

WILLIAM WORDSWORTH

FOLLOW-UP

1. Relate a recent experience you had involving nature, such as a hike in the wilderness, a camping trip, or a storm that you were caught in. Write about the experience in either short story or lyric poem form. Concentrate on creating vivid details and on capturing feelings.

[1]Proteus: a sea god who could assume any shape.
[2]Triton: demigod of the sea who blew a trumpet made of a conch shell.

2. If you are musically inclined and play an instrument, write a ballad about a local or an historical event. You should be familiar with the people and places described either through experience or through your reading. Record the song on tape and play it for the class.
3. Be someone else, real or imaginary. Assume that your character has recently had an experience that was contrary to his or her nature; for example, your character might be an elderly woman who recently found herself driving a Mack truck, or a man who knows nothing about sports but who was talked into going to a game.

   Write a dramatic monologue—what your character would say as he or she tells about the experience to a silent friend. Perform your poem in front of a small group, or, if you wish, the class. See if your audience can guess the situation, who the speaker is, and who he or she is talking to.
4. Do some research and find a folk song which makes a social comment (suggested recording artists: Bob Dylan, Simon and Garfunkel, Joan Baez, Randy Newman, Valdy, Murray McLauchlan, Gordon Lightfoot, Tom Waits, Buffy Ste. Marie, and Ian and Sylvia Tyson).

   Play the song for the class and talk about the aspects of society being criticized, the solutions proposed in the song, and your reactions to the solutions.
5. Do some research and find a satirical poem by a poet like Ogden Nash, Earle Birney, or Lawrence Ferlinghetti. Copy it out on a separate page. Then on another page, tell a) what is being satirized, and b) why you feel the selection is a reasonable example of satire.
6. Pair up with another student. Individually, make up a series of test questions based on the material of this chapter. Then try to answer each other's questions.

RELATED POEMS IN CHAPTER 8:

Jabberwocky, (Lewis Carroll), p. 165
My Last Duchess, (Robert Browning), p. 193
Low Tide on Grand Pré, (Bliss Carman), p. 215
Midnight, (Archibald Lampman), p. 222
A Kite is a Victim, (Leonard Cohen), p. 248
Because I could not stop for Death, (Emily Dickinson), p. 282
Death, Be Not Proud, (John Donne), p. 284
Dreams, (Langston Hughes), p. 290

CHAPTER 5

POETRY: YOU CAN DO IT

Now that we have looked at the reading of poetry and discussed it as a form of literature, the next step is to examine the art of writing poetry. When they think about writing poetry, many people imagine themselves hunched over a paper, laboring to find a rhyme, checking the meter of a line, or searching in vain for an idea worth writing about. For other people, writing poetry is associated with peaceful reflection and the satisfaction of having produced a work that uses words in the best way possible.

Why, other than for people who want to become poets or songwriters, should the study of poetry include some writing of it? We have seen that poetry is present to a great degree in our lives, and we have seen, too, that it has a special appropriateness for communicating emotional, personal views or experiences. Poetry is important because we are exposed to it often and have occasion to use it.

Writing poetry is challenging, but it is also rewarding. Searching for the starting idea, finding the right words, and capturing an effective rhythm is hard work, but the satisfaction of reading one's own work and seeing that all the parts - every word and image - work together to communicate in the best way possible is immense. This is especially so when this satisfying feeling is combined with the realization that the poem expresses something that is hard to say. One high school student voiced it in these plain words: "Writing poetry can be a very useful outlet for your emotions and can give you a chance to convey feelings that you might otherwise not be able to express."

And, finally, writing poetry enables us to recognize and appreciate more fully the thoughts and techniques other poets used in

Truth

creating their own poems. Those people who have tried their hand at writing poetry tend to be at ease with it as a form of writing because they have an understanding of the craft.

I. Writing a Free Verse Image Poem

Where should we begin in writing a poem? Let's start with a form that is easily mastered because it requires no regular rhythm or rhyme patterns: free verse. Free verse is called "free" because it places no real restrictions on the poet; it allows the writer more freedom in choosing words, using sounds, and arranging lines for effect than do the conventional, older forms, such as the ballad and the sonnet.

Included below are three examples of free verse poetry. Study each for its rhythm and sound.

The Lonely Land

Cedar and jagged fir
uplift sharp barbs
against the gray
and cloud-piled sky;
and in the bay
blown spume and windrift
and thin, bitter spray
snap
at the whirling sky;
and the pine trees
lean one way.

A wild duck calls
to her mate,
and the ragged
and passionate tones
stagger and fall,
and recover,
and stagger and fall,
on these stones—
are lost

in the lapping of water
on smooth, flat stones.

This is a beauty
of dissonance,
this resonance
of stony strand,
this smoky cry
curled over a black pine
like a broken
and wind-battered branch
when the wind
bends the tops of the pines
and curdles the sky
from the north.

This is the beauty
of strength
broken by strength
and still strong.

A.J.M. SMITH

This Is Just to Say

I have eaten
the plums
that were in
the icebox

and which
you were probably
saving
for breakfast

Forgive me
they were delicious
so sweet
and so cold

WILLIAM CARLOS WILLIAMS

Portrait

Book-thin behind the desk
with fingers rigid as pencils she stamps
stacks returns, read or unread
she cares not.

Bloodless as paper she, and lifeless
as dead words on dull binding are her eyes,
looking not in nor out, only seeing
date-print on card and flyleaf;
and mute
as volumes never off the shelves her tongue—
the rubbered pencil used to point
the novel overdue, the scanty fine.
O life—love—something—burst the resisting doors—
ignore the silence sign—vault the tall desk
and on her locked blank pages
write a living tale.

ANNE MARRIOTT

EXERCISES

1. Which poem makes some use of rhyme? Are the rhymes noticeable on first reading the poem? Comment.
2. Find two examples of special line arrangements that add emphasis. What did the poet want to emphasize? Was it effective? Explain.
3. Which poem makes the most effective use of sound? Comment.
4. How does Williams' poem differ from a casual note that a husband might write to his wife?
5. What techniques did Marriott use to link together all the parts of her poem?

From the three examples, we can see that free verse poetry allows the poet considerable freedom in word choice and line arrangement; this flexibility means that poets can emphasize important words and images and can use sounds in the best way possible. Before a poet can write a good free verse poem, however, he or she must have an idea, situation, or image in mind. The first challenge of this chapter is to write a type of free verse poem called an image poem.

If we return for a moment to A.J.M. Smith's poem, "The Lonely Land" we can see that it is concerned mostly with creating a mood, or impression, while capturing a scene for the reader. Many writers who see something moving or beautiful paint it in words simply to preserve the richness, immediacy, and intensity of the moment. Often, such poems are deceptively simple. George

Bowering's poem "CPR Window" brings out mixed reactions from readers:

CPR Window
For Raymond Souster

The night train
across the prairies

passes small villages
with their few trees

plowed snow of streets
& is gone again

into the next hundred miles
of dark snow.

GEORGE BOWERING

All that Bowering is saying is this: from the train's window, the small villages seem almost overwhelmed by winter. The few trees are meagre protection, and the villages have to struggle to keep nature at bay by plowing the streets. Bowering captures the desolation and tentativeness of winter life in the small villages along the rail line. In just a few lines, he recreates and shares with the reader both the scene and his reactions to it.

Let's look at three more free verse image poems, one of which stands also as a song:

Neighbors

They live alone
together,

she with her wide hind
and bird face,
he with his hung belly
and crewcut.

They never talk
but keep busy.

Today they are
washing windows

(each window together)
she on the inside
he on the outside.
He squirts Windex
at her face:
she squirts Windex
at his face.

Now they are waving
to each other
with rags.

not smiling.

DAVID ALLAN EVANS

Silver Wheels

High speed drift on a prairie road
Hot tires sing like a string being bowed
Sudden town rears up then explodes
Fragments resolve into white line code
Whirl on Silver Wheels

Black earth energy receptor fields
Undulate under a grey cloud shield
We outrun a river colour brick red mud
That cleaves apart hills soil rich as blood

Highway squeeze . . . construction steam
Stop caution hard hat yellow insect machines
Silver steel towers stalk rolling land
Toward distant stacks that shout
"Feed on demand"

100 miles later the sky has changed
Urban anticipation—we get 4 lanes
Redorange furnace sphere notches down
Throws up silhouette skyline in brown

Sundogs flare on windshield glass
Sudden swoop skyward iron horse overpass
Pass a man walking like the man in the moon
Walking like his head's full of irish fiddle tunes

The skin around every city looks the same
Miles of flat neon spelling well-known names

USED TRUCKS DIRTY DONUTS YOU YOU'RE
THE ONE
Fat wheeled cars squeal into the sun

Radio speakers gargle top 10 trash
Muzak sound track to slow collapse
Planet engines pulsate in sidereal time
If you listen close you can hear the whine

BRUCE COCKBURN

Weasel

Thin as death,
the dark brown weasel slides
like smoke through night's hard silence.
The worlds of the small are still. He glides
beneath the chicken house. Bird life
above him sleeps in feathers as he creeps
among the stones, small nose testing every board
for opening, a hole small as an eye, a fallen knot,
a crack where time has broken through.
His sharp teeth chatter.
Again and again he quests the darkness
below the sleeping birds. A mouse freezes,
small mouth caught by silence in the wood.
His life is quick. He slips into his hole.
Thin as death, the dark brown weasel slides
like smoke. His needles worry wood.
The night is long.
Above him bird blood beats.

PATRICK LANE

EXERCISES

1. What mood dominates "Silver Wheels"? How does the author create that mood?
2. What verbs are used in "Weasel"? What effect do the verbs create?
3. Evans' poem paints a clear picture of an everyday sight. What statement does the poem make? How does this single scene work to reveal the relationship between the neighbors? Comment on the importance of the last line.

All three selections are respected as image poems because they each create a clear picture in vivid, concrete, concise wording. Rereading them carefully will reveal no elaborate figures of speech and little unusual vocabulary. The selections gain their strength from their simplicity, from the vividness of the moment on which they focus, and from the implied meaning attached to the scene being described.

As we mentioned already, the first challenge of this chapter is for the readers to write a free verse image poem. The main goal is to describe a scene in words that are vivid and precise. In deciding what scene to describe, you might wish to consider some guidelines on what to write about and how to proceed.

A. Getting Started

Image poems work best when the poet starts with a striking, specific image. Choose a scene or a moment – a close-up on the world – that is fresh and focused. It may be something familiar that is often overlooked, or it may be something unusual. Avoid standard, over-worked images, such as sunsets, flowers, and clouds.

Image poems are more effective, as well, when they are specific and concrete. Create your scene in words that are precise and vivid. Avoid empty, colorless words such as "beautiful" and "nice"; avoid, too, generalizations that do not create a specific picture, such as "old man" or "dog." Consider the following "apple ladder":

Life — General, Abstract
Basic Needs
Nourishment
Food
Fruit
Apple — Specific, Concrete

Keep your descriptive words at the bottom of the ladder. That will help you to create in words a picture as clear as a painting.

Finally, an image poem works best when the image is allowed to speak for itself. Avoid injecting emotional words such as "happy," "angry," and "sad." Instead, show the readers details that suggest the emotion. Simply put, the rule here is show, rather than tell.

B. Planning The Poem

Choose an experience that you want to write about. It may be from your childhood, from last week, or from the immediate present – but it should be memorable. Here are some suggestions to consider:

- Your earliest memory of school
- Your favorite place
- A visit with a stranger
- A child at play
- A moment of triumph
- Extreme tiredness

Once you have decided on the experience you are going to describe, list as many words or phrases – images – as you can that concretely describe the subject of your poem. Use several specific nouns and adjectives.

Once you have completed a list of images, organize it in some order, such as according to time sequence (chronological), location (spatial), or significance (climactic). You might decide, at this point, how the poem will end. Some image poems conclude with the strongest image; some end with a generalization about the details that were described; and others have a surprising or unusual ending. Study the poem that follows:

Canadian January Night

Ice storm: the hill
a pyramid of black crystal
down which the cars
slide like phosphorescent beetles
while I, walking backwards in obedience
to the wind, am possessed
of the fearful knowledge
my compatriots share
but almost never utter:
this is a country
where a man can die
simply from being
caught outside.

ALDEN NOWLAN

EXERCISES

1. Which type of ending does the poem have? Is it effective? Why?
2. What type of ending does each of the following have?
   (a) "Silver Wheels" by Bruce Cockburn
   (b) "Weasel" by Patrick Lane
   (c) "Neighbors" by David A. Evans
3. Consider "Canadian January Night" and the three poems listed above. Which do you prefer? Why?

After you have organized the images and decided on the poem's ending, study the images further and convert them into more complete phrases or full, rhythmical sentences by adding prepositions, joining words, and forceful verbs in the active voice. Start with your opening image; the rest will follow naturally.

Study the resulting poem; read it aloud to hear its rhythm. Change words and rearrange lines to make the images clearer and more vivid, and to make the poem read more fluently (a thesaurus and a dictionary may be helpful).

At this point, you will be ready to finalize the line breaks in your poems. In studying the lines, you might ask yourself where you should break each line and how long a free verse line should be. Here are some guidelines:

1. Free verse lines are often a group of words comfortable for reading in one sweep of the eyes.
2. Lines can be broken to emphasize key images or words. Return for a moment to the poem "Weasel." Which images are most important? How does the poet use line breaks to emphasize those images?
3. Some poets use line breaks to create a pause and substitute for a form of punctuation. If we return again to "Silver Wheels," "Weasel," and "Neighbors," what examples can you find of line breaks used as a substitute for punctuation? We should note at this point, then, that punctuation and capitalization can be omitted if the poet uses other devices to substitute for them or wishes to create a special effect. The question as to whether a poet should use punctuation and capitalization or not is important only when use of either will help or hinder the poet in communicating his message effectively.

Note: See Glen Kirkland's essay "Line Divisions in Free Verse Poetry", p. 326.

Reread the resulting poem a final time to check once more your impression of it as a total poem. Make any small changes you wish and then write out a good copy with a suitable title.

Congratulations! You have produced a free verse image poem. You might consider sharing your work with others.

II. Writing a Parody

Now that you have tried your hand at free verse, which involves very precise consideration of word choice and word arrangement, you are ready to try the second challenge in this chapter: writing a parody. Before we proceed, let's consider the definition of a parody, as it applies to poetry. A parody is a poem that imitates the rhythm and structure of another, more recognizable poem. Sometimes, the author of a parody wishes to make fun of the work he is imitating; often, though, the parody is used as a vehicle for satire.

Read the poems that follow and see if you can recite the original work each poem is parodying:

Hey Diddle Diddle

Hey diddle diddle,
The physicists fiddle,
   The Bleep jumped over the moon.
The little dog laughed to see such fun
   And died the following June.

PAUL DEHN

Little Miss Muffet

   Little Miss Muffet
   Crouched on a tuffet,
Collecting her shell-shocked wits.
   There dropped (from a glider)
   An H-bomb beside her—
Which frightened Miss Muffet to bits.

PAUL DEHN

Variations on a Theme by
William Carlos Williams

1

I chopped down the house that you had been saving
    to live in next summer.
I am sorry, but it was morning, and I had nothing to do
and its wooden beams were so inviting.

2

We laughed at the hollyhocks together
and then I sprayed them with lye.
Forgive me. I simply do not know what I am doing.

3

I gave away the money that you had been saving to
    live on for the next ten years.
The man who asked for it was shabby
and the firm March wind on the porch was so juicy and cold.

4

Last evening we went dancing and I broke your leg.
Forgive me. I was clumsy. And
I wanted you here in the wards, where I am the doctor!

KENNETH KOCH

EXERCISES

1. Which parody is the most humorous? Explain the source of the humor.
2. What common statement do Dehn's poems make?
3. Study Williams' poem, "This Is Just to Say" and then read Koch's parody. Does Koch's poem make fun of Williams'? What criticism does it make?

As the examples illustrate, parodies are enjoyable to read. The familiar rhythm, rhyme, and wording patterns give added impact to the humorous or satirical thought in the poem.

Your second challenge, then, is to write a parody of a familiar poem.

A. Getting Started

Start by selecting the poem on which your parody will be based. Choose a nursery rhyme or a well-known poem with which your familiar. You might write a new parody based on "Hey Diddle Diddle," "Little Miss Muffet," or "This Is Just to Say," or you might choose one of the following:

- Little Jack Horner
- Hickory, Dickory Dock
- Baa Baa Black Sheep
- Twinkle, Twinkle Little Star
- Mary Had a Little Lamb
- The Tiger, by William Blake (p. 111)
- Stopping by Woods, by Robert Frost (p. 126)

Write out the original version of the poem if you know it by heart. If you are not certain of the exact wording, check in the school library. Above all, have the original version in front of you before you start.

B. The Actual Writing

Begin by reading the original version of the poem you will be parodying. Get the feel of its rhythm. Note which lines rhyme, if any.

Once you feel comfortable working with the poem, decide on the subject of the parody. You might mock or satirize technology or the arms race, as did Paul Dehn, or you might try one of the following topics:

- a political or social issue
- an historial figure
- a fashion trend
- a recent movie
- a popular television show

Once you have selected your topic, give it some thought. Note down possible statements or angles you might use. Select one statement or approach and return to the original poem. Reread the poem and attempt to substitute your own words in place of the first line. Work from there, line by line, until you have completed the poem and created your parody.

The difficult task will be to keep the same rhythm as the original poem. Each time you write a new line, read it over several times and then read the original line that it will be replacing. Listen for any difference. If you have difficulty discovering why a new line does not quite work, count the number of syllables in it and mark those that would be stressed if it were read aloud. Do the same for the original line and compare the two. Any differences in syllables and stresses will point out wording that needs to be adjusted if the parody is to work.

Be patient. It will take some time, but the results will be worthwhile. When you have completed your parody, read it aloud one final time and listen carefully to its rhythm and its rhymes. Follow this by reading the original and comparing the two versions. Make any small adjustments that you feel are necessary. Write out a good copy of your parody.

"I gotta write a poem about Dad. What rhymes with 'el dummo'?"

III. Writing a Limerick

Another form of poetry that is often humorous is the limerick. So popular and easily memorized is it that many people can easily recite a favorite. As a form, it consists of five lines in mixed iambic and anapestic meter with a rhyme scheme of AABBA. The first two lines and the fifth are written in trimeter (three units or feet), while the third and fourth lines are in dactylic dimeter (two units or feet). The resulting poem is a fast-paced, rhythmical verse that is easy to remember. Some limericks are nonsensical and some are off-colored, but most are intended to be humorous.

Here are some examples of the limerick – the first by Rudyard Kipling, and the second and third by John Robert Colombo.

There was a young man of Quebec
Who was frozen in snow to his neck,
    When asked, "Are you Friz?"
    He replied, "Yes I is,
But we don't call this cold in Quebec."

There was a young man of South Bay,
Making fireworks one summer day,
    He dropped his cigar
    In the gunpowder jar . . .
There *was* a young man of South Bay.

A poet from Winnipeg, Man.,
Wrote verses that never would scan,
    When asked why this was,
    He replied, "Well, because
I always try to fit in as many words to a line as I can."

EXERCISES

1. Limericks sometimes take liberties with spelling and grammar in order to rhyme. Point out two examples in the three limericks printed above. Are they effective? Why?
2. Which of the three limericks do you prefer? Why?

The limerick, then, differs from the parody in that the limerick has a set form and is usually more light or witty than satirical. The next challenge in this chapter is to write a limerick that uses in it the name of a familiar town or city, as was done in the last two examples.

A. Getting Started

The difficulties in writing a limerick will be to capture the rhythm and to find rhymes that work. Study the examples again to be certain that you have the feel of the limerick as a form.

You might begin by making a list of towns or cities that you would be interested in using.

B. The Actual Writing

From your list, select a place-name that you want to work with. Jot down as many words as you can that rhyme with the place-name. Study the rhyming words until you discover a way of using them in the second and fifth lines. The rhymes in the third and fourth lines, being independent of the other lines, are easier to find.

You should now be ready to write the first line. Once you have penned it, scan the line to check the meter and, if it works, try the second line. If you work line-by-line and keep an eye on the rhythm each time, the poem will unfold, slowly but definitely.

Once you have drafted the limerick, read it aloud and listen to its flow. Check the rhythm and the rhymes, and make any adjustments that will help the poem read smoothly and clearly. Write out a good copy and try it out on a classmate or friend.

This chapter asked you to write three poems. The first focused mostly on imagery; the second focused on imitating the flavor of a recognized poem; and the third asked you to work within a set pattern of rhythm and rhyme. The experiences should have given you some new thoughts about poetry. You may wish to share these by responding to the questions that follow.

EXERCISES

1. Which poem did you most enjoy writing? Why?
2. Which poem do you think is your best? Why?

3. What observations can you make about the poems your classmates wrote and shared?

AN EXERCISE IN REVISION

The poem printed below is a rough draft and needs to have several changes made to improve it. Read the poem carefully and revise it in whatever way you feel would be an improvement. This might involve adding more specific details, using more concrete words, rearranging images in a more effective sequence, or omitting unnecessary details. Compare your results with poems produced by others in your class. Be prepared to justify your changes.

Small Town Sunday

First the green sign—
1 kilometer to go—
and then the Corporate Limits sign,
upside-down and full of bullet holes.

Next,
a little church, empty and white
against the dark green grass
and tall trees.

On the main street,
a small boy pedals past vacant lots
toward the railroad station,
where a lone man unloads boxes
from a grey pick-up truck.

The corner garage is closed down—
an old car sits next to the
empty pumps.

Dark houses, dust-covered,
are hidden behind
bushy hedges.

Near the curling rink's foundations,
an old man walks slowly,
alone.

Suddenly,
the noon siren rings and
a lone black dog
in the ditch by the graveyard
lifts its head and howls.

QUESTIONS TO CONSIDER WHILE REVISING

1. What single impression about the small town does the author wish to emphasize? Does every image add to that impression? Should any be omitted?
2. Study the images. Could any details be added? Could the wording of any be made sharper or more concrete?
3. Does the poem end with a powerful image? Should any of the images be rearranged?
4. Study the line breaks. Should any lines be shortened? Lengthened? Are important words given proper emphasis?

FOLLOW-UP

first draft of **Anthem for Doomed Youth**

What mind's bells for these who die so fast?
—Only the monstrous anger of our guns.
Let the majestic insults of their iron mouths
Be as the priests' words at their burials.
Of choristers and holy music, none,
Nor any voice of mourning, save the wail,
The long-drawn wail of high, far-sailing shells.
What candles may we hold for these lost souls?
Not in the hands of boys, but in their eyes.
Shall many candles shine, and He will light them:
Women's wide-spreaded arms shall be their wreaths,
And pallor of girls' cheeks shall be their palls.
The flowers, the tenderness of old men's minds,
And every dusk, a drawing down of blinds.

WILFRED OWEN

Anthem for Doomed Youth

What passing-bells for these who die as cattle?
  Only the monstrous anger of the guns.
  Only the stuttering rifles' rapid rattle
Can patter out their hasty orisons.
No mockeries now for them; no prayers nor bells,
  Nor any voice of mourning save the choirs,—
The shrill, demented choirs of wailing shells;
  And bugles calling for them from sad shires.

What candles may be held to speed them all?
  Not in the hands of boys, but in their eyes

Shall shine the holy glimmers of good-byes.
  The pallor of girls' brows shall be their pall;
Their flowers the tenderness of patient minds,
And each slow dusk a drawing-down of blinds.

WILFRED OWEN

EXERCISES

1. Working from the final version, summarize in your own words what Owen is saying.
2. Study the first draft and the final version. Did Owen alter his message at all?
3. In lines 3 and 4 of his first draft, Owen personifies the sounds. In his final version, those same lines have been changed significantly. Explain why lines 3 and 4 in the final version are more effective.
4. The last seven lines of the first draft compare to the last six lines of the final version. Identify two changes Owen made - something he added, eliminated, or altered - and explain how the changes improved his poem.
5. We have seen that the basic message of both versions is the same, yet there are significant reasons why the final version is better. Compare the two versions for differences in:
   (a) rhyme patterns
   (b) word choice; use of sound
   (c) development of the poem's thought.

RELATED POEMS IN CHAPTER 8:

There was a young lady of Gimli, (Walter Kirkconnell), p. 152
There was a young man from Perth, (John Robert Colombo), p. 153
Lord Randal, (Anonymous), p. 153
After the Ballad "Lord Randall, My Son", (Anne Wilkinson), p. 154
Thaw, (Margaret Avison), p. 207
Bright Morning, (Sid Marty), p. 220
Rain Song, (Roo Borson), p. 221
Song of the Open Road, (Ogden Nash), p. 258

THIS LAND
IS YOUR LAND
EEP THIS LAND
PRETTY

CHAPTER 6

THE EYE OF THE BEHOLDER

By the time you have reached your last year of high school, you will have been exposed to a large number of poems; this is especially so if we count poetry in its many forms. Some of you will develop poetry writing skills, and will see poetry from the point of view of a craftsman, or poet. However extensive your background, all of you will be asked to become critical readers of poetry. In order to understand further the nature of poetry and how to talk about individual poems, we should stop and consider poetry from the three perspectives mentioned in this paragraph: those of the poet, the general reader, and the critical reader.

Since poets produce the works that are read and criticized, we will begin with their perspectives. In order to understand how poets see poetry, we have to consider why they write.

I. Why Poets Write

Poetry involves a magical linking of sound, image, thought, and emotion. Because poetry requires that language be used in a fine, precise, artistic manner, all poets have in common a love of language that makes writing poetry almost a compulsion. The following poem, by Deborah Gore, describes this drive to write poetry:

This is Not

this is not
            my poetry
i do not conceive

then
write it.
it is the work
of a
small inexhaustible demon
who grinds my bones
into verse.

DEBORAH GORE

While some poets may, at times, write for the pleasure of working with words, probably every poet will have other, additional reasons for being committed to writing poetry.

EXERCISE

At this point, you might stop to consider why poets write. What reasons can you suggest?

THE WIZARD OF ID by Brant parker and Johnny hart

By permission of Johnny Hart and News Group Chicago, Inc.

Other reasons poets might give to explain why they write can be viewed from three general perspectives. At times, poets may write because writing poetry does something important for themselves; at other times, poets might write mostly for others; and finally, on occasion, poets might write for the sake of art. These three perspectives are very general; a poet's reasons for writing might fall into one, two, or all three categories.

A major reason for poetry-writing was suggested by the students whose opinions on poetry were quoted in Chapter 3 (p. 37). They said that poets write to express themselves, to gain emotional release. This view is supported by the poets themselves. Robert Frost explained how an emotion might move a poet to write:

> A poem starts with a lump in the throat, a homesickness or a lovesickness. It is a reaching out toward expression, an effort to find fulfillment.

For some poets, then, poetry, because it is so well-suited to expressing the emotions, provides a medium for capturing, expressing, and exploring their feelings.

In addition to helping poets understand and express their emotions, poetry can help them learn more about themselves. By capturing and examining their own emotions, thoughts, and experiences in poetry, poets are able to understand themselves better, to develop a clearer sense of their identities and uniqueness. Canadian poet Bill Howell expressed it this way:

> [I] wonder who I am. And that is the starting point, the need to find out what's coming and going inside myself, and in the world around me . . . So I write as an act of faith, I guess, so I can believe in myself. More and more I find I have to live up to what I'm writing.

Clearly, then, poetry, for many writers, does much more than put feelings into words. Poetry is an important medium through which individuals can better understand themselves.

Most poets, though, are not moved to write only for themselves; they are very much aware of their readers. Those poets know that, just as their poems help them to understand themselves and their world, those same poems might help others in a similar way. Another Canadian poet, Ian Young, explained his relationship with his readers in this way:

> My primary reason for writing is to bring into consciousness, to establish connections, and so to gain more control of my reality, and to help whoever reads my work to gain control of his.

We know, then, that poets, whether they write for themselves or others, have a readership in mind. Because they are human and concerned with understanding what that means, poets, in being emotional, thoughtful, or descriptive, are communicating something worth listening to. Indeed, it is helpful to remember that the poet once occupied a special place in primitive societies as a prophet or shaman.

Though he acknowledged his readers, Ian Young still indicated that he writes poetry mainly because it helps himself. Other poets have said that they write mostly to communicate with others. David Helwig said, "My poetry is what I write in case there's somebody listening." Poets like Helwig think of the poem as a way to reach other human beings. Whether they are describing an experience, satirizing a social weakness, telling a story, or expressing thought or emotion, these poets are mainly concerned with sharing something they feel needs to be shared.

What other reasons remain to explain poets' motives for writing? So far, we have looked at reasons that were rooted in the personal. If we look beyond those, two other reasons for writing emerge, and both concern themselves with poetry as a high-level art form.

Some poets write to crystallize ideas or vision into works of art that will withstand the test of time. Shakespeare expressed this in the sonnet that follows:

Shall I compare thee to a summer's day?

Shall I compare thee to a summer's day?
Thou art more lovely and more temperate;
Rough winds do shake the darling buds of May,
And summer's lease hath all too short a date;
Sometime too hot the eye of heaven shines,
And often is his gold complexion dimmed;
And every fair from fair sometime declines,
By chance, or nature's changing course untrimmed.

But thy eternal summer shall not fade,
Nor lose possession of that fair thou owest,
Nor shall death brag thou wander'st in his shade
When in eternal lines to time thou growest:
  So long as men can breathe, or eyes can see,
  So long lives this, and this gives life to thee.

WILLIAM SHAKESPEARE

For such poets, poetry is an art form that immortalizes the subjects on which the poet writes.

Other poets, at times, write for other non-personal interests or values, such as to serve the society of mankind. In his poem "War Poet," Donald Bain explains an important function of the poet in society:

War Poet

We in our haste can only see the small components of the
  scene
We cannot tell what incidents will focus on the final
  screen.
A barrage of disruptive sound, a petal on a sleeping face,
Both must be noted, both must have their place;
It may be that our later selves or else our unborn sons
Will search for meaning in the dust of long deserted guns,
We only watch, and indicate and make our scribbled pencil
  notes.
We do not wish to moralize, only to ease our dusty throats.

DONALD BAIN

As Bain points out, poets help reveal the meaning of major social events by recording them faithfully and sensitively; if we extend this further, we can say, too, that some poets write to help better our society by pointing out its strengths and weaknesses.

In considering why poets write, we have come to understand more about what poetry does for individuals – both the poet and the reader. We have also observed that poetry moves beyond private communication into social communication and art.

EXERCISES

1. Do any poets write for money or fame? Comment.
2. Can you think of any reasons for writing poetry other than those we discussed?
3. Consider, for a moment, Bain's poem "War Poet." What does the poem suggest is the difference between the role of the poet and the role of the historian?
4. What roles do poets play in our society? A character in *Our Town*, a play by Thornton Wilder, said that the only people who really see into life are saints and poets. Do you agree? Comment.

II. Poetry and the General Reader

We have examined poetry from the poet's perspective. Let's turn now to those people who read what poets write: the general readers. If we look at how they see poetry, we will come to understand even better what value poetry has for its audience.

When asked why they like to read poetry, two students wrote the following answers:

> The thing I like most about poetry is that when I read it, it takes me into another part of myself that I don't really use very much.
>
> I like poetry because it gives me a chance to understand my feelings better by reading about how other people feel. My imagination thrives on poetry.

Both students indicated that they benefited from reading poetry because poems are enjoyable and stimulating. Poetry gives much to the reader who takes time to read it actively.

Let's look a little more closely at why poetry is enjoyable. On one level, poetry delights and entertains through its sounds and rhythms, its story-telling, and its refreshing descriptions of the familiar. Readers are pleased, especially, to discover a poem that touches their world, that is a part of their experience. John Keats described this encounter when he wrote that poetry ". . . should strike a reader as a wording of his own highest thoughts and appear almost a remembrance." The general reader, then, finds enjoyment in the entertaining aspects of poetry and in discovering familiar thoughts and experiences described in a fresh, vivid manner.

This leaves us with having a look at why poetry is stimulating. Hand-in-hand with the pleasure that poetry brings is the understanding it opens up for its readers. Both students pointed out that poetry takes them places or changes them. The journeys they refer to are travels into the self in which they, as readers, test their own feelings and thoughts against those described in the poem. Poetry, then, creates a feeling of oneness with not only the poem but with things or people outside of the reader.

In its power to teach its reader, poetry gains the power to reveal and to revitalize. Poetry gives readers new insights and helps them to find out more about themselves, to get to know themselves better. These insights bring alive inert potential, clarifying what readers may have felt dimly but never realized before. This instructive quality of poetry brings enjoyment to readers who experience such revelations. Matthew Arnold described this benefit when he said:

> The grand power of poetry is its . . . power of so dealing with things as to awaken in us a wonderfully full, new and intimate sense of them.

Readers who enjoy the entertaining and instructive qualities of poetry value each poem for the experience it holds. The act of reading brings to life the experience of a poem and leaves the readers affected, similar to the way in which they might be affected by a real-life experience. In his poem "Ars Poetica," Archibald MacLeish described the essential experiential quality of poetry:

Ars Poetica[1]

A poem should be palpable and mute
As a globed fruit,

Dumb
As old medallions to the thumb,

Silent as the sleeve-worn stone
Of casement ledges where the moss has grown—

[1]Ars Poetica: The Art of Poetry; also the title of a work by the 8th century Roman poet Horace.

A poem should be wordless
As the flight of birds.

•

A poem should be motionless in time
As the moon climbs,

Leaving, as the moon releases
Twig by twig the night-entangled trees,

Leaving, as the moon behind the winter leaves,
Memory by memory the mind—

A poem should be motionless in time
As the moon climbs.

•

A poem should be equal to:
Not true.

For all the history of grief
An empty doorway and a maple leaf.

For love
The leaning grasses and two lights above the sea—

A poem should not mean
But be.

ARCHIBALD MACLEISH

According to MacLeish, a poem should be "wordless" because the words should rise above being mere words or babble – they should become, as much as possible, the reality that the poem is describing. The true, basic value of poetry is found, then, in its power to create an intense experience for its readers.

EXERCISES

1. How important is the general reader's life experience and poetry experience (i.e. experience in reading poems) in enjoying, understanding, and appreciating poetry?
2. Can you suggest any other ways in which a reader might benefit from reading poetry?
3. Of the many poems you have read, which one stands out most? What does that poem cause you to feel as you read it? What qualities of the poem do you find appealing or moving?

4. Some poems, though they are recognized as being classics, leave some readers completely unaffected. What reasons can you give to explain this?
5. Reflect for a moment on MacLeish's poem. After you are satisfied that you know what MacLeish is saying about poetry, try writing your own poem about poetry. If you wish, you might, instead, write a poem answering or offering a rebuttal to "Ars Poetica".
6. Is it more important for a poem to have a message ("mean") or for it to provide an experience to be responded to by the reader ("be")?

III. Poetry and the Critical Reader

Now that we have examined poetry from the perspective of the poet and the general reader, we are left with one more perspective that must be explored if we are to consider poetry fully: that of the critical reader. Before reading this chapter, each of you knew already that many people write poetry and still more people read it. Probably most of you have written poetry and, certainly, everyone has read and listened to it. Only in your later years of schooling were you introduced to reading critically.

As a critical reader you read at a number of different levels. You read not only for delight, for the experience, and for the emotional qualities of a poem, but also for the instruction, the message, and the thoughtful qualities of a poem. For the critical reader, poetry is a rich vein to be mined at many levels.

Such a reader realizes the experience of the poem does not end with the individual reader, but that it is meant to be shared, understood, discussed, interpreted, and, finally, appreciated with others. This active interaction with poetry and with other readers helps you to develop yourself, to establish your identity, and to convey your ideas. Because of this interaction, you have as much potential for growth as the poet and much more potential than the general, uncritical, or inexperienced reader.

In addition to reading at different levels and actively exploring your own and others' views of poetry, you must also recognize that poetry is an art form and, as such, uses certain artistic strategies peculiar to poetry (such as sound patterns and imagery). In recognizing this, you acknowledge that a fuller experience – in the sense of intensity, richness, and complexity – can be had by close readings which uncover or demystify some of the sources of the poem's power. Sensible analysis will not destroy, but rather enhance or fine-tune your perceptions and appreciation of the poem.

Critical reading is a natural, evolutionary stage that comes with more life and poem experience. As readers gain experience with life, they gain access to the meaning of more poems. For this reason, many poems are difficult or meaningless for people prior to their high school years. As readers read more poetry, they develop literary experience that allows them reasonably to compare, contrast, judge, and evaluate. The two in combination – life and poem experience – are the foundation on which we as critical readers build our reactions to new poems.

In the next chapter, you will be asked to do some critical reading. When you are practising criticism, it is important not to lose perspective on some basic points we have discussed in this chapter:

1. A poet is an individual speaking to other individuals – a flesh and blood person who desires to and is attempting to communicate with readers who share the same humanity.
2. Although sharing a perspective or thought, the poet is also expressing feelings or emotions. Never lose track of the author's tone (his or her feelings or attitude toward the subject).
3. Although poems can be interpreted, discussed, or explained by critical readers, teachers, and students, they exist foremost as literary or imaginative experience (as pointed out by MacLeish). There are times when good poems themselves must have the final say and even critical readers must be silent and hold back their urges to explain or make comment. At such moments, all readers defer to the poem and rest in awe of its power and depth.
4. No matter how many interpretations or meanings you can give of a poem, the truly good poem itself will have a mystical chemistry or magic that will be present with each rereading and will intensify the mystery of life. Emily Dickinson described the impact of real poetry when she wrote:

   If I read a [poem] and it makes my whole body so cold no fire can ever warm me, I know that it is poetry. If I feel physically as if the top of my head were taken off, I know *that* is poetry.

In closing this chapter's discussion, we return again to the poets – this time to Marianne Moore, who insists that regardless of who you are (general or critical reader, or poet) and no matter what you do with or to poetry, it will remain "useful" only as long as the reader recognizes that the "raw material" of life provides the inspiration for poetry, and as long as the poem itself deals with "the genuine": what we might call the essentially important matters or experience of life.

Poetry

I, too, dislike it: there are things that are important
beyond all this fiddle.
Reading it, however, with a perfect contempt for it, one
discovers in
it after all, a place for the genuine.
Hands that can grasp, eyes
that can dilate, hair that can rise
if it must, these things are important not because a

high-sounding interpretation can be put upon them but
because they are
useful. When they become so derivative as to become
unintelligible,
the same thing may be said for all of us, that we
do not admire what
we cannot understand: the bat
holding on upside down or in quest of something to

eat, elephants pushing, a wild horse taking a roll, a tireless
wolf under
a tree, the immovable critic twitching his skin like a
horse that feels a flea, the base-
ball fan, the statistician—
nor is it valid
to discriminate against 'business documents and

school-books'; all these phenomena are important. One
must make a distinction
however: when dragged into prominence by half poets,
the result is not poetry,

nor till the poets among us can be
'literalists of
the imagination'—above
insolence and triviality and can present

for inspection, "imaginary gardens with real toads in them",
shall we have
it. In the meantime, if you demand on the one hand,
the raw material of poetry in
all its rawness and
that which is on the other hand
genuine, then you are interested in poetry.

MARIANNE MOORE

For Better or For Worse®

EXERCISES

1. How does a person become a critical reader of poetry?
2. What are some ideas general readers might have about poetry?
3. How does studying the characteristics of poetry as an art form help the critical reader?
4. If you were asked to talk to a group of ten-year-olds about the value of poetry, what would you say to them?
5. Can analysis of poetry be overdone? At what point might critical reading ruin or "kill" a poem? What gets lost in over-analysis?

FOLLOW-UP

1. Interview five people in the working world about their attitudes toward poetry. Summarize your findings for the class; in your report, offer some explanations to account for the attitudes held by those people you interviewed.
2. Interview a poet to discover his or her reasons for writing. If the poet is unable to come in and speak to the class, bring back the interview on tape or as a transcript and present it to the class.
3. Select a short poem that is challenging for most readers. Ask three people outside of school to read the poem and tell you their opinion of it. Summarize each person's thoughts in a report and conclude by offering your own observations about responses to poetry. In other words, try to account for any differences in the responses to the poem.
4. You have read many poems by poets who were expressing their feelings and thoughts about poetry. Find a song lyric that makes a comment on songs or song-writing. Present the song to the class and give a commentary that summarizes the main thoughts it suggests about the power of songs.
5. An editorial in a local paper has called for the removal of poetry from all school English courses, claiming that poetry has no value, that it is nothing more than word puzzles, and that the time would be better spent on learning practical skills such as letter writing and spelling. Write a letter to the editor in which you agree or disagree with the editorial.

RELATED POEMS IN CHAPTER 8:

Pullman Porter, (Robert Service), p. 155
This Poem Leaves No Survivors, (Robert Hilles), p. 156
Poetry for Intellectuals, (Louis Dudek), p. 168
The Memory of a Poem, (Michael Bullock), p. 247
More Intricate, (Milton Acorn), p. 248
Trees, (Joyce Kilmer), p. 258
Such is the power of the lover's sonnet, (Stephen Hume), p. 269
On His Blindness, (John Milton), p. 298

CHAPTER 7

BECOMING A CRITICAL READER

I. Critical Analysis: What and Why?

It is natural and logical for a general reader to want to go from contemplating or experiencing a poem to explaining or articulating his or her responses to it. Critical response helps readers express and explain what they understand when they read a poem.

Analysis allows the reader to explore poems beyond his or her own immediate responses and experiences, and to communicate feelings and thoughts about the poem to others through discussion and writing. This sharing of views, in turn, leads to further insights about the poem, oneself and others.

Critical analysis also activates the reader's mind or intellect in addition to already awakened feelings, memories, and associations. Through analysis, initial, vague, unformed "gut responses" or intuitions become clearer, and, as a result, critical responses carry greater weight in communications about the poem.

Having considered some of the benefits of analysis, we might now go on to list some typical activities that go into the critical analysis of poetry.

1. The critical reader is usually willing to consider alternate possibilities of meaning.
2. The critical reader reads with an open mind.
3. The critical reader looks for patterns and deliberately asks questions about any troublesome parts of the poem.
4. The critical reader reads in these ways, knowing that such approaches yield payoffs in enjoyment, understanding, and appreciation.

Read the following poem and note your immediate impressions:

The Tiger

Tiger! Tiger! burning bright
In the forests of the night,
What immortal hand or eye
Could frame thy fearful symmetry?

In what distant deeps or skies
Burnt the fire of thine eyes?
On what wings dare he aspire?
What the hand dare seize the fire?

And what shoulder, and what art,
Could twist the sinews of thy heart?
And when thy heart began to beat,
What dread hand forged thy dread feet?

What the hammer? what the chain?
In what furnace was thy brain?
What the anvil? what dread grasp
Dare its deadly terrors clasp?

When the stars threw down their spears,
And watered heaven with their tears,
Did he smile his work to see?
Did he who made the Lamb make thee?

Tiger! Tiger! burning bright
In the forests of the night,
What immortal hand or eye
Dare frame thy fearful symmetry?

WILLIAM BLAKE

You, the student, are probably familiar with tigers through a combination of reading, television or film, and actual experience. After reading Blake's poem, you may be a little surprised or confused by the unexpected information about anvils, hammers, and so forth.

A general reader might well ask, "What does all this furnace stuff have to do with tigers?" and feel that the poem has somehow failed to make sense. A critical reader, on the other hand, would ask a different question: "What *might* all this furnace stuff have to do with the subject?"

As a critical reader, your attitude to what you read changes somewhat. Let's say your curiosity has been piqued by the apparently irrelevant furnace descriptions. Begin to explore the poem, but on *its* terms, not yours. Try to view the poem as an interesting mystery of possibilities, instead of a baffling piece of pointless writing that does not match your knowledge and experience.

Search for any patterns that would assist you in understanding what puzzles and intrigues you. For instance, observe that the tiger is consistently described in terms of fire and various tools associated with fire (e.g. "hammer," "anvil," "chain"), commonly found in a blacksmith's shop or, on a larger scale, an industrial factory.

Begin to ask questions – and Blake's poem invites many – such as the following:

> "Who is the 'he' of stanza 5?"
> "Is the 'he' related to the shoulder which seems to create the tiger in the third stanza?"
> "What is the poet's purpose in describing the tiger with images of fire?"
> "What is the poet's purpose in repeating the first stanza with the exception of one word: 'dare'?"

Questioning of this kind helps the reader to focus more on the parts of the poem, to see a *context* (a specific background, situation, or plot) which brings the whole poem into perspective.

Lost in the confusion of a first reading and mired in the expectation that every poem must make immediate sense, the general reader may become a closed-minded reader who does not make much headway with the poem. An unwillingness to compromise one's views and imagine other understandings of the poem leads to an unsatisfactory closed reading. Conversely, the critical reader arrives at a more positive understanding and appreciation of Blake's energetic descriptions of the tiger's creation and the poet's questions regarding the nature of the mysterious creator and his creations.

It is apparent, then, that the general reader who chooses not to use natural mental processes such as curiosity and imagination to explore and develop preliminary responses is deprived of layers of meaning, especially when working with intriguing poems, like "The Tiger," which pose stimulating philosophical questions about life.

EXERCISES

1. Choose a poem from "Poems for Further Study" (Chapter 8) and do the following:
   a) Read it until you are satisfied that you understand it.
   b) Write down what you think of the poem.
   c) In a small group, present your selected poem to the other group members. Tell them what you think of it and ask for their opinions.
   d) After everyone has had a turn presenting a poem, take time to reread the one you chose. Write down what you think of it, now that others have discussed it with you. Has your opinion changed at all?
2. Working alone or with a partner, construct a one-minute television advertisement aimed at teaching viewers how to appreciate a poem. Be prepared to present your advertisement to the class.
3. Make a board game based on a challenging poem. Your aim would be to have the players demonstrate their understanding of the poem's parts before they can make any forward moves. Explain the rules and play the game as a demonstration to the class.
4. Plan a one-period lesson for a grade six class that is studying poetry. Your goal would be to teach them in forty minutes, the difference between the way a closed-minded reader and a critical reader view poetry.

II. Levels of Response: Engagement

Because poetry, like any other form of written communication, can be responded to in a number of ways, depending on the reader, we would like to examine four levels of response to poetry which, together, form a logical sequence for reading and analysing poetry. These four levels are: a) engagement or first reading, b) understanding content, c) understanding how form (techniques and style) develops content, and d) evaluation or critical judgment.

ENGAGEMENT takes place on your first contact with the poem, usually a silent reading, when you attempt to relate to what the poem says or presents; to form a mental image of what the poem is describing or talking about. If you are fortunate, you may already be familiar with the subject, the poet, or, possibly, the poem itself. This first reading, in any case, entails the reader's unstudied acceptance of what the poem has to say, without stopping to ponder difficult lines or to evaluate the worth of what he or she has just read.

After this initial reading, you will notice that you have had a number of immediate responses: that is, you may be amused, saddened, confused, disgusted, exhilarated, indifferent, etc.

Although many poems are an encounter with the familiar (subjects about which we know something from past experience), some may leave us confused or troubled because they contain peculiar insights. As you recall, when you began to read "The Tiger," you probably felt as if you were treading on familiar ground; but, by the end of the reading, you may not have been so sure anymore.

You may have been tempted to call the poem "sick," "dumb," or "weird" even before you explored or understood it. It is important to resist this impulse to dismiss what, at first, seems obscure, difficult, or out-of-the-ordinary.

How many times have we dismissed a person, a book, or an experience on the narrow basis of first contact - that superficial first impression - only to find out later that we made an error in judgment? It is easy to pass judgment, but much more difficult to judge accurately. For this reason, it is especially important for us to suspend judgments until a later stage of evaluation when we *know* the poem and are, therefore, capable of a truly informed response.

THE IMPORTANCE OF READER BACKGROUND should not be underestimated. As said earlier, each reader should be aware that he or she brings to the poem a unique background of life and literary experience. This background can be a positive influence and can assist you in your acceptance of what the poem says. For instance, you may know something about eels - that they are edible, but that you, personally, would prefer not to eat one. Then you might read a poem about this subject, of which you have some knowledge or an opinion:

The Eel

I don't mind eels
Except as meals.

OGDEN NASH

Because of your previous knowledge and preferences, you can more easily identify with the poet's point of view and appreciate his attitude than someone who does not know what an eel looks like or its use as food.

What happens sometimes, though, is that what you know and like can be handicaps unless you focus your knowledge or keep your preferences in check. When reading "The Tiger," you would have to be aware of a certain fact – that tigers can be cruel, destructive creatures – to gain even a tentative foothold in understanding Blake's poem.

Similarly, you would have to set aside certain attitudes or preferences – say, for rhyming poems that make immediate sense – in order to enjoy selections such as the following:

Return

No moon.
My boots crunch on the iced-over path.
The woods are still.
I have nowhere to go.

Then from a dark place
you jump out and throw yourself on my shoulders.
You've come back.

I will carry you,
strange rider.

LOU LIPSITZ

As readers, we need to become more conscious of our knowledge and prejudices, and how they can favorably or adversely affect our response to poetry.

EXERCISES

1. "I don't like poems that don't rhyme."
   "I don't like poems longer than one page."
   "Anything written prior to the 1980's is crummy."
   a) Why are these critical attitudes unreasonable?
   b) What are some other unreasonable reader predispositions and prejudices that might hinder reader response to poetry?
2. The text suggests that evaluation must logically occur follow-

ing understanding and appreciation. Do you agree? Why or why not?

3. If a poem is about a topic already familiar to you (e.g. love, animals), should you bother to read it?
4. Select one of the following poems dealing with uncommon topics and do the following:
   a) Identify the uncommon topic.
   b) Read the poem and indicate what you learned about the subject from reading and thinking about the poem.
   c) Tell how you feel about the subject as a result of reading the poem. Quote lines from the poem to support your explanation.

Silences

There is no silence upon earth or under the earth like the silence under the sea;
No cries announcing birth,
No sounds declaring death.
There is silence when the milt is laid on the spawn in the weeds and fungus of the rock-clefts;
And silence in the growth and struggle for life.
The bonitoes pounce upon the mackerel,
And are themselves caught by the barracudas,
The sharks kill the barracudas,
And the great molluscs rend the sharks,
And all noiselessly—
Though swift be the action and final the conflict,
The drama is silent.

There is no fury upon the earth like the fury under the sea.
For growl and cough and snarl are the tokens of spendthrifts who know not the ultimate economy of rage.
Moreover, the pace of the blood is too fast.
But under the waves the blood is sluggard and has the same temperature as that of the sea.

There is something pre-reptilian about a silent kill.

Two men may end their hostilities just with their battlecries.
"The devil take you," says one.
"I'll see you in hell first," says the other.

And these introductory salutes followed by a hail of gutturals and sibilants are often the beginning of friendship, for who would not prefer to be lustily damned than to be half-heartedly blessed?
No one need fear oaths that are properly enunciated, for they belong to the inheritance of just men made perfect, and, for all we know, of such may be the Kingdom of Heaven.
But let silent hate be put away for it feeds upon the heart of the hater.
Today I watched two pairs of eyes. One pair was black and the other grey. And while the owners thereof, for the space of five seconds, walked past each other, the grey snapped at the black and the black riddled the grey.
One looked to say—"The cat,"
And the other—"The cur."
But no words were spoken;
Not so much as a hiss or a murmur came through the perfect enamel of the teeth; not so much as a gesture of enmity.
If the right upper lip curled over the canine, it went unnoticed.
The lashes veiled the eyes not for an instant in the passing.
And as between the two in respect to candour of intention or eternity of wish, there was no choice, for the stare was mutual and absolute.
A word would have dulled the exquisite edge of the feeling,
An oath would have flawed the crystallization of the hate.
For only such culture could grow in a climate of silence,—
Away back before the emergence of fur or feather, back to the unvocal sea and down deep where the darkness spills its wash on the threshold of light, where the lids never close upon the eyes, where the inhabitants slay in silence and are as silently slain.

E.J. PRATT

How to Tell a Tornado

Listen for noises.
If you do not live
near railroad tracks,

the freight train you hear
is not the Northern Pacific
lost in the storm:
that is a tornado
doing imitations of itself.
One of its favorite sounds
is no sound.
After the high wind, and
before the freight train,
there is a pocket of nothing:
this is when you think
everything has stopped:
do not be fooled.
Leave it all behind
except for a candle
and take to the cellar.

Afterwards
if straws are imbedded
in trees without leave,
and your house—except
for the unbroken bathroom mirror—
has vanished
without a trace,
and you are naked
except for the right leg
of your pants,
you can safely assume
that a tornado
has gone through your life
without touching it.

HOWARD MOHR

The Three Fates

At the instant of drowning he invoked the three sisters.
It was a mistake, an aberration, to cry out for
life everlasting.

He came up like a cork and back to the river-bank,
put on his clothes in reverse order,
returned to the house.

He suffered the enormous agonies of passion
writing poems from the end backwards,

brushing away tears that had not yet fallen.

Loving her wildly as the day regressed towards morning
he watched her wringing in the garden, growing younger,
barefoot, straw-hatted.

And when she was gone and the house and the swing and daylight
there was an instant's pause before it began all over,
the reel unrolling towards the river.

ROSEMARY DOBSON

III. Levels of Response: Understanding Content

The second step in analyzing a poem occurs after the initial open-minded reading (the step we called engagement). The reader returns to the poem and rereads it, attempting to process and understand what it says, its content (subject matter, context, purpose and theme). Understanding content has two main parts to it: *clarifying the unknown* and *understanding purpose.*

A. Clarifying the Unknown

These are four logical steps in going about this:

- Check the title
- Define unfamiliar words
- Find the allusions
- Paraphrase difficult lines

CHECKING THE TITLE offers us a place to start our analysis; it is a helpful signpost which may contain key words, ideas, and images that describe the subject or give clues as to tone, mood, or the author's purpose. As a critical reader you should ask yourself questions about titles. For instance, does a title such as "Alligator Pie" foreshadow presentation of a serious or humorous subject? Would a poem called "Graduation Evening" give clues as to setting? Could a title such as "The World Is a Beautiful Place to Be Born Into" be ironic in tone?

Reprinted by permission of Meadowbrook Press and Simon & Schuster, Inc.

Titles generally do one of four things that are worth remembering:

- They clearly indicate the subject matter (e.g. "Don Quixote," "Adolescence").
- They foreshadow first, central, or recurring lines (e.g. "Because I Could Not Stop for Death," "King of Pain").
- They present necessary background information (e.g. "This Is a Photograph of Me," "5 p.m./july/the city").
- They indicate an intended audience (e.g. "To an Athlete Dying Young," "To Kate, Skating Better Than Her Date").

DEFINING UNFAMILIAR WORDS: after you have explored the title, reread the poem itself, looking up any unfamiliar words in a dictionary. It is important to be aware that most words have more than one meaning. That the 500 most commonly used English words, together, have over 14,000 meanings clearly illustrates that the primary and secondary definitions of a word may not necessarily be the ones which the poet intended. Words, incidentally, should always be defined according to how they are used in a line or sentence.

FINDING ALLUSIONS is a skill that develops as your familiarity with literature grows.

Many poems, even modern ones, may contain *allusions* (references to someone or something famous from history, myth, religion, or literature). These should be looked up in dictionaries of classical mythology[1]. Much hangs in the balance if you neglect to look up the meaning of even one unfamiliar word or allusion: a phrase, sentence, stanza, or the poem as a whole can remain unintelligible or incompletely known.

EXERCISES

1. Titles are signposts. a) What might you expect from the following titles?
   "Wondering Where the Lions Are"
   "With Age Wisdom"
   "A Narrow Fellow in the Grass"
   "To a Skylark"
   "Island Estate at St. Andrew's"
   "Frosted"
   "The Listeners"

   b) After you have stated your impressions, turn to the index to find the page numbers for these poems. c) Read them; then compare your initial expectations with the actual content of the poems. d) Make some observations about the usefulness of titles in comprehension of poetry.
2. Read the following poems and compose suitable titles for them. Compare your titles with the actual titles in the table of contents.

[1]Consult a) Zimmerman, *Dictionary of Classical Mythology*, Harper and Row; b) Jobes, G., *Dictionary of Myth, Folklore and Symbols*, Scarecrow; c) dictionaries of biblical allusions (i.e., Hastings, James, *Dictionary of the Bible*, Charles Scribner's Sons); d) general encyclopedias and literary encyclopedias (i.e., Benet, William Rose, *Reader's Encyclopedia*, Crowell). If these books fail to answer your questions about an allusion, ask your teacher or librarian to assist you.

you are reading to me

you spread the newspaper out
across your knees
it crackles dully as you fold back the pages

your heavy thumbs
pressing along the creases
leave a grey smear

PLANE DOWN ON THE BARRENS
you read

BOY TORN BY HUSKIES

TWO PERISH IN BLIZZARD

your voice is warm and exultant

I have been dead all winter
no one has noticed it
my bones, sewed up in a cheerful
print sack, balanced on the seat of a chair
answer all your questions

I shuffle into the kitchen to make tea
soft dust rises from the floor
I pour and pour
the cups remain empty

ANNE SZUMIGALSKI

(on an ancient manuscript)

Dear Aunty May,
Last week after the news I sent off some
express letters.
I sent them to

The Human Inhabitant, The White House, USA,
The Human Inhabitant, The Kremlin, USSR and
The Human Inhabitant, 10 Downing Street, UK.

Inside the letters I wrote: You must not send
people to the wars because they have told me
they don't want to kill a species they

haven't seen.
The Post Office
returned the letters to me unopened.

On the envelope they wrote: Address Unknown.

So then I sent express letters to all the Human
Inhabitants, in all the houses in the world.
Inside the letters I wrote:
STOP PRESS: If you don't want to go to the wars
(like you keep telling me) then you needn't.
There are no longer Human Inhabitants

governing the world.
The Post Office
returned all those letters to me as well:
Address Unknown.

That's how I discovered it.
The Post Office wouldn't lie.
There aren't any Human Inhabitants in the world.

There are a lot of explosions around the stars.
I feel lonely.

In case of miracles like you used to believe in
I am going to put this letter into a bottle
and throw it into the sea. Love from Eve.

JENI COUZYN

Vertigo is my territory. Man
only another movement, another shift
in the arrangement of shadows beneath my shadow,
angular, thick-boned, cumbersome, and bad meat.

I do not trouble him or the larger kind,
having no love of eating on the ground;
I kill what I can bring into my height,
what I can raise up until, terror-stunned,

they watch the dwindling of their day, perceive
the small earth small, self-cancelling, and share
the shock that is the last discovery; here
they learn abandonment of every word

and are self-rent before I rend and eat
what they already have forgotten, locked
on fear and splendour. Image me as God.
I am the final judgement and the rock.

ROBIN SKELTON

3. Read the following poem.
   a) Then discuss what meanings, associations, and effects the reader would miss by not knowing the meanings of the following words: "Sampler," "fragrant," "oblivion," "dust-bin," "open stock."
   b) What kind of "sampler" is Finch describing?
   c) Make some observations about the importance of understanding all words in an individual poem.

Sampler

You dip the tips of your fingers in other lives
As in bowls of fragrant liquid,
If the perfume displeases, you wipe the tips of your fingers
On a delicate towel of oblivion, woven over
A pattern of years, from similar disappointments.
How many bowls you have sent crashing
From the table of remembrance
To the dustbin of once upon a time!
All, happily,
open stock.

ROBERT FINCH

4. a) What myths are alluded to in the following poems?
   b) Why did Mandel use these allusions? What do they add to his poems?

Minotaur Poems

I

It has been hours in these rooms,
the opening to which, door or sash,
I have lost. I have gone from room to room
asking the janitors who were sweeping up
the brains that lay on the floors,
the bones shining in the wastebaskets,
and once I asked a suit of clothes
that collapsed at my breath and bundled
and crawled on the floor like a coward.
Finally, after several stories,
in the staired and eyed hall,
I came upon a man with the face of a bull.

II

My father was always out in the garage
building a shining wing, a wing
that curved and flew along the edge of blue air
in that streamed and sunlit room
that smelled of oil and engines
and crankcase grease, and especially
the lemon smell of polish and cedar.
Outside there were sharp rocks, and trees,
cold air where birds fell like rocks
and screams, hawks, kites, and cranes.
The air was filled with a buzzing and flying
and the invisible hum of a bee's wings was honey
in my father's framed and engined mind.
Last Saturday we saw him at the horizon
screaming like a hawk as he fell into the sun.

ELI MANDEL

PARAPHRASING DIFFICULT LINES: Another basic aspect of content that the student occasionally has to cope with is the *syntax* (the arrangement of words to form phrases, clauses, sentences). Poets sometimes make grammatical shifts or use uncommon sentence structure to gain emphasis, to organize ideas, or to develop a unique style. If you have studied some of Shakespeare's plays, you are already familiar with unusual or difficult syntax patterns in poetry.

As the following poem by e.e. cummings illustrates, some modern poetry makes similar shifts in word order which may temporarily baffle general readers:

since feeling is first

since feeling is first
who pays any attention
to the syntax of things
will never wholly kiss you;

wholly to be a fool
while Spring is in the world

my blood approves,
and kisses are a better fate
than wisdom

lady i swear by all flowers. Don't cry
—the best gesture of my brain is less than
your eyelids' flutter which says

we are for each other: then
laugh, leaning back in my arms
for life's not a paragraph

And death i think is no parenthesis

e.e. cummings

If your first reading of this poem left you completely confused, you might begin by paraphrasing the bits you do understand, and then attempting to connect or relate them:

since feeling is first who pays any attention to the syntax of things will never wholly kiss you;	feeling is more important than logic and reason
and kisses are a better fate than wisdom	love is more rewarding than knowledge
And death i think is no parenthesis	death is no limitation in the face of great love

If you stick with it, the poem will gradually untangle itself as your paraphrase becomes more complete.

It is important when paraphrasing to make certain that we are getting the gist or meaning of individual parts of the poem. The only way to test this is to compare our paraphrase with the original and to alter the wording of the paraphrase until we feel it is an accurate restatement of what the poem says.

Incidentally, this technique works well with all poems, even the more traditional four-line stanza poems which present sequence of thoughts, feelings, and experiences for our perusal:

Stopping by Woods on a Snowy Evening

Whose woods these are I think I know.
His house is in the village though;
He will not see me stopping here
To watch his woods fill up with snow.

My little horse must think it queer
To stop without a farmhouse near
Between the woods and frozen lake
The darkest evening of the year.

He gives his harness bells a shake
To ask if there is some mistake.
The only other sound's the sweep
Of easy wind and downy flake.

The woods are lovely, dark and deep,
But I have promises to keep,
And miles to go before I sleep,
And miles to go before I sleep.

ROBERT FROST

Frost's famous poem might be paraphrased one stanza at a time in the following manner:

> The speaker is uncertain whether he should be stopping on someone else's property to watch a snowfall, but decides that it does not really matter much because the owner lives in the village.
>
> He imagines the horse's parallel uncertainty about the wisdom of stopping by the woods during the dead of winter.
>
> The speaker continues to project his uncertainty about stopping, on the horse, but continues listening to the sounds of snowfall and wind.
>
> The speaker remains fascinated with the woods until he overcomes his inertia with the decision to continue on his journey.

As we can see from the above, paraphrasing gives us insight into not only the literal meaning of what is going on, but, in many cases, the main ideas, events, or movements of the poem.

EXERCISES

1. "Genuine poetry can communicate before it is understood."
   - T.S. ELIOT

   Agree or disagree with Eliot's statement.
2. Working individually, paraphrase one of the following poems. After completing the paraphrase, move into groups and com-

pare your work. Have each group vote on the best paraphrase and give the reasons for their choice.

Let me not to the marriage of true minds

Let me not to the marriage of true minds
Admit impediments. Love is not love
Which alters when it alteration finds,
Or bends with the remover to remove.
O no! it is an ever-fixèd mark
That looks on tempests and is never shaken;
It is the star to every wandering bark,
Whose worth's unknown, although his height be taken.
Love's not Time's fool, though rosy lips and cheeks
Within his bending sickle's compass come;
Love alters not with his brief hours and weeks,
But bears it out even to the edge of doom.
 If this be error and upon me proved,
 I never writ, nor no man ever loved.

WILLIAM SHAKESPEARE

The Second Coming

Turning and turning in the widening gyre
The falcon cannot hear the falconer;
Things fall apart; the center cannot hold;
Mere anarchy is loosed upon the world.
The blood-dimmed tide is loosed, and everywhere
The ceremony of innocence is drowned;
The best lack all conviction, while the worst
Are full of passionate intensity.

Surely some revelation is at hand;
Surely the Second Coming is at hand.
The Second Coming! Hardly are those words out
When a vast image out of *Spiritus Mundi*[1]
Troubles my sight: somewhere in sands of the desert
A shape with lion body and the head of a man,
A gaze blank and pitiless as the sun,
Is moving its slow thighs, while all about it
Reel shadows of the indignant desert birds.
The darkness drops again; but now I know
That twenty centuries of stony sleep

[1]Spiritus Mundi: the spirit of the universe; a "great memory" or subconscious connecting all human souls.

Were vexed to nightmare by a rocking cradle,
And what rough beast, its hour come round at last,
Slouches towards Bethlehem to be born?

WILLIAM BUTLER YEATS

Understanding the content of a poem really begins with an understanding of every part of the poem, whether these parts be titles, words, allusions, or lines and sentences. Without a thorough understanding of the parts, a reader's knowledge of the whole poem remains fragmented and incomplete. In this last section, we have outlined four simple, effective ways to increase mastery of poem content. Once the unknown has been clarified, we can move to our second phase in coming to terms with a poem's meaning.

B. Understanding Purpose

Further entry into a poem is gained by understanding what the writer's purpose is. In this next section, we are going to look at four elements that clarify what the purpose of a poem is. They are:

- Context
- Mood
- Tone
- Theme

CONTEXT (background, plot or situation) becomes clear with rereading and analysis. As we know, paraphrasing can be helpful in opening up a poem's context and meaning. The paraphrase we did of Frost's "Stopping by Woods" revealed most of the pertinent details about the poem's context and enabled us to see what was, literally, going on: a man stops his horse-drawn sleigh to watch a snowfall in secluded woods on a December evening.

But understanding context also includes such matters as identifying the speaker[1] and possible audiences. In Frost's poem, who is the speaker? It is difficult to tell, as no details of characterization are given. Therefore, the imagined speaker comes across as a general type - the harried adult who secretly longs to escape his responsibilities, whatever they might be - a person most teenage and adult readers can identify with.

The only apparent audience in the poem is the general reader, an

[1]not to be confused with the term "poet." A speaker is an imaginary character in the poem, a voice or mask which presents ideas and feelings which are not necessarily those of the poet.

invisible watcher who observes the speaker from a distance, yet who vicariously participates in his moral dilemma.

On the basis of our paraphrase and study of context, we can see that Frost wants to present an experience which explores life and death, responsibility and escape from responsibility. He presents this experience through a lyric poem which focuses on the man's and horse's responses to the natural setting.

Another example might serve to illustrate the importance of understanding contexts with speakers and audiences as a valid means of recognizing author purpose:

Getting It On

This is Sam the Man Spenser again
back for another 55 fantastic minutes
While the news was on ladies and laddies
I had one sick fella on the phone
Wanted me to play that John R. Cash song
How high's the water Momma?
Five feet high and risin
With the crest still to hit River Park
we'll have none of that   No siree
It's golden oldies all weekend
the best of early fifties rock
taking you back to where it all began
But first a public-service message
on behalf of the guys at EMO
Puh-lease stay off the telephones
at least whenever possible
Our man at Sask. Tel.
reports lines burning up
They can hardly handle the load
Guess everybody's phoning
to see how high the water is
So you take it to heart
out there in radio land
Now let's get it on again
with the hot songs from the cool fifties
If you've got a favourite
give us a call right here
at the key to the world's breadbasket
CKCB in Moose Jaw

ROBERT CURRIE

Surely the main point to grasp in reading this poem is its context. The reader must understand that he or she is listening with other imagined radio listeners to Sam the Man Spenser, a colorful radio station disc jockey, who continues to do his program during a flood in Moose Jaw.

The poem is apparently a dramatic monologue; the speaker is allowed to talk by himself without any interruptions by the poet or other imagined characters (in this case, his radio audience). Robert Currie was obviously intrigued by this type of disc jockey and his witty patter to the point that he wrote this poem. His main purpose seems to be to share an interesting, offbeat character with the readers of his poem.

TONE (the poet's or speaker's attitude toward subject or audience) can clarify what the author's purpose is. We might assume that, in "Stopping by Woods," for instance, Frost's own attitude is similar to the speaker's (i.e. that he is weary with living and tempted by the prospect of death) because there are no counterpoints to the speaker's position, and because Frost designed the poem to function as an attractive experience for speaker and reader alike.

In the poem "Getting It On," it is not absolutely clear what Currie's attitude is toward Sam the Man, but given the latter's uninterrupted running commentary, and its odd juxtapositions in serious and humorous lines and images, we might assume that the poet finds the announcer to be a personable, entertaining character who is unflappable in a crisis.

MOOD (the state of mind or feelings created in the reader by a poem) also contributes to a sense of the poem's purpose. In "Stopping by Woods," the poem's lines cast a drowsy, almost hypnotic spell over the reader as well as the speaker, reinforcing the latter's desire to rest and enjoy the seductive but deadly beauty of the snowfall in the woods.

In contrast, the mood in "Getting It On" is one of light humor. We recognize the sort of person being described and smile, or chuckle if we have never encountered anyone like this before.

Understanding mood and tone, perceiving speakers, audiences, and poem types are all essential, related activities in the comprehension of a poem's purpose or context. There is also another component which may help us to understand the poem even better – theme.

THEME is a central idea or message. The themes of most poems can be concisely worded in a sentence or two, called the thematic statement. The thematic statement is a general point about some aspect of life or the human condition addressed by the poem. Similar to writing paraphrases, writing thematic statements provides opportunities for the student to compose a personal interpretation of what he or she has read.

Thematic statements can be derived in a number of ways. Sometimes it helps to jot down key words, fragments, phrases, or associations as we reread a poem, sort of an outline of our impressions of its meaning. For "Stopping by Woods," we might have composed a list of notes as follows:

> "stopping"
> stopping "queer"
> "Mistake" - error: to do what? stop?
> "dark" repeated - dark-what? death? stopping?
> "promises" such as? promises-what? responsibilities? Obligations?
> "miles", "sleep" repeated
> "miles"-road to travel, life to live (travelling)
> "sleep"-go to sleep, death (stopping)

Such a list can be a resource to assist us in putting our thoughts and feelings together in a generalized statement covering the entire poem: although we sometimes desire release from our human obligations, we are more likely to choose to carry on with life and its burdens than give in to the tempting prospects of death and its peace. Composing thematic statements can help clarify a poet's purpose: it can also clarify our own innermost feelings and thoughts about a poem.

So, to summarize, our second level of response, understanding content, depends on the following:

1. *Clarifying the Unknown*
   a. Checking the Title
   b. Defining Unfamiliar Words
   c. Finding Allusions
   d. Paraphrasing Difficult Lines

2. *Understanding Purpose*
   a. Context
   b. Tone

c. Mood
d. Theme

EXERCISES

1. Why do readers often disagree on what a poem means? What factors can lead to different interpretations?
2. What factors could make one interpretation more valid than another?
3. Should the reader take the poet's life into consideration in interpreting a poem?
4. What advice would you have for someone who says he or she "does not" understand poetry"?
5. Identify the a) poem type, b) context, c) mood, d) tone, and e) theme of the following poems:

The White Buffalo

The indian warriors
are brown photographs
of battlefields

bleached altars telling
with soft wooden words

how the eagle soars
over the skull of the snake

how the thunder of bison
will crack the earth
like clay

how the scales of the dragon
are sown as corn
and grow tall
in the hearts of the brave

They color their faces
with earth warpaint

they wait in the snow
outside their tents
for dawn to creep
from under the claw
of the night

They went into battle
armed with the curse
of a mad shaman

they crumbled
as the birch falls

in a fire of feathers
and screaming ponies

SUSAN LANDELL

To Autumn

I

Season of mists and mellow fruitfulness,
Close bosom-friend of the maturing sun;
Conspiring with him how to load and bless
With fruit the vines that round the thatch-eves run;
To bend with apples the moss'd cottage-trees,
And fill all fruit with ripeness to the core;
To swell the gourd, and plump the hazel shells
With a sweet kernel; to set budding more,
And still more, later flowers for the bees,
Until they think warm days will never cease,
For Summer has o'er-brimm'd their clammy cells.

II

Who hath not seen thee oft amid thy store?
Sometimes whoever seeks abroad may find
Thee sitting careless on a granary floor,
Thy hair soft-lifted by the winnowing wind;
Or on a half-reap'd furrow sound asleep,
Drowsed with the fume of poppies, while thy hook
Spares the next swath and all its twinèd flowers:
And sometimes like a gleaner thou dost keep
Steady thy laden head across a brook;
Or by a cyder-press, with patient look,
Thou watchest the last oozings hours by hours.

III

Where are the songs of Spring? Ay, where are they?
Think not of them, thou hast thy music too,—
While barred clouds bloom the soft-dying day,
And touch the stubble-plains with rosy hue;
Then in a wailful choir the small gnats mourn
Among the river sallows, borne aloft

Or sinking as the light wind lives or dies;
And full-grown lambs loud bleat from hilly bourn;
Hedge-crickets sing; and now with treble soft
The red-breast whistles from a garden-croft;
And gathering swallows twitter in the skies.

JOHN KEATS

IV. Levels of Response: Form Develops Content

Assuming we can identify the *content* of the poem (the "what" of the communication; the subject matter), we might now go on to look at some of the features that make the poem work – the *form* (the "how" which develops the "what"). If we understand how form reinforces content, we begin to appreciate some of the art and craftmanship that went into the creation of the poem.

For the writer, form is a means to an end; it is how the purpose of writing is accomplished. To write a humorous poem, a poet might use a limerick form or hyperbole. To tell a story, he or she will probably opt for the ballad format with its four-line rhyming stanzas.

In our consideration of form, you will encounter several terms or concepts used to describe techniques poets use. These terms or concepts are meaningful only when they are used as tools to help us understand a poem and talk or write about it. In other words, they should not be learned for their own sake; rather, students should attempt to understand the proper terms by actively using them while discussing poems.

A. Technique

Technique refers to the basic methods used by the poet to organize a poem; it includes selection of and order of subject matter.

SELECTION OF SUBJECT MATTER is an important stage in the artistic process. In "Stopping by Woods," on page 126, what does Frost choose to show? What does he leave out?

The first significant thing to note is that Frost has chosen a

The first significant thing to note is that Frost has chosen a middleman (the speaker) to present personal feelings about the scene. The reason for this is that we can more easily identify with the unknown traveller who describes the scene and how he feels about it than we might with Frost's own personal observations about a snowfall and obligations.

Everything Frost says about the speaker is purposely vague. The specific destination of the traveller is never indicated, making it easier for us vicariously to imagine both Frost's and the speaker's destinations, which, in turn, results in a closer identification between us and the poem.

The beauty and mystery of the scene give rise to the speaker's feelings which are a key feature of the poem ("The woods are lovely, dark, and deep"). The poet also wants to emphasize the solitude and drama of the scene, so he mentions the horse's anxious reactions which, of course, form a counterpoint to the speaker's desire for rest. Another detail that reinforces the feeling of solitude is the very brief mention of the owner who lives in the village, which means that the speaker is quite free to stop and revel in the woods' loveliness as long as he wishes.

ORDER OF SUBJECT MATTER is a second important consideration in looking at technique. Does the poet use a *chronological* (based on time), *spatial* (based on space or place), or *ennumerative* order (most important to least important or vice-versa)? Is comparison-contrast used? What line structure does the poet use? How has the poem been divided? What form of poetry has been used? Free verse? Four-line stanzas? Why? Answers to questions like these about order naturally depend again upon the writer's purpose.

In "Stopping by Woods," Frost uses both chronological and spatial orders. In treating the speaker's experiences in their order of occurrence, he uses a chronological arrangement. The use of a spatial order is also evident in the poem's movement from the speaker to the horse, then back to the speaker. Rhyming four-line stanzas develop the seductive sounds of the snowfall by the forest, impel the reader toward the conclusion, and eventually approximate the speaker's thoughts, especially in the repeated lines of the last stanza which emphasize the speaker's weary resolve to carry on with living.

Poets enhance their writing through the techniques of order and selection of subject matter. Similarly, style is another aspect of form which can add to the presentation of a poem.

B. Style

Style refers to the unique way in which the poet writes, as reflected in the use of a) diction, b) figurative devices, c) rhythm, and d) sound.

DICTION is choice of words. Diction helps create or reinforce a poem's mood and tone. Word choice can operate on a number of levels: simple/complex, formal/colloquial, denotative/connotative, literal/figural.

In "Stopping by Woods," Frost uses simple, one or two syllable nouns (e.g. "woods," "house," "horse," "lake") to convey a sense of the natural setting's simplicity, starkness, and solitude ("He will not see me stopping here/To watch his woods fill up with snow").

He introduces adjectives very sparingly. In stanza two, "frozen" and "darkest" are used to emphasize the coldness of the evening and season. In addition to carefully selected nouns and adjectives, Frost uses key connotative words such as "dark," "mistake," "promises," "miles," and "sleep" to reinforce the various moods and tensions of the speaker's mind.

FIGURATIVE DEVICES are another ingredient of style. The "woods" of Frost's poem, for instance, are a symbol; they represent a stopping place or retreat from life, possibly death. Travelling, on the other hand, seems to be identified with life in the speaker's and the critical reader's minds. The personification of the horse is a clever stroke designed to emphasize the solitude of the horse and its master from the company of others. The personification and symbols, like any figures of speech, add a richness and depth to the deceptively simple surface situation of the poem.

RHYTHM is yet another facet of style. The predominant iambic rhythm of "Stopping by Woods" creates a lulling effect on the reader similar to that created on the speaker by the scene he watches. This rhythm reinforces the attractive, dreamy quality of Frost's poem. Later, the repeated rhythms of the last two lines simultaneously suggest the speaker's tiredness and resignation.

SOUND is the final, but by no means least, component of style. Frost creates the effects of foreshadowing (notice how "here" in stanza 1 anticipates the predominant rhymes in stanza 2), suspense (about whether the "deep" woods will override the promises to "keep"), and climax (in the repetition of "sleep") through his deliberately planned end-line rhyme structure. The last stanza's rhymes, along with the "e" assonance, support the general impression that the speaker is weary with life. Other sounds such as the "d" consonance (eg. "woods," "dark," deep") in the last stanza contribute to the reader's sense of the dreamy seductiveness of the woods.

Diction, figures of speech, rhythm, and sound are all key formal elements of style in poetry. As the discussion and examples for each element pointed out, the critical reader should always take care to consider single stylistic features in terms of their overall purpose within a poem.

EXERCISES

1. What other elements of style not identified in the chapter do you notice in "since feeling is first," and "Getting It On"?
2. Take one of the following poems and analyze it in terms of form (techniques and style). You will have to decide first what the poem is about before you can accomplish your task, so pair up with another student to share your initial impressions of content first.

The Back Road Farm

This house is built within a sheltering
Sweep of the hills. You will not find the sea
From attic windows; and the seasons bring
No lift and change of tide, here in the lee
Of the land's high windbreak, where the buffeting
Onshore wind is tripped on the mountain's knee.
No mist of blowing salt is flung to sting
The trusting flesh. You will not find the sea.

This property is private. Drifting rain
Beats on its shingles and its native stone;
The wind of August on its leaning grain
Is dark with a shadow, and the leaves are blown
To a soft thunder. But the hills remain;
Their strength is certain and their purpose known.
Only at night, in the stillness, low and plain
You can hear the far deep rumor of sea on stone.

CHARLES BRUCE

Pioneer

He laboured, starved, and ploughed:
In these last days
Cities roar where his voice
In lonely wilderness first sang out praise.

Out of the forest, walls,
From rock, the wheat:
Winters to chill the heart
That slowly withers in the summer's heat.

Out of the fight, desire
Re-born each spring
To leave some mark behind—
High harvest for the autumn's gathering.

What labourer could dream
The axe's chime
And swiftly builded house
Would mean a city in so brief a time

He sits with folded hands
And burns to see
How he has ravaged earth
Of her last stone, her last, most stubborn tree.

DOROTHY LIVESAY

V. Levels of Response: Evaluation

Evaluation is an informed verdict on the effectiveness, relevance, and overall value of a poem. It is properly reached after steps II, III and IV have been completed. Evaluation gives you a chance to synthesize your thoughts about the poem, to put them together following analysis. It can be done in a number of ways. Here are four suggestions:

- Using your past life experience, relate the poem to yourself and others, establishing its relevance and value.
- If you already know the poet's work, compare the poem to others by the same poet.

- Compare the poem to others written by the poet's contemporaries, or to other works (including drama and fiction) on the same subject written by authors of any time or place.
- Evaluate the poem according to certain personal criteria or standards of what makes good poetry, literature, or art.

Using the above suggestions, here are some concluding remarks about the Frost poem:

1. The poem echoes real feelings and wishes that we all periodically have of wanting to retreat from life's cares, problems, and responsibilities.
2. If we compare this poem to certain others by Frost (e.g. "Out, Out –" p. 283; "Departmental" p. 69; or "Birches" in the following Exercises), we notice that the poet is preoccupied with the subject of death.
3. We might compare the poem to others which cover the subject, say Leonard Cohen's "The Bus" or James Dickey's "Inside the River," both printed in the following Exercises, and conclude that escape into nature from urban life seems to be a recurrent idea in modern poetry.
4. We might comment on the richness of the poem's associations or the poet's uncanny ability to draw the reader into the poem, making him or her feel what the speaker feels.

EXERCISES

1. Compare and contrast Frost's "Birches" with "Stopping by Woods" according to: a) views on life and b) attitudes toward nature and human society.

Birches

When I see birches bend to left and right
Across the lines of straighter darker trees,
I like to think some boy's been swinging them.
But swinging doesn't bend them down to stay
As ice-storms do. Often you must have seen them
Loaded with ice a sunny winter morning
After a rain. They click upon themselves
As the breeze rises, and turn many-colored
As the stir cracks and crazes their enamel.
Soon the sun's warmth makes them shed crystal shells

Shattering and avalanching on the snow-crust—
Such heaps of broken glass to sweep away
You'd think the inner dome of heaven had fallen.
They are dragged to the withered bracken by the load,
And they seem not to break; though once they are bowed
So low for long, they never right themselves:
You may see their trunks arching in the woods
Years afterwards, trailing their leaves on the ground
Like girls on hands and knees that throw their hair
Before them over their heads to dry in the sun.
But I was going to say when Truth broke in
With all her matter-of-fact about the ice-storm
I should prefer to have some boy bend them
As he went out and in to fetch the cows—
Some boy too far from town to learn baseball,
Whose only play was what he found himself,
Summer or winter, and could play alone.
One by one he subdued his father's trees
By riding them down over and over again
Until he took the stiffness out of them,
And not one but hung limp, not one was left
For him to conquer. He learned all there was
To learn about not launching out too soon
And so not carrying the tree away
Clear to the ground. He always kept his poise
To the top branches, climbing carefully
With the same pains you use to fill a cup
Up to the brim, and even above the brim.
Then he flung outward, feet first, with a swish,
Kicking his way down through the air to the ground.
So was I once myself a swinger of birches.
And so I dream of going back to be.
It's when I'm weary of considerations,
And life is too much like a pathless wood
Where your face burns and tickles with the cobwebs
Broken across it, and one eye is weeping
From a twig's having lashed across it open.
I'd like to get away from earth awhile
And then come back to it and begin over.
May no fate willfully misunderstand me
And half grant what I wish and snatch me away
Not to return. Earth's the right place for love:
I don't know where it's likely to go better.
I'd like to go by climbing a birch tree,
And climb black branches up a snow-white trunk

Toward heaven, till the tree could bear no more,
But dipped its top and set me down again.
That would be good both going and coming back.
One could do worse than be a swinger of birches.

ROBERT FROST

2. Compare what "Stopping by Woods" and the following two poems have to say about: a) life in cities and towns, (b) escape into nature, and c) the consequences of such escapes.

The Bus

I was the last passenger of the day,
I was alone on the bus,
I was glad they were spending all that money
just getting me up Eighth Avenue.
Driver! I shouted, it's you and me tonight,
let's run away from this big city
to a smaller city more suitable to the heart,
let's drive past the swimming pools of Miami Beach,
you in the driver's seat, me several seats back,
but in the racial cities we'll change places
so as to show how well you've done up North,
and let us find ourselves some tiny American fishing village
in unknown Florida
and park right at the edge of the sand,
a huge bus pointing out,
metallic, painted, solitary,
with New York plates.

LEONARD COHEN

Inside the River

Dark, deeply. A red.
All levels moving
A given surface.
Break this. Step down.
Follow your right
Foot nakedly in
To another body.
Put on the river

Like a fleeing coat,
A garment of motion,
Tremendous, immortal.
Find a still root

To hold you in it.
Let flowing create
A new, inner being:
As the source in the mountain
Gives water in pulses,
These can be felt at
The heart of the current.
And here it is only
One wandering step
Forth, to the sea.
Your freed hair floating
Out of your brain,

Wait for a coming
And swimming idea.
Live like the dead
In their flying feeling.
Loom as a ghost
When life pours through it.
Crouch in the secret
Released underground
With the earth of the fields
All around you, gone
Into purposeful grains
That stream like dust

In a holy hallway.
Weight more changed
Than that of one
Now being born,
Let go the root.
Move with the world
As the deep dead move,
Opposed to nothing.
Release. Enter the sea
Like a winding wind.
No. Rise, Draw breath.
Sing. See no one.

JAMES DICKEY

3. Write a two or three paragraph evaluation of any other poem which appeared in this chapter. Write your evaluation so that it might be delivered as a special feature of C.B.C. radio.
4. Can a reader say a poem is excellent, but still dislike it strongly? Comment.

VI. Some Last Words on Analysis

We have now reached the end of our discussion of the stages of analysis. In the process, you have seen a fairly close reading of one poem in detail, the classic "Stopping by Woods on a Snowy Evening." A question remains: what do we have at the end of the procedure?

Obviously, we have dealt with the poem at a rational level and have developed a reasonable explanation of the poem's meaning – a typical by-product of critical reading. This does not mean, however, that we have somehow captured the poem's "essence" in our thematic statement or paraphrase.

In fact, if you stop to compare any of the paraphrases or thematic statements in this chapter to the original poems, you will notice that something is missing: a certain richness of language and intensity of experience, thought, and feeling that can only be truly conveyed by the poem's own words themselves. Dylan Thomas said that, "You can tear a poem apart to see what makes it technically tick . . . [but you always come] back [to] the mystery of having been moved by words."

As Archibald MacLeish and the authors pointed out in Chapter 6, a poem must "be" as well as mean. It must be read as an experience as well as a source of critical analysis. It has other dimensions which ultimately and inevitably elude our presumptuous attempts at analysis. Nowhere is this fact more plain than when we ponder the classics, written by literary giants such as Shakespeare and Blake. At such times we may begin to feel that analysis seems to be a pointless, somewhat absurd exercise. In the presence of something larger than us, we are often not so much the judges as the ones being judged.

Sometimes our critical questions such as "Is this a good poem?" need to be set aside in favor of more realistic ones such as "Do *we* measure up to the poem's greatness and largeness of vision?" or "What do our readings tell us about ourselves?" Such humility keeps our critical responses within the bounds of reason, and our analysis of poetry in its proper perspective.

FOLLOW-UP

I. Critical Analysis: What and Why?

1. A recent letter to the editor in your local paper spoke out against the time devoted to analyzing poetry in senior English classes. The author maintained that good poetry was art to be appreciated, not analyzed. Write a letter to the editor arguing against or supporting the writer's stand.
2. Select any poem from Chapter 8, "Poems for Further Study," and read it through. As you read, note any questions that come to mind. Pair up with someone else in class and exchange poems as well as questions. Study your partner's selected poem and try to answer his or her questions. After you have both finished,

exchange views on the poems until you are satisfied that you both understand each selection. In a paragraph, record your thoughts about the experience.

II. Levels of Response: Engagement

3. Choose a poem from Chapter 8. Read it through until you are satisfied you understand it, then do the following:
   a. Explain what you think of the poem and why,
   b. Tell what your father or mother might think of it and why,
   c. Explain how a nine-year-old might feel about the poem and why,
   d. Comment on whether the poem you picked would appeal only to a certain kind of person.

III. Levels of Response: Understanding Content

4. Choose a poem from Chapter 8:
   a. analyze the significance of the title,
   b. look up any unfamiliar words and allusions,
   c. paraphrase any difficult lines,
   d. draw some conclusions about the poem's purpose and meaning.
5. Choose a poem from Chapter 8 and
   a. describe the context,
   b. comment on the tone,
   c. comment on the mood,
   d. compose a thematic statement.

IV. Levels of Response: Form Develops Content

6. Comment on how the following elements develop the content of a poem of your choice from Chapter 8:
   a. Technique
      - Selection of Subject Matter
      - Order of Subject Matter
   b. Style
      - Diction
      - Figurative Devices
      - Rhythm
      - Sound

V. Levels of Response: Evaluation

7. The United Nations has decided to preserve for the future, examples of fine world literature. They have asked for the

general public to submit briefs defending particular works. Choose a poem that you think deserves to be preserved as a significant work of art and write a brief giving reasons for your choice.

VI. Some Last Words on Analysis

8. Have a debate in class on whether beauty is something residing in the eye of the beholder or in the individual poem.
9. In this chapter section, it was suggested that analyzing poetry of great writers is a presumptuous activity. In his famous book *Walden,* Henry David Thoreau stated that "the works of great poets have never yet been read by mankind, for only great poets can read them."

   Imagine that this quotation has been used by a supporter of Thoreau's comment in a magazine article. Write a letter to the editor, agreeing or disagreeing with Thoreau's view. Make it clear how you think poetry by great writers should be regarded by general and critical readers.

RELATED POEMS IN CHAPTER 8:

CHAPTER 8

POEMS FOR FURTHER STUDY

Wit and Humor

You Held Out the Light

You held out the light to light my cigarette
But when I leaned down to the flame
It singed my eyebrows and my hair;
Now it is always the same—no matter where
We meet, you burn me.
I must always stop and rub my eyes
And beat the living fire from my hair.

GWENDOLYN MACEWEN

1. Explain the appropriateness of the image in the poem's opening line.
2. The poem uses fire imagery to describe a relationship. How is the speaker affected by the "you" she refers to?
3. In what way is the effect of this poem largely dependent upon surprise and arrangement of images in order of impact?
4. Working in small groups, compare the imagery used in this poem with that used in "Paper Matches" by Paulette Jiles. What similarities are there? Which do you prefer?
5. Write a poem from the perspective of the "you" in the poem. How does that person see the poem's speaker?

Frosted

Standing on the bus stop bench
arms vined they
kick in unison like
two from a can-can line
slicing exhaust-filled air
with melody.

"Probably" says the waiting man
leather coat clutched
against their winter show,
"probably they're high on drugs."

CAROLYN REDL-HLUS

1. In what way do the two dancers contrast with their environment?
2. What does the waiting man reveal about his character? Is his reaction a typical one? Comment.
3. Explain the pun in the poem's title.
4. What feelings does the speaker have about the dancers and the man?
5. Write a sequel to this poem, called "Defrosted", in which the waiting man learns something about people.
6. Improvise the circumstances of this poem and carry it further to show the conversation that develops between the speaker and the waiting man. You might involve the dancers, too.

A Glass of Beer

The lanky hank of a she in the inn over there
Nearly killed me for asking the loan of a glass of beer;
May the devil grip the whey-faced slut by the hair,
And beat bad manners out of her skin for a year.

That parboiled ape, with the toughest jaw you will see
On virtue's path, and a voice that would rasp the dead,
Came roaring and raging the minute she looked at me,
And threw me out of the house on the back of my head!

If I asked her master he'd give me a cask a day;
But she, with the beer at hand, not a gill would arrange!

May she marry a ghost and bear him a kitten, and may
The High King of Glory permit her to get the mange.

JAMES STEPHENS

1. What emotion dominates the poem?
2. How does the author use imagery and sounds to convey that emotion?
3. What caused the speaker to be in such a mood?
4. Explain the irony that gives the poem its humor.
5. Script a scene in which the "waitress" explains to her "master" that she threw the speaker out of the inn.

Epitaph intended for his wife

Here lies my wife: here let her lie!
Now she's at rest, and so am I.

JOHN DRYDEN

1. What does this couplet suggest about the relationship between the speaker and his wife?
2. What emotion does the couplet express?
3. Explain the pun in the poem's second line.
4. What is an epitaph? How does the title add to the poem's irreverent humor?
5. Soon, you will be finished this stage of your schooling. Write an epitaph for your high school years. What would you like said about you as a student?

There was a young lady of Gimli

There was a young lady of Gimli
Who sought to walk slender and slimly.
    She won her heart's wish
    On a diet of fish
And the gravedigger smiled rather grimly.

WALTER KIRKCONNELL

There was a young man from Perth

There was a young man from Perth,
Who was born on the day of his birth.
He was wed, so they say,
On his wife's wedding day,
And he died on his last day on earth.

JOHN ROBERT COLUMBO

1. Which limerick requires the reader to draw an inference? What is the inference? What is the irony in the limerick?
2. What is the appeal of the second limerick?
3. Comment on the effectiveness of the words "slender and slimly" and "grimly" in the first limerick.
4. Which limerick can be seen as satirical? Explain.
5. Compose an original limerick that (a) summarizes a fictional character's life, as in the second limerick, or (b) makes fun of a current fad or fashion, as in the first limerick.

Lord Randal

"O where ha you been, Lord Randal, my son?
And where ha you been, my handsome young man?
"I ha been at the greenwood; mother, mak my bed soon,
For I'm wearied wi hunting, and fain[1] wad lie down."

"An wha met ye there, Lord Randal, my son?
An wha met you there, my handsome young man?"
"O I met wi my true-love; mother, mak my bed soon,
For I'm wearied wi huntin, an fain wad lie down."

"And what did she give you, Lord Randal, my son?
And what did she give you, my handsome young man?"
"Eels fried in a pan; mother, mak my bed soon,
For I'm wearied wi huntin, and fain wad lie down."

"And wha gat your leavins[2], Lord Randal, my son?
And wha gat your leavins, my handsome young man?"
"My hawks and my hounds; mother, mak my bed soon,
For I'm wearied wi hunting, and fain wad lie down."

"And what becam of them Lord Randal, my son?
And what becam of them, my handsome young man?"

[1]fain: willingly, gladly
[2]leavins: leftovers, remnants

"They stretched their legs out an died; mother, mak my bed soon,
For I'm wearied wi huntin, and fain wad lie down."

"O I fear you are poisoned, Lord Randal, my son!
I fear you are poisoned, my handsome young man!"
"O yes, I am poisoned; mother, mak my bed soon,
For I'm sick at the heart, and I fain wad lie down."

"What d'ye leave to your mother, Lord Randal, my son?
What d'ye leave to your mother, my handsome young man?"
"Four and twenty milk kye[2]; mother, mak my bed soon,
For I'm sick at the heart, and I fain wad lie down."

"What d'ye leave to your sister, Lord Randal, my son?
What d'ye leave to your sister, my handsome young man?"
"My gold and my silver; mother, mak my bed soon,
For I'm sick at the heart, an I fain wad lie down."

"What d'ye leave to your brother, Lord Randal, my son?
What d'ye leave to your brother, my handsome young man?"
"My houses and my lands; mother, mak my bed soon,
For I'm sick at the heart, and I fain wad lie down."

"What d'ye leave to your true-love, Lord Randal, my son?
What d'ye leave to your true-love, my handsome young man?"
"I leave her hell and fire; mother, mak my bed soon,
For I'm sick at the heart, and I fain wad lie down."

ANONYMOUS

After the Ballad "Lord Randall, My Son"

"O where have you been, my baby, my son?
O who scratched your face, my poor little one?"
"The rose tore my cheek; Mother wrap me up warm
And hold me and rock me and keep me from harm."

"You're bruised near to dying, my school-boy, my son,
Your nose is all bloody; who bullied my man?"
"The girls are so rough; Mother, wash my face clean
And stay close beside me and feed me ice-cream."

"What makes you so sad, my young man, my son
Who dares to refuse you, my handsome one?"

[2]kye: cattle

"She laughed at my love; Mother make my bed soon
And kiss me good-night for I fain would lie down."

"You'll not go to war, my only, my son?
Your heart has a murmur, you're barely full grown."
"You cut off my feet, Mother, stumps cannot stand,
And look, they still bleed for you're licking your hand."

ANNE WILKINSON

1. Study the original version of "Lord Randal." In your own words, summarize the plot.
2. The original version is a traditional ballad, originally composed to be sung. What features does the poem have that would make it easy to sing?
3. Traditional ballads were handed down through many generations. In order for a poem to survive through centuries, it must have a strong appeal. What is appealing about the original version of "Lord Randal"?
4. Study "After the Ballad 'Lord Randall, My Son'." What point is Wilkinson making through her parody?
5. What similarities are there between the original version and the parody?
6. What advantages did Wilkinson gain by parodying "Lord Randal"? Is her poem effective? Comment.

Pullman Porter

The porter in the Pullman car
Was charming, as they sometimes are.
He scanned my baggage tags: "Are you
The man who wrote of Lady Lou?"
When I said "yes" he made a fuss—
Oh, he was most assiduous;:
And I was pleased to think that he
Enjoyed my brand of poetry.

He was forever at my call.
So when we got to Montreal
And he had brushed me off, I said:
"I'm glad my poems you have read.
I feel quite flattered, I confess,
And if you give me your address
I'll send you (autographed, of course)
One of my little books of verse."

He smiled—his teeth were white as milk:
He spoke—his voice was soft was silk.
I recognized, despite his skin,
The perfect gentleman within.
Then courteously he made reply:
"I thank you kindly, Sir, but I
With many other cherished tome
Have all your books of verse at home.

"When I was quite a little boy
I used to savour them with joy;
And now my daughter, aged three,
Can tell the tale of Sam McGee;
While Tom, my son, that's only two,
Has heard the yarn of Dan McGrew. . . .
Don't think your stuff I'm not applaudin'"—
My taste is Eliot and Auden."

So as we gravely bade adieu
I felt quite snubbed—and so would you.
And yet I shook him by the hand,
Impressed that he could understand
The works of those two tops I mention.
So far beyond *my* comprehension—
A humble bard of boys and barmen.
Disdained, alas! by Pullman carmen.

ROBERT SERVICE

1. What were the duties of a porter in a Pullman car? How did this porter do in carrying out his duties?
2. What assumption did the author make about the porter's interest in his poetry? How did the author react to the porter's preference for Eliot and Auden?
3. According to the porter, what appeal does the author's writing have?
4. Is the porter a general or a critical reader? What has shaped his taste in poetry?

This Poem Leaves No Survivors

this poem collects
things but it
leaves no survivors.

it's not surprising that
you come here
expecting the worst
since we all
carry murder around
like baby pictures in a wallet.
it's too late to scream
this poem is soundproof
and if you try
to tear your
eyes away the page
will wrench them
back.
i didn't want to
resort to this but
you stood too long
jingling your change.

ROBERT HILLES

1. What "things" does the poem collect? How does it collect?
2. In what way does the poem leave "no survivors"?
3. What does the reader expect from this poem, according to the speaker?
4. What attitude is suggested by the phrase "jingling your change"? Why would the speaker resort to a hypnotic, almost violent approach to capture the attention of a reader who stands too long jingling his change?
5. What does this poem have to saying about the relationship between the reader, the writer, and the poem?
6. Write a poem of your own in which you assume the voice of someone who has been captured and imprisoned inside a book of poetry.

WIT AND HUMOR

1. Write a parody of "You Held Out the Light" based on another chivalrous action, such as opening a car door or pulling out a dining-table chair.
2. Which poem in this section is the most humorous? What makes it so funny?

3. "Epitaph intended for his wife" is both an epitaph and a couplet. What other humorous epitaphs or couplets have you heard? Compose an epitaph the wife might have written had their positions been reversed.
4. Which poem's humor is based on the absurd? What is appealing about absurdity?
5. Research and find a humorous poem you would like to see included in this unit of study. Working with a small group, record your poem with those of the other group members. As the tape is played for the class, each group member might introduce his or her poem.

Puzzle Poems

The Griesly Wife

"Lie still, my newly married wife,
  Lie easy as you can.
You're young and ill accustomed yet
  To sleeping with a man."

The snow lay thick, the moon was full
  And shone across the floor.
The young wife went with never a word
  Barefooted to the door.

He up and followed sure and fast,
  The moon shone clear and white.
But before his coat was on his back
  His wife was out of sight.

He trod the trail wherever it turned
  By many a mound and scree,[1]
And still the barefoot track led on,
  And an angry man was he.

He followed fast, he followed slow,
  And still he called her name,
But only the dingoes of the hills
  Yowled back at him again.

---

[1]*scree*—steep, rocky slope

His hair stood up along his neck,
  His angry mind was gone,
For the track of the two bare feet gave out
  And a four-foot track went on.

Her nightgown lay upon the snow
  As it might upon the sheet,
But the track that led from where it lay
  Was never of human feet.

His heart turned over in his chest,
  He looked from side to side,
And he thought more of his gumwood fire
  Than he did of his griesly[2] bride.

And first he started walking back
  And then began to run,
And his quarry wheeled at the end of her track
  And hunted him in turn.

Oh, long the fire may burn for him
  And open stand the door,
And long the bed may wait empty:
  He'll not be back any more.

JOHN MANIFOLD

1. Where is the poem set? How do you know?
2. In your own words, tell about the events of each stanza.
3. Look up the characteristics of the *ballad* in the glossary (p. 334) and tell which ballad features this poem has.
4. "Like most good writing, poetry's subject matter is a blend of the familiar and the unfamiliar." Discuss this statement with references to this poem.

A narrow Fellow in the Grass

A narrow Fellow in the Grass
Occasionally rides—
You may have met Him—did you not
His notice sudden is—

---

[2]*griesly*—frightful, ghastly

The Grass divides as with a Comb—
A spotted shaft is seen—
And then it closes at your feet
And opens further on—

He likes a Boggy Acre
A Floor too cool for Corn—
Yet when a Boy, and Barefoot—
I more than once at Noon
Have passed, I thought, a Whip lash
Unbraiding in the Sun
When stooping to secure it
It wrinkled, and was gone—

Several of Nature's People
I know, and they know me—
I feel for them a transport
Of cordiality—

But never met this Fellow
Attended, or alone
Without a tighter breathing
And Zero at the Bone—

EMILY DICKINSON

1. Who or what is the "narrow fellow"?
   What lines and images support your opinion?
2. What is meant by "His notice sudden is"?
3. Compose a riddle about another of "nature's people." See if anyone in class can guess which creature you are describing.

In the pond in the park
all things are doubled:
Long buildings hang and
wriggle gently. Chimneys
are bent legs bouncing
on clouds below. A flag
wags like a fishhook
down there in the sky.

The arched stone bridge
is an eye, with underlid
in the water. In its lens
dip crinkled heads with hats

that don't fall off. Dogs go by,
barking on their backs.
A baby, taken to feed the
ducks, dangles upside-down,
a pink balloon for a buoy.

Treetops deploy a haze of
cherry bloom for roots,
Where birds coast belly-up
in the glass bowl of a hill;
from its bottom a bunch
of peanut-munching children
is suspended by their
sneakers, waveringly.

A swan, with twin necks
forming the figure three,
steers between two dimpled
towers doubled. Fondly
hissing, she kisses herself,
and all the scene is troubled:
water-windows splinter,
tree-limbs tangle, the bridge
folds like a fan.

MAY SWENSON

1. What does the poem describe?
2. Compose a suitable title for this selection (the poem's actual title is in the table of contents).
3. Select three or four lines that you like. Tell what you like about these lines.

Oh No

If you wander far enough
you will come to it
and when you get there
they will give you a place to sit

for yourself only, in a nice chair
and all your friends will be there
with smiles on their faces
and they will likewise all have places.

ROBERT CREELEY

1. Where is "there"?
2. Why is the poem called "Oh No"?
3. In your opinion, is this a good poem? Explain.

Seven Natural Songs

1 Awoke and stretched in all the bodies
lofted on sinewy air. Clipped out
beak-shaped cries and skinned the mist
from the morning.

2 Stood wooden, wiggled in earth way under.
A toenail scraped a mammoth's tusk.
Jounced and jittered all these lippy leaves.

3 Slicked along meddling with rocks. Tore
their ears off gradually. Sparkling made
them hop and holler down a slate-cold throat.

4 Humped up, sucked in all my thongs
belly-deep to the roaring core. Recoiled
for a big yellow bloom. Burst and hurled
wide open pods of light everywhere.

5 Loosened and lolled elongate in hammocks
of blue. Evasive of shape and the eggshell's
curve. Without taint or tint or substance
dissolved in fleecy sloth.

6 Pricked up out of each pore, urgent, ambitious,
itching to be even. Scurried and spread
so all is kept level. Forever unfinished
my mass fernal mystery. Ants read its roots,
tell its juices to sand.

7 Once cloud, now all memory my motion.
Amorphous creeping slow as sleep to a full
black gulping flood. The small five fingered
blot enlarged beyond identity. Heavy, unslaked,
still hunting form. The hiding place,
the necessary horror.

MAY SWENSON

1. Working in small groups of two or three students, identify the different aspects or phenomena of nature being described.

2. Using simple images and figures of speech, make your own "natural song" about some aspect of nature or an animal. Everyone will submit a "natural song" which will be collected in a class booklet which can be traded with another class for a similar booklet. Both classes will try to guess the solutions for the various "songs."
3. Write a description of an ordinary, everyday scene that is distorted to the human eye: e.g. your reflection in a water tap, the view through a fish-eye camera lens, the view in a distorting rear-view car mirror. Read your description to the class and see if anyone can identify the scene.

NEWFOUNDLAND

(for E.J. Pratt)

n ***e*** w f o u n ***d*** l a n d
n e w ***f*** ***o*** ***u*** ***n*** ***d*** l a n d
n ***e*** ***w*** f o u n d ***l*** ***a*** ***n*** ***d***
n e w f ***o*** u ***n*** d l a n d
n e w f ***o*** u n d ***l*** a n ***d***
n e w ***f*** ***o*** u n d ***l*** a n ***d***
n e w f o u n d l ***a*** ***n*** ***d***
n e ***w*** f o u n d l ***a*** ***n*** d
n e ***w*** f ***o*** u n d ***l*** a n ***d***
n e w ***f*** ***o*** ***u*** ***n*** ***d*** l a n d
n ***e*** w f o u n d ***l*** ***a*** ***n*** d
n e w f o u n d l ***a*** ***n*** ***d***
n e w f ***o*** ***u*** ***n*** d l a n d
n e w ***f*** o ***u*** ***n*** d l ***a*** ***n*** ***d***
n e ***w*** f ***o*** u ***n*** d l ***a*** ***n*** d
n ***e*** w f ***o*** u ***n*** d l a n d
n ***e*** w f o u n d l a ***n*** ***d***

EARLE BIRNEY

1. a) This poem contains a message. What is it?
   b) Look up any words in the message you are not familiar with. What secondary meanings and associations does the poem convey?
   (Note: Ned is an allusion to famous Newfoundland writer E.J. ("Ned") Pratt, considered to be one of Canada's foremost 20th century poets.)
2. Using "Newfoundland" as a model, write your own concrete poem based on a Canadian place name.

Jabberwocky

'Twas brillig, and the slithy toves
  Did gyre and gimble in the wabe;
All mimsy were the borogoves,
  And the mome raths outgrabe.

"Beware the Jabberwock, my son!
  The jaws that bite, the claws that catch!
Beware the Jubjub bird, and shun
  The frumious Bandersnatch!"

He took his vorpal sword in hand:
  Long time the manxome foe he sought—
So rested he by the Tumtum tree,
  And stood awhile in thought.

And, as in uffish thought he stood,
  The Jabberwock, with eyes of flame,
Came whiffling through the tulgey wood,
  And burbled as it came!

One, two! One, two! And through and through
  The vorpal blade went snicker-snack!
He left it dead, and with its head
  He went galumphing back.

"And hast thou slain the Jabberwock?
  Come to my arms my beamish boy!
O frabjous day! Callooh! Callay!"
  He chortled in his joy.

'Twas brillig, and the slithy toves
  Did gyre and gimble in the wabe;
All mimsy were the borogoves,
  And the mome raths outgrabe.

LEWIS CARROLL

1. Check a definition of *light verse* in the glossary. Discuss how "Jabberwocky" fits this definition.
2. "Jabberwocky" is made up of *portmanteau words* (new words which are formed from combinations of familiar words; e.g. "brillig" is made up of "brilliant," "light," "bright," etc). Analyze the portmanteau words of the poem.
3. a) In your own words, clarify the "hidden story" of "Jabberwocky."
   b) Does it remind you of any other famous stories?

4. What would be lost if this poem was written using nothing but familiar English words?
5. Carroll was a mathematician who was fond of word puzzles and games. His famous books, *Alice's Adventures in Wonderland* and *Through the Looking Glass*, contain other witty verses you may want to explore on your own.
6. Write your own portmanteau word poem based on a familiar story, perhaps a disguised version of an Aesop's Fable or a Mother Goose poem.

The Listeners

"Is there anybody there?" said the Traveller,
  Knocking on the moonlit door;
And his horse in the silence champed the grasses
  Of the forest's ferny floor:
And a bird flew up out of the turret,
  Above the Traveller's head:
And he smote upon the door again a second time;
  "Is there anybody there?" he said.
But no one descended to the Traveller;
  No head from the leaf-fringed sill
Leaned over and looked into his grey eyes,
  Where he stood perplexed and still.
But only a host of phantom listeners
  That dwelt in the lone house then
Stood listening in the quiet of the moonlight
  To that voice from the world of men:
Stood thronging the faint moonbeams on the dark stair,
  That goes down to the empty hall,
Hearkening in an air stirred and shaken
  By the lonely Traveller's call.
And he felt in his heart their strangeness,
  Their stillness answering his cry,
While his horse moved, cropping the dark turf,
  'Neath the starred and leafy sky;
For he suddenly smote on the door, even
  Louder, and lifted his head:—
"Tell them I came, and no one answered,
  That I kept my word," he said.
Never the least stir made the listeners,
  Though every word he spake
Fell echoing through the shadowiness of the still house
  From the one man left awake:

Ay, they heard his foot upon the stirrup,
  And the sound of iron on stone,
And how the silence surged softly backward.
  When the plunging hoofs were gone.

WALTER DE LA MARE

1. In your own words, describe the situation of the poem, indicating who the following are: the Traveller, the listeners, "them".
2. What is interesting about the horse's reaction to the above situation?
3. Draw a sketch of the scene in the poem.
4. Tape record a lively reading of the poem with background music and sound effects.

This Is a Photograph of Me

It was taken some time ago.
At first it seems to be
a smeared
print: blurred lines and grey flecks
blended with the paper;

then, as you scan
it, you see in the left-hand corner
a thing that is like a branch: part of a tree
(balsam or spruce) emerging
and, to the right, halfway up
what ought to be a gentle
slope, a small frame house

In the background there is a lake,
and beyond that, some low hills.

(The photograph was taken
the day after I drowned.

I am in the lake, in the center
of the picture, just under the surface.

It is difficult to say where
precisely, or to say
how large or small I am:
the effect of water
on light is a distortion

but if you look long enough,
eventually
you will be able to see me.)

MARGARET ATWOOD

1. What is the mood of this poem? How does Atwood use vocabulary to establish this mood?
2. Why did the poet enclose the second half of the poem in parentheses? What effect does this have?
3. Write a two page essay on this poem entitled "Appearance vs. Reality."
4. What is the puzzle in this poem? What makes it odd? Does the oddness work? Discuss.

Poetry for Intellectuals

If you say in a poem "grass is green",
They all ask, "What did you mean?"

"That nature is ignorant," you reply.
"And on a deeper level—youth must die."

If you say in a poem "grass is red",
They understand what you have said.

LOUIS DUDEK

1. What important message does this poem have for the critical reader of poetry?
2. What irony is Dudek pointing out? Is he criticizing all readers? Explain.
3. How does a reader know when an interpretation of a poem is right? What guidelines would you suggest for a reader who wants to know how to interpret a symbol in a poem?

PUZZLE POEMS

1. a) What characteristics do puzzle poems share with games or puzzles?

b) Despite these similarities, what makes this unit's selections poems rather than something else?

2. Compose your own puzzle poem. The class will then set up a bulletin board display of everyone's (teacher included) original puzzle poem.
3. As a class, make an illustrated children's book of original puzzle poems intended for an audience of grade three's. Deliver the finished book to a grade three class in your district. Ask for a reaction.
4. In your library, find a poem that is intriguing but difficult to understand. Working in small groups, "solve" the others' poems and yours.
5. Does nature play a prominent role in these puzzle poems? Discuss.
6. Write two or three paragraphs explaining which poems were the easiest to solve, and which were the most difficult.

Birds and Beasts

Catalogue

Cats sleep fat and walk thin.
Cats when they sleep, slump;
When they wake, pull in—
And where plump's been
There's skin.
Cats walk thin.

Cats wait in a lump,
Jump in a streak.
Cats, when they jump, are sleek
As a grape slipping its skin—
They have technique.
Oh, cats don't creak.
They sneak.

Cats sleep fat.
They spread comfort beneath them
Like a good mat,
As if they picked the place

And then sat.
You walk around one
As if he were the City Hall
After that.

If male,
A cat is apt to sing on a major scale;
This concert is for everybody, this
Is wholesale.
For a baton, he wields a tail.
(He is also found
When happy, to resound
With an enclosed and private sound.)

A cat condenses.
He pulls in his tail to go under bridges,
And himself to go under fences.
Cats fit
In any size box or kit;
And if a large pumpkin grew under one,
He could arch over it.

When everybody else is just ready to go out,
The cat is just ready to come in.
He's not where he's been.
Cats sleep fat and walk thin.

ROSALIE MOORE

1. Comment on the suitability of the poem's title. Can you think of any alternative titles?
2. What is meant by the line, "Cats sleep fat and walk thin."?
3. On the basis of rhyme, quote the rhyming lines that most appealed to you. Tell why you enjoyed them or found them effective.
4. Write a rhyming poem or three paragraphs describing your favorite pet or animal. At the top of your page, draw a picture or paste a photograph of your subject.

The Beautiful Tiger

parting of grasses—beautiful tiger—flutter of fern—beautiful tiger—moving through green through green his orange through green—beautiful tiger—moving through green through green through green his orange—beautiful tiger—under the vine—beautiful tiger—over the brush—beautiful tiger—branches of brown and brown his orange by branches of brown—beautiful tiger—branches of brown and brown by branches of brown his orange—beautiful tiger—loping a stream—beautiful tiger—gliding through tangle—beautiful tiger—gliding through tangle his orange through tangle his tangle through orange his orange through tangle —beautiful tiger—path to a clearing—beautiful tiger-whispering feet —beautiful tiger—disguised as an edge—beautiful tiger—looking:

KEITH GUNDERSON

1. What effect is the poet trying to achieve with use of hyphens and repeated words?
2. Gunderson had fun writing this and wants us to have fun reading it. How can you tell?
3. Comment on the effectiveness of the last word and colon.

The Prize Cat

Pure blood domestic, guaranteed,
Soft-mannered, musical in purr,
The ribbon had declared the breed,
Gentility was in the fur.

Such feline culture in the gads,
No anger ever arched her back—
What distance since those velvet pads
Departed from the leopard's track!

And when I mused how Time had thinned
The jungle strains within the cells,
How human hands had disciplined
Those prowling optic parallels;

I saw the generations pass
Along the reflex of a spring,
A bird had rustled in the grass,
The tab had caught it on the wing:

Behind the leap so furtive-wild
Was such ignition in the gleam,
I thought an Abyssinian child
Had cried out in the whitethroat's scream.

E.J. PRATT

1. Working in small groups of 3-4 students, brainstorm the meanings for each of the poem's stanzas. (You may have to use a dictionary to define some unfamiliar words.)

   Each individual should then write his or her analysis of the poem in essay form according to the following three subsections: content, form, evaluation.
2. What is the conflict in the poem? Quote three images that effectively reveal this conflict.
3. What do the last two lines mean?
4. Why does the poem's subject have to do with a prize cat rather than a tomcat or a kitten?
5. a) What other wild animals has man successfully domesticated?

   b) Can domesticated animals ever be fully tamed?
6. Do some library research on some of the basic instinctive characteristics or behavior that house cats share with larger undomesticated members of the cat family. Write a report on your findings.

Lynx in Winnipeg

His stiff fur
Bristles. He looks neither to left
Nor right. His feet
Scuff dust dropped from chimneys.
Over the years, his forests have grown houses.
Unable to tell what
Is his, he has come to reclaim it,
To see if boards will remember how to sprout branches.
In an hour his daily dream of rabbits
Will be lost in the white snarl of dogs
As he crouches in a tree without leaves.
A bullet will open his chest,
Releasing ten thousand memories of frogs
On the soft edges of streams, snow turning purple
With night, warm blood after a long hunt.
All this will be lost.
At the last, he will draw back, his yellow coat
As hard as quills, his mouth
Defiant, his claws rending the air.
His body will back itself into the distance
As though he would climb for heaven or a new world

Of tree tops and blue sky. His death will not come
Easily. Out of his place, he will drive
Others out of their lives until
A young man with a wife and two children
To whom he is kind, will ease himself
From his car, raise his heavy rifle,
Nestle wood to cheek.
Hedges are forests grown impotent.

W.D. VALGARDSON

1. Describe the context or situation of the poem.
2. a) From whose point of view is the poem written?
   b) Why?
3. Comment on the effects created by the following images:
   "His feet/Scuff dust dropped from chimneys."
   "his forests have grown houses"
   "he has come to reclaim it,/To see if boards will remember how to sprout branches"
   "ten thousand memories of frogs"
   "he will drive/Others out of their lives."
   "Hedges are forests grown impotent."
4. What social comments are made by this poem?
5. Would this poem have worked better in stanza form with rhyme? Comment.

Three Bears

1.
In early September, yellow light
as snow was falling
and he was alone
returning from woodcutting
plans of putting up wood
for a long winter
In the blizzard without warning
he crossed the silvertip's trail
old sow and cubs, and she charged
out of that swirling light
tearing, tearing him

In the snow he woke up later
(this surmised from the signs found

and she again, feeding nearby
was on him
but seeing no threat
allowed him passage of a kind
under a tree
where he stuffed his sash
a style he wore
into the hole in his side
terrible wound in that cold
and there, he died

2.
In September's fading colours
riding home
three bears, the fatal number
charged the horse which threw him hard
on the downed timber
breaking pelvis and thigh bones
out cold for a time
and coming to, he carved
handholds of sharp stakes
and crawled a mile to his cabin

Piling boxes one on the other
in the intervals of consciousness
he reached the phone
which happened to be working
so they saved him that time

Now he drinks beer in Edson
lives in the old folks home
And they say around the ruin
of that old cabin
there's a bottle of rum he buried
in the roots of an old spruce
But I never could find it

3.
Three weeks passed, and no other voice
but the whiskyjack's mockery round the cabin
I changed my shirt, and rode to Moosehorn Lakes
but the campground was empty

Indian paintbrush flowers
cover the trail
as if rust burst forth in blooms
lulling the senses

I think of Andy Suknaski
baiting a hook with the ochre flower
faithful as a child,
casting it out with a ripple
catching a perfect silver trout
The only fish we caught that day

How we are beguiled

The wind lifts toward the east
to brush these petals
when suddenly, from round a corner
swinging his head from side to side
a Grizzly Bear, silvertip
five, six hundred pounder
coming on so quickly
that motion would be useless

He sounds me, stops at twenty paces
to consider the next move

Speak to this bear
for he may know you,
said a voice
in my frozen senses

So I spoke softly
in his fierce hiatus
a deep and secret language
of love and claws,
a fluency I had only suspected
did make me wonder,
while he reared to his hind legs
in judgement

He swept the air once
with his claws, and hesitated
Dropping to all fours, he grunted
and moving aside
ascended the hill

But I am reminded
I am not at home
Here where I live
only at hazard

There is a darkness
along the bright petals

SID MARTY

Note: Andy Suknaski is a Canadian poet best known for *Wood Mountain Poems*. See his poem, "Hitch-Hiking", p. 234.

1. a) Why is the poem divided into three sections?
   b) What progressions, transitions, and changes do you notice in the three sections?
2. Give reasons for the outcomes of the three episodes.
3. What is the significance of the poem's title?
4. Comment on the meaning of the last two lines.
5. What makes "Three Bears" a poem?
6. Do some research on Sid Marty. How have his jobs and experiences affected his career as a writer?

The Giant Bear

There once was a giant bear
who followed people for his prey.
He was so big he swallowed them whole:
Then they smothered to death inside him
if they hadn't already died of fright.

Either the bear attacked them on the run,
or if they crawled into a cave
where he could not squeeze his enormous body in,
he stabbed them with his whiskers like toothpicks,
drawing them out one by one,
and gulped them down.

No one knew what to do
until a wise man went out and let the bear swallow him,
sliding right down his throat into the big, dark, hot, slimy stomach.

And once inside there, he took his knife
and simply cut him open,
killing him of course.

He carved a door in the bear's belly
and threw out those who had been eaten before,
and then he stepped out himself
and went home to get help with the butchering.

Everyone lived on bear meat for a long time.
That's the way it goes:
Monster one minute, food the next.

KIAKSHUK

1. What does this poem reveal about Inuit life?
2. Though this story is somewhat grotesque, it does contain humor. What is the source of the humor?
3. Many cultures have preserved myths in the poetic form, making them easy to recall and share. What is appealing about this story? What important lesson might it teach a child?
4. Working in groups, translate the poem into a pantomime. Perform the mime for the class while one student acts as narrator.
5. Using a series of cartoon-style frames or separate sheets of paper, draw the various scenes from the poem. Print at the bottom of each drawing the appropriate lines to explain the picture.

View of a Pig

The pig lay on a barrow dead.
It weighed, they said, as much as three men.
Its eyes closed, pink white eyelashes.
Its trotters stuck straight out.

Such weight and thick pink bulk
Set in death seemed not just dead.
It was less than lifeless, further off.
It was like a sack of wheat.

I thumped it without feeling remorse.
One feels guilty insulting the dead,
Walking on graves. But this pig
Did not seem able to accuse.

It was too dead. Just so much
A poundage of lard and pork.
Its last dignity had entirely gone.
It was not a figure of fun.

Too dead now to pity.
To remember its life, din, stronghold
Of earthly pleasure as it had been,
Seemed a false effort, and off the point.

Too deadly factual. Its weight
Oppressed me—how could it be moved?
And the trouble of cutting it up!
The gash in its throat was shocking, but not pathetic.

Once I ran a fair in the noise
To catch a greased piglet
That was faster and nimbler than a cat,
Its squeal was the rending of metal.

Pigs must have hot blood, they feel like ovens.
Their bite is worse than a horse's—
They chop a half-moon clean out.
They eat cinders, dead cats.

Distinctions and admirations such
As this one was long finished with.
I stared at it a long time. They were going to scald it,
Scald it and scour it like a doorstep.

TED HUGHES

1. Quote one example for each of the following figures of speech and explain what each example adds to our view of the pig: a) simile, b) metaphor, c) personification.
2. What imagery types are used by the poet to describe the pig? (You may have to check the list of imagery types on p. 46.)
3. How does the speaker feel about the pig? Quote lines to support your opinions.
4. Although this poem has four line stanzas, it does not rhyme. Would it have been a better poem with rhyme? Comment.
5. Using all the different image types and some figures of speech, write a prose description of a vivid memory from your past experience.

The Bull Calf

The thing could barely stand. Yet taken
from his mother and the barn smells
he still impressed with his pride,
with the promise of sovereignty in the way
his head moved to take us in.
The fierce sunlight tugging the maize from the ground
licked at his shapely flanks.
He was too young for all that pride.
I thought of the deposed Richard II.

"No money in bull calves," Freeman had said.
The visiting clergyman rubbed the nostrils
now snuffing pathetically at the windless day.

"A pity," he sighed.
My gaze slipped off his hat toward the empty sky
that circled over the black knot of men,
over us and the calf waiting for the first blow.

Struck,
the bull calf drew in his thin forelegs
as if gathering strength for a mad rush . . .
tottered . . . raised his darkening eyes to us,
and I saw we were at the far end
of his frightened look, growing smaller and smaller
till we were only the ponderous mallet
that flicked his bleeding ear
and pushed him over on his side, stiffly,
like a block of wood.

Below the hill's crest
the river snuffled on the improvised beach.
We dug a deep pit and threw the dead calf into it.
It made a wet sound, a sepulchral gurgle,
as the warm sides bulged and flattened.
Settled, the bull calf lay as if asleep,
one foreleg over the other,
bereft of pride and so beautiful now,
without movement, perfectly still in the cool pit.
I turned away and wept.

IRVING LAYTON

1. a) How many witnesses are there to the death of the bull calf? Identify them.
   b) What are their reactions to the calf's death?
2. Why do you think Layton wrote this poem? What was he trying to get the reader to see?
3. What roles do imagery, figures of speech, and point of view play in creating sympathy for the bull calf?
4. Do some research on Richard II of England. (Check references to Shakespeare's play *Richard II* as well as to the real Richard II).
   a) Who was he?
   b) What was he like as a person?
   c) What is the purpose of the allusion?
5. Would an essay about the slaughter of useless farm animals have had the same effect as the poem? Why or why not?

Snake

A snake came to my water-trough
On a hot, hot day, and I in pyjamas for the heat,
To drink there.

In the deep, strange-scented shade of the great dark carab-tree
I came down the steps with my pitcher
And must wait, must stand and wait, for there he was at the trough before me.

He reached down from a fissure in the earth-wall in the gloom
And trailed his yellow-brown slackness soft-bellied down, over the edge of the stone trough
And rested his throat upon the stonebottom,
And where the water had dripped from the tap, in a small clearness,
He sipped with his straight mouth,
Softly drank through his straight gums, into his slack long body,
Silently.

Someone was before me at my water-trough,
And I, like a second comer, waiting.

He lifted his head from his drinking, as cattle do,
And looked at me vaguely, as drinking cattle do,
And flickered his two-forked tongue from his lips, and mused a moment,
And stooped and drank a little more,
Being earth-brown, earth-golden from the burning bowels of the earth
On the day of Sicilian July, with Etna smoking.

The voice of my education said to me
He must be killed,
For in Sicily the black, black snakes are innocent, the gold are venomous.

And voices in me said, If you were a man
You would take a stick and break him now, and finish him off.
But must I confess how I liked him,
How glad I was he had come like a guest in quiet, to drink at my water-trough
And depart peaceful, pacified, and thankless,
Into the burning bowels of this earth!

Was it cowardice, that I dared not kill him?
Was it perversity, that I longed to talk to him?
Was it humility, to feel honoured?

And yet those voices:
If you were not afraid, you would kill him!

And truly I was afraid, I was most afraid,
But even so, honoured still more
That he should seek my hospitality
From out the dark door of the secret earth.

He drank enough
And lifted his head, dreamily, as one who has drunken,
And flickered his tongue like a forked night on the air, so black,
Seeming to lick his lips,
And looked around like a god, unseeing, into the air,
And slowly turned his head,
And slowly, very slowly, as if thrice adream,
Proceeded to draw his slow length curving round
And climb again the broken bank of my wall-face.

And as he put his head into that dreadful hole,
And as he slowly drew up, snake-easing his shoulders, and entered
farther,
A sort of horror, a sort of protest against his withdrawing into that
horrid black hole,
Deliberately going into the blackness, and slowly drawing himself
after,
Overcame me now his back was turned.

I looked round, I put down my pitcher,
I picked up a clumsy log,
And threw it at the water-trough with a clatter.

I think it did not hit him,
But suddenly that part of him that was left behind convulsed in
undignified haste,
Writhed like lightning, and was gone
Into the black hole, the earth-lipped fissure in the wall-front,
At which, the intense still noon, I stared with fascination.

And immediately I regretted it.
I thought how paltry, how vulgar, what a mean act!
I despised myself and the voices of my accurséd human education.

And I thought of the albatross,
And I wished he would come back, my snake.

For he seemed to me again like a king,
Like a king in exile, uncrowned in the underworld,
Now due to be crowned again.

And so, I missed my chance with one of the lords
Of life.
And I have something to expiate;
A pettiness.

D.H. LAWRENCE

1. What was the speaker's initial reaction to the snake?
2. What causes him to change his views?
3. Why does he throw the log?
4. Why does he later regret throwing the log?
5. a) Of which albatross is the speaker thinking?
   b) What is the purpose of this allusion?
6. Comment on the way in which the poem is written. Do you consider it to be effective? Why or why not?
7. In a one page paper, describe a conflict you once had between your original instinctive feelings and the "voices of your education". Tell whether or not you would react the same way as you did then and why.
8. Do a survey of myths your classmates, family, and friends have about snakes. Then do some library research on snakes. Compare the findings of your survey with those from your reading. Compile a report, drawing some conclusions about the nature of snakes and man-made myths about these animals.

The Blue Heron

In a green place lanced through
With amber and gold and blue;
A place of water and weeds
And roses pinker than dawn,
And ranks of lush young reeds,
And grasses straightly withdrawn
From graven ripples of sands,
The still blue heron stands.

Smoke-blue he is, and grey
As embers of yesterday.
Still he is, as death;
Like stone, or shadow of stone,
Without a pulse or breath,
Motionless and alone

There in the lily stems:
But his eyes are alive like gems.

Still as a shadow; still
Grey feather and yellow bill:
Still as an image made
Of mist and smoke half hid
By windless sunshine and shade,
Save when a yellow lid
Slides and is gone like a breath:
Death-still—and sudden as death!

THEODORE GOODRIDGE ROBERTS

1. What is the rhyme scheme of this poem?
2. The poet repeats one word six times. Which word is it, and what effect does this repetition have on the mood and pace of the poem?
3. There are many colour words in this poem. Write a one page essay discussing how these words are used to create an atmosphere, and what they suggest about the poet's view of his subject.

To a Skylark

1

Hail to thee, blithe Spirit!
Bird thou never wert,
That from Heaven, or near it,
Pourest thy full heart
In profuse strains of unpremeditated art.

2

Higher still and higher
From the earth thou springest
Like a cloud of fire;
The blue deep thou wingest.
And singing still dost soar, and soaring ever singest.

3

In the golden lightning
Of the sunken Sun,
O'er which clouds are brightning,
Thou dost float and run;
Like an unbodied joy whose race is just begun.

4

The pale purple even
  Melts around thy flight;
Like a star of Heaven,
  In the broad day-light
Thou art unseen, but yet I hear thy shrill delight.

5

Keen as are the arrows
  Of that silver sphere,
Whose intense lamp narrows
  In the white dawn clear,
Until we hardly see, we feel that it is there.

6

All in the earth and air
  With thy voice is loud,
As, when Night is bare,
  From one lonely cloud
The moon rains out her beams, and Heaven is overflowed.

7

What thou art we know not;
  What is most like thee?
From rainbow clouds there flow not
  Drops so bright to see,
As from thy presence showers a rain of melody.

8

Like a poet hidden
  In the light of thought,
Singing hymns unbidden,
  Till the world is wrought
To sympathy with hopes and fears it heeded not:

9

Like a high-born maiden
  In a palace-tower,
Soothing her love-laden
  Soul in secret hour
With music sweet as love, which overflows her bower:

10

Like a glow-worm golden
  In a dell of dew,
Scattering unbeholden
  Its aërial hue
Among the flowers and grass, which screen it from the view:

11

Like a rose embowered
  In its own green leaves,
By warm winds deflowered,
  Till the scent it gives
Makes faint with too much sweet those heavy-winged thieves:

12

Sound of vernal showers
  On the twinkling grass,
Rain-awakened flowers,
  All that ever was
Joyous, and clear, and fresh, thy music doth surpass.

13

Teach us, Sprite or Bird,
  What sweet thoughts are thine:
I have never heard
  Praise of love or wine
That panted forth a flood of rapture so divine.

14

Chorus Hymeneal,
  Or triumphal chaunt,
Matched with thine would be all
  But an empty vaunt,
A thing wherein we feel there is some hidden want.

15

What objects are the fountains
  Of thy happy strain?
What fields, or waves, or mountains?
  What shapes of sky or plain?
What love of thine own kind? what ignorance of pain?

16

With thy clear keen joyance
  Languor cannot be:
Shadow of annoyance
  Never came near thee:
Thou lovest; but ne'er knew love's sad satiety.

17

Waking or asleep,
  Thou of death must deem
Things more true and deep
  Than we mortals dream,
Or how could thy notes flow in such a crystal stream?

18

We look before and after,
  And pine for what is not:
Our sincerest laughter
  With some pain is fraught;
Our sweetest songs are those that tell of saddest thought.

19

Yet if we could scorn
  Hate, and pride, and fear;
If we were things born
  Not to shed a tear,
I know not how thy joy we ever should come near.

20

Better than all measures
  Of delightful sound,
Better than all treasures
  That in books are found,
Thy skill to poet were, thou scorner of the ground!

21

Teach me half the gladness
  That thy brain must know,
Such harmonious madness
  From my lips would flow,
The world should listen then, as I am listening now.

PERCY BYSSHE SHELLEY

1. This is an *ode*. Look up a definition of the term in your glossary. Does this poem qualify as an example of this poetic form? Comment.
2. Quote your three favorite similes used to describe the skylark and its song.
   What do these devices add to the poem's portrayal of the bird?
3. In what sense is the skylark's song "unpremeditated art"?
4. a) Quote three references to the elusiveness of the bird.
   b) Quote three references to the divinity of the bird.
5. Do you agree with Shelley's views in stanza 18?
6. What wish does Shelley express in stanza 21?
7. If you enjoyed this poem, you may also like to read a poem written by one of Shelley's friends, John Keats, entitled "Ode to a Nightingale".

BIRDS AND BEASTS

1. For review, make a crossword puzzle consisting of: authors' names, poem titles, animals, allusions, images, and examples of figures of speech from the selections on this theme.
2. Summarize what all the speakers and authors learned from their various encounters with animals. You may wish to conclude with your own observations about what you learned from studying this unit.
3. Describe the situation of "Snake" or "Three Bears" from the point of view of the animal. Be sure to react to the presence and actions of the speakers or authors.
4. Describe the myths or assumptions about the various animals in all five poems.
5. Write a parody based on one of the poems in this unit.
6. For class discussion: Which poems did the best job of representing the animals described?
7. What views of human beings are presented by the unit poems?

Characters

My mistress' eyes are nothing like the sun

My mistress' eyes are nothing like the sun;
Coral is far more red than her lips' red:
If snow be white, why then her breasts are dun[1];
If hairs we wires, black wires grow on her head.
I have seen roses damasked[2], red and white,
But no such roses see I in her cheeks;
And in some perfumes is there more delight
Than in the breath that from my mistress reeks.
I love to hear her speak, yet well I know
That music hath a far more pleasing sound:

[1]dun: dark, drab.
[2]damasked: variegated,

I grant I never saw a goddess go,—
My mistress, when she walks, treads on the ground.
And yet, by heaven, I think my love as rare
As any she belied[3] with false compare.[4]

WILLIAM SHAKESPEARE

1. How does Shakespeare's mistress differ from the ideal beautiful woman of his time?
2. How does he feel about her?
3. a) What important points is Shakespeare making about physical appearances?
   b) Do you agree with his points?
4. Do a paraphrase of the rhyming couplet.
5. Is the poem serious in tone? Which words reinforce this tone?
6. Imitating Shakespeare's style and tone, write a description or poem about your boyfriend or girlfriend.
7. Write the dialogue for a scene in which Shakespeare's mistress indicates her feelings to him about the poem being published.

She's Always a Woman to Me

She can kill with a smile
She can wound with her eyes
She can ruin your faith
With her casual lies
And she only reveals
What she wants you to see
She hides like a child
But she's always a woman to me

She'll lead you to love
She can take you or leave you
She can ask for the truth
But she'll never believe you
And she'll take what you give her
As long as it's free
Yes, she steals like a thief
But she's always a woman to me

Chorus:
Oh—she takes care of herself

---

[3]belied: give a false impression of; misrepresent
[4]with false compare: by false comparison

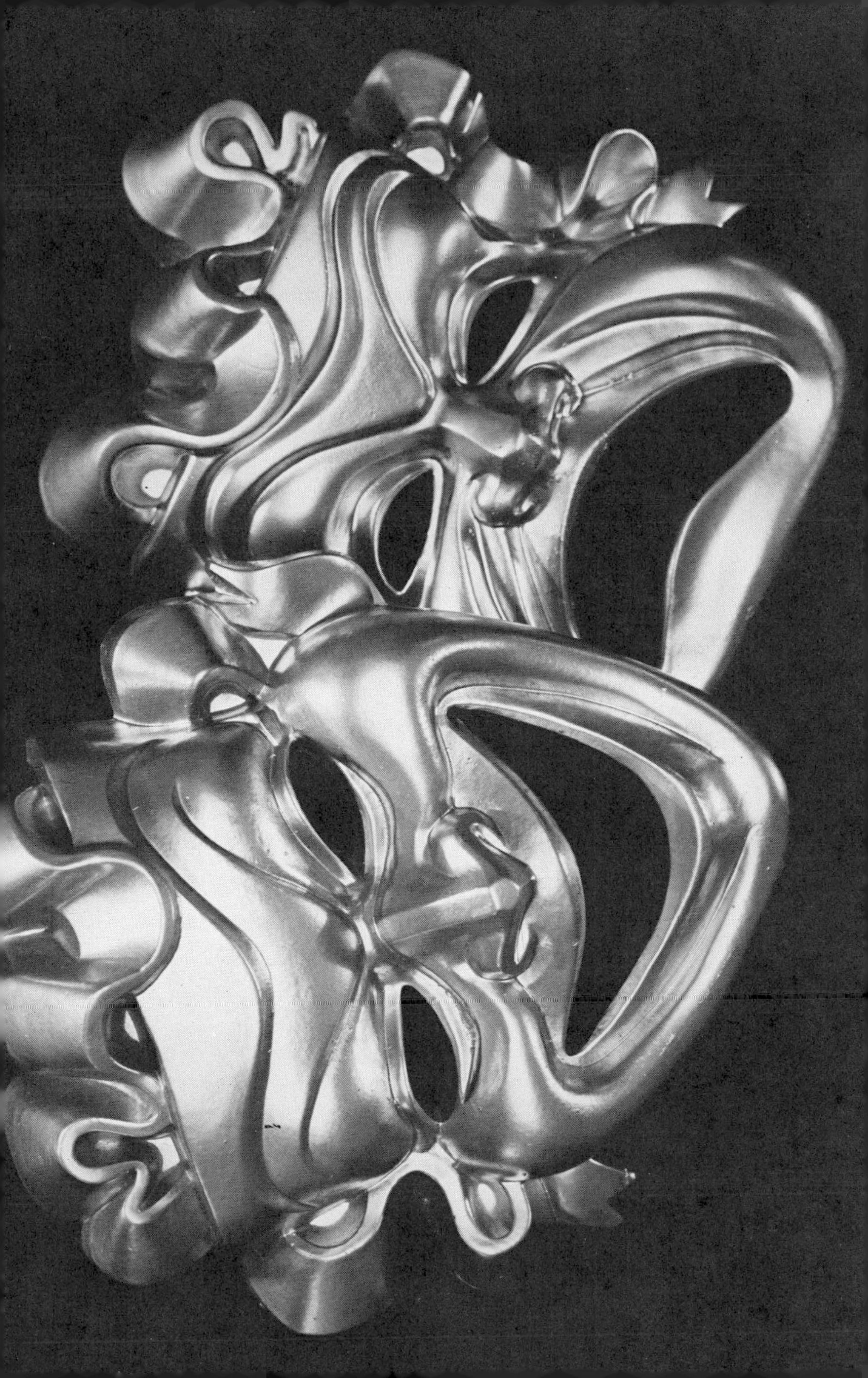

She can wait if she wants
She's ahead of her time
Oh—and she never gives out
And she never gives in
She just changes her mind

She will promise you more
Than the Garden of Eden
Then she'll carelessly cut you
And laugh while you're bleedin'
But she'll bring out the best
And the worst you can be
Blame it all on yourself
'Cause she's always a woman to me

She is frequently kind
And she's suddenly cruel
She can do as she pleases
She's nobody's fool
But she can't be convicted
She's earned her degree
And the most she will do
Is throw shadows at you
But she's always a woman to me

BILLY JOEL

1. Using adjectives and nouns, write a character sketch of the woman.
2. Describe the tone of the song, in particular the writer's feelings about the woman.
3. What is meant by the following lines?
   a) "She can ruin your faith/With her casual lies"
   b) "She can ask for the truth/But she'll never believe you"
   c) "She will promise you more/Than the Garden of Eden"
   d) "And the most she will do/Is throw shadows at you"
4. What figures of speech are used? What do they add to the portrait of the woman?
5. Are people as complex as Joel seems to indicate in this song lyric? Discuss.
6. Write a character sketch describing the most intriguing person you know or ever met.

My Last Duchess
Ferrara[1]

That's my last Duchess painted on the wall,
Looking as if she were alive. I call
That piece a wonder, now: Frà Pandolf's hands
Worked busily a day, and there she stands.
Will't please you sit and look at her? I said
"Frà Pandolf" by design, for never read
Strangers like you that pictured countenance,
The depth and passion of its earnest glance,
But to myself they turned (since none puts by
The curtain I have drawn for you, but I)
And seemed as they would ask me, if they durst,
How such a glance came there; so, not the first
Are you to turn and ask thus. Sir, 'twas not
Her husband's presence only, called that spot
Of joy into the Duchess' cheek: perhaps
Frà Pandolf chanced to say "Her mantle laps
"Over my Lady's wrist too much," or "Paint
"Must never hope to reproduce the faint
"Half-flush that dies along her throat:" such stuff
Was courtesy, she thought, and cause enough
For calling up that spot of joy. She had
A heart—how shall I say?—too soon made glad,
Too easily impressed; she liked whate'er,
She looked on, and her looks went everywhere.
Sir, 'twas all one! My favour at her breast,
The dropping of the daylight in the West,
The bough of cherries some officious fool
Broke in the orchard for her, the white mule
She rode with round the terrace—all and each
Would draw from her alike the approving speech,
Or blush, at least. She thanked men,—good! but thanked
Somehow—I know not how—as if she ranked
My gift of a nine hundred years old name
With anybody's gift. Who'd stoop to blame
This sort of trifling? Even had you skill
In speech—(which I have not)—to make your will
Quite clear to such an one, and say "Just this
"Or that in you disgusts me; here you miss,
"Or there exceed the mark"—and if she let
Herself be lessoned so, nor plainly set

[1]Ferrara: a city in Italy important during the Renaissance.

Her wits to yours, forsooth, and made excuse,
—E'en then would be some stooping, and I choose
Never to stoop. Oh, Sir, she smiled, no doubt
Whene'er I passed her; but who passed without
Much the same smile? This grew; I gave commands;
Then all smiles stopped together. There she stands
As if alive. Will't please you rise? We'll meet
The company below, then. I repeat,
The Count your Master's known munificence
Is ample warrant that no just pretence
Of mine for dowry will be disallowed;
Though his fair daughter's self, as I avowed
At starting, is my object. Nay, we'll go
Together down, Sir! Notice Neptune, tho',
Taming a sea-horse, thought a rarity,
Which Claus of Innsbruck cast in bronze for me.

ROBERT BROWNING

1. Who is the speaker of this dramatic monologue? What is he like?
2. Who was Frà Pandolf? How can you tell?
3. a) What is the "spot of joy"?
   b) How does the speaker account for it?
4. a) What was the Duchess like?
   b) What happened to her?
5. a) Who is the "you" of the poem?
   b) Why is he with the speaker?
6. a) Is it possible that some things said in the poem may be untruths?
   b) Would this affect your answers to 3 b) and 4 a)?
7. What does the imagery of the last 3 lines reveal about the character of the speaker?
8. Put the speaker on trial. The charge is murder.
9. Script the follow-up conversation between the messenger and the Count.

Housewife

What can be wrong
That some days I hug this house
Around me like a shawl, and feel

Each window like a tatter in its skin,
Or worse, bright eyes I must not look through?

Now my husband stands above me
As high as ever my father did,
And I am in that house of dolls, which,
When young I could not shrink to.

I feel the shrinkage in each bone.
No matter what I do, my two girls
Spoil like fruit. Already they push us back
Like too-full plates. They play with us
Like dolls.

The road before the house is like a wish
That stretches out and out and will not
Stop, and the smallest hills are built
Like steps to the slippery moon,
But I
Circle this lit house like any moth
And see the day open its fingers
To disclose the stone—which hand?
Which hand? and the stone in both.

Once, I drove my car into a tree.
The bottles in the back
Burst like tubular glass beasts,
Giving up the ghost. My husband
Thought it was the road. It was.
In the rear-view mirror, it curved and curled,
Longer and stronger than the road ahead,
A question of perspective, I thought then.
I watched it till it turned, and I did not.
I breathed in pain like air,
As if I, the rib, had cracked.

I did not feel this pain, not then,
Almost in my mouth. I wiggled this life
And find it loose. Like my girls,
I would pull it out, would watch
Something new and white
Push like mushrooms from the rich red soil.
But there is just this hole, this bone.

So I live inside my wedding ring,
Inside its arch,
Multiplying the tables of my days,
Rehearsing the lessons of this dish, that sleeve,

Wanting the book that no one wrote,
Loving my husband, my children, my home,
Wanting to go.

Do others feel like this? Where do they go?

SUSAN FROMBERG SCHAEFFER

1. a) Referring to the various metaphors and similes, tell how the housewife feels about herself and others.
   b) What makes her feel this way?
2. What patterns are repeated in the housewife's life?
3. Comment on the symbolic significance of the following:
   a) "the house of dolls" (stanza 2),
   b) "the shrinkage in each bone" (stanza 3),
   c) the stone image (stanza 4),
   d) the broken bottles (stanza 5),
   e) "this hole, this bone" (stanza 6),
   f) "Wanting the book that no one wrote" (stanza 7), and
   g) the final two questions.
4. a) Are there patterns in the lives of housewives and working husbands? Comment.
   b) Do you feel that this poem presents an accurate description of the feelings of housewives?
   c) Have you seen movies or read novels that present the same or similar viewpoints?

A Small Room

little lady
sitting on a park bench
small straw purse
clutched against her side
staring through weary eyes
at the life
around

home is a small room
dusty with memories
noisy with traffic going somewhere
on the second-hand bureau
are photographs
sisten Ellen at graduation

a young bride and groom
Mickey when he was ten

eveyone is dead now
everyone except the bride

over the sink hangs
a calendar
with spaces to fill in
events of importance
and every space
is empty.

MELODIE CORRIGALL

1. What does the poem show about the life of the little lady? What images support this view?
2. How does the lady view life? Why does she see it this way?
3. Who is the bride?
4. Write a short story about a day in the life of the lady.
5. Listen to Paul Simon's "A Most Peculiar Man" (on Simon and Garfunkel's *Sounds of Silence* album – Columbia) and Lennon and McCartney's "Eleanor Rigby" (on the Beatles' *Revolver* album – Capitol). How do these songs compare with "A Small Room"?

Leader of the Band

An only child
Alone and wild
A cabinet maker's son
His hands were meant
For different work
And his heart was known
  To none—
He left his home
And went his lone
And solitary way
And he gave to me
A gift I know I never
  can repay.

A quiet man of music
Denied a simpler fate
He tried to be a soldier once
But his music wouldn't wait

He earned his love
  Through discipline
A thundering, velvet hand
His gentle means of sculpting souls
Took me years to understand.

The leader of the band is tired
And his eyes are growing old
But his blood runs through
  My instrument
And his song is in my soul—
My life has been a poor attempt
To imitate the man
I'm just a living legacy
To the leader of the band.

My brothers' lives were
  different
For they heard another call
One went to Chicago
And the other to St. Paul
And I'm in Colorado
When I'm not in some hotel
Living out this life I've chose
And come to know so well.

I thank you for the music
And your stories of the road
I thank you for the freedom
When it came my time to go—
I thank you for the kindness
And the times when you got tough
And, papa, I don't think I
Said 'I love you' near enough—

The leader of the band is tired
And his eyes are growing old
But his blood runs through
  my instrument
And his song is in my soul—
My life has been a poor attempt
To imitate the man
I'm just a living legacy
To the leader of the band.
I am the living legacy to
The leader of the band.

DAN FOGELBERG

1. a) Who is the "leader of the band"?
   b) Why is he called that?
2. Why do you think Fogelberg wrote this song?
3. Quote two poetic-sounding lines and explain why you consider these lines to be poetic in tone.
4. Write a poem or song lyric dedicated to someone who has influenced your life.

Pinball Wizard

Ever since I was a young boy
I played the silver ball;
From Soho down to Brighton
I must have played 'em all
But I ain't seen nothin' like him
In any amusement hall.
That deaf, dumb and blind kid
Sure plays a mean pinball.

He stands like a statue,
Becomes part of the machine,
Feelin' all the bumpers,
Always playin' clean,
Plays by intuition,
The digit counters fall
That deaf, dumb and blind kid
Sure plays a mean pinball.

He's a pinball wizard
has to be a twist,
A pinball wizard
Got such a supple wrist

How do you think he does it?
I don't know.
What makes him so good?

Ain't got no distractions,
Can't hear those buzzes and bells,
Don't see no lights a-flashin',
Plays by sense of smell,
Always gets the replay,
Never seen him fall,
That deaf, dumb and blind kid
Sure plays a mean pinball.

I thought I was
The body table king,
But I just handed
My pinball crown to him.

Even on my fav'rite table
He can beat my best.
His disciples lead him in
And he just does the rest.
He's got crazy flippin' fingers,
Never seen him fall.
That deaf, dumb and blind kid
Sure plays a mean pinball.

PETER TOWNSHEND

1. a) Why do you think Townshend chose to write about the pinball wizard?
   b) What is remarkable about the wizard?
2. a) Who is the speaker of the song lyric?
   b) What can you tell about his background from his diction?
3. Who are the "disciples"?
4. Who are the speakers of the dialogue midway through the poem?
5. Write a humorous personal essay about how to spot a video game addict.

The Parson

There was a good man of religion
who was a poor Parson of a town;
but he was rich in holy thoughts and works.
He was also a learned man, a clerk,
who would truly preach Christ's gospel;
he would teach his parishioners devoutly.
He was benign, and wonderfully diligent,
and most patient in adversity,
and had been proved to be such many times.
He was loath to excommunicate for his tithes,
but would, without a doubt, rather give
his poor parishioners thereabouts
part of his own offerings and property.
He was satisfied with very little.

His parish was wide and its houses far apart,
but he never neglected—for rain or thunder,
sickness or trouble—to visit on foot,
with a staff in his hand,
the furthest in his parish, great or humble.
He gave this noble example to his sheep:
that he practiced first and preached afterwards.
He took this motto from the Gospel
and further added this saying:
that if gold rusts, what shall iron do?
For if a priest in whom we trust be corrupt,
it is no wonder if an ignorant man go to rust.
And it is indeed shameful (if a priest will but note)
to find a filthy shepherd and a clean sheep.
Surely a priest ought to give an example,
by his own spotlessness, of how his sheep should live.
He did not hire out his benefice
and leave his sheep encumbered in the mire
while he ran off to London, to Saint Paul's,
to find himself a chantry for souls
or be shut up with a religious order,
but stayed at home and kept his fold well,
so that the wolf could not harm it:
he was a shepherd and not a mercenary.
And although he was holy and virtuous,
he was not scornful to sinful men,
or haughty and proud in his speech,
but discreet and benign in his teaching.
To draw folk to heaven by fair behavior
and good example—that was his business.
But if any person were obstinate,
whoever he was, of high or low degree,
he would scold him sharply on that occasion.
I believe there is no better priest anywhere.
He did not look for pomp and reverence,
nor affect an overly scrupulous conscience;
he taught the lore of Christ and his twelve
Apostles—but first he followed it himself.

GEOFFREY CHAUCER

1. How does the parson show himself to be a good clergyman?
2. Who are his "sheep"? Who is the "wolf"?
3. What is the meaning of the "gold rusts" saying?

4. What might the parson have done if he was less conscientious?
5. Imagine you are the parson's superior who has just completed an inspection tour of the parson's parish. Write his progress report on the state of the parish and the character of the parson.

The Pardoner[1]

With him there rode a gentle Pardoner
of Rouncivalle; he was the Summoner's[2] friend and
comrade, who had come straight from the court of
Rome. Loudly he sang, "Come hither, love, to me,"
and the Summoner accompanied him powerfully—
never did a trumpet make half so great a sound.
The Pardoner had hair as yellow as wax,
but it hung as smoothly as a hank of flax;
wisp by wisp his locks hung down,
and he had spread them over his shoulders—
but they lay thinly, in strands, one by one;
however, for sport, he wore no hood;
it was trussed up in his pack.
He thought he rode all in the latest style;
with his hair down, he rode bareheaded except for his cap.
He had staring eyes just like a hare's.
He had sewed a veronica on his cap;
his bag was in his lap before him,
brimful of pardons, all come hot from Rome.
He had a voice as thin as a goat's;
no beard did he have, nor would ever have—
his face was as smooth as if he just shaved;
I expect he was a gelding or a mare.
But to speak of his craft, from Berwick to Ware
there was no other such pardoner;
for in his bag he had a pillowcase
which, he said, was Our Lady's veil;
he said he had a piece of the sail
Saint Peter had when he sailed
on the sea, until Jesus Christ took him;
he had a cross of brass, set with stones,
and in a glass he had pigs' bones;
but with these "relics," whenever he found

[1]Pardoner: a usually corrupt clergyman who sold pardons (for sins) from the Pope.
[2]Summoner: an officer of the church who summoned delinquents to appear before an ecclesiastical court

a poor country parson,
he in one day got himself more money
than the parson got in two months.
And thus, with false flattery and tricks,
he made monkeys of the parson and the people.
But in the end, to do him justice,
in church he was a noble ecclesiastic.
He could read a lesson or a history beautifully,
but best of all he sang an offertory;
for well he knew that when that song was sung
he must preach and smooth his tongue
to win silver, as he indeed could do—
therefore he sang the more merrily and the louder.

GEOFFREY CHAUCER

1. How does the pardoner's physical appearance support Chaucer's description of his character?
2. What is the purpose in comparing the pardoner to a gelding, a mare, and a goat?
3. Comment on the quality of the "relics."
4. How well-off is the pardoner compared to the parson?
5. How and why is the pardoner a "noble ecclesiastic" in church?
6. Of the parson and the pardoner, which of the two did you:
   a) find more interesting and why,
   b) consider to be the more intelligent and why, and
   c) admire and why?

W. L. M. K.

How shall we speak of Canada,
Mackenzie King dead?
The Mother's boy in the lonely room
With his dog, his medium, and his ruins?

He blunted us.

We had no shape
Because he never took sides,
And no sides
Because he never allowed them to take shape.

He skilfully avoided what was wrong
Without saying what was right,

And never let his on the one hand
Know what his on the other hand was doing.

The height of his ambition
Was to pile a Parliamentary Committee on a Royal
  Commission.
To have "conscription if necessary
But not necessarily conscription",
To let Parliament decide—
Later.

Postpone, postpone, abstain.

Only one thread was certain:
After World War I
Business as usual,
After World War II
Orderly decontrol.
Always he led us back to where we were before.

He seemed to be in the centre
Because we had no centre,
No vision
To pierce the smoke-screen of his politics.

Truly he will be remembered
Wherever men honour ingenuity,
Ambiguity, inactivity, and political longevity.

Let us raise up a temple
To the cult of mediocrity,
Do nothing by halves
Which can be done by quarters.

F.R. SCOTT

1. Who was W.L.M.K.? Using the library and available Canadian history books, find information about this famous Canadian politician.
   a) What were his accomplishments? b) How was he regarded by Canadians of his time? c) How does the poet regard him?
2. What is the purpose of Scott's poem? Quote words and lines from the poem to support your views.
3. Referring to the poem, describe W.L.M.K.'s style of politics. How does he compare with politicians of our day?
4. Write your own satirical poem about a local, provincial, or federal political figure.

Houdini

This poem is Houdini's water tank trick,
The one he died performing on Halloween,
Fever clutching his abdomen, strength gone,
With nothing left to pick the locks
& time running out, light emanating
From the carved pumpkin's head.
It is the curtained place where he hung
Suspended by the ankles, immersed,
Water demanding entry to his lungs,
& he waiting, helpless, for someone with an axe
To break him out. This poem
Is the shattered glass of the rescue
That comes too late.

KEN NORRIS

1. Check the accuracy of the information in the poem with the facts of Houdini's death.
2. What image of Houdini do we get from reading this poem?
3. Comment on the effects of the last sentence and the last two words.
4. Why did Norris write this poem?
5. Imagine and write Houdini's thoughts as he performs the water tank trick.

CHARACTERS

1. Discuss the portraits of women in this unit's poems. Which one is:
   a) the most surprising?
   b) the most pathetic?
   c) the most honest?
   d) the most impressive?
   e) the most charming?
2. Which of the male characters did you like best and least? Why?
3. As a class, videotape your version of a personality interview talk show. Guests, roleplayed by various students in the class, are the various characters from this unit or any character poems from elsewhere in the text.
4. Discuss the various influences that helped shape the personality of three characters in this unit.
5. Write three diary entries for one character in this unit.

Landscapes and Locales

Preludes

I

The winter evening settles down
With smell of steaks in passageways.
Six o'clock.
The burnt-out ends of smoky days.
And now a gusty shower wraps
The grimy scraps
Of withered leaves about your feet
And newspapers from vacant lots;
The showers beat
On broken blinds and chimney-pots,
And at the corner of the street
A lonely cab-horse steams and stamps.
And then the lighting of the lamps.

II

The morning comes to consciousness
Of faint stale smells of beer
From the sawdust-trampled street
With all its muddy feet that press
To early coffee-stands.
With the other masquerades
That time resumes,
One thinks of all the hands
That are raising dingy shades
In a thousand furnished rooms.

III

You tossed a blanket from the bed,
You lay upon your back, and waited;
You dozed, and watched the night revealing
The thousand sordid images
Of which your soul was constituted;
They flickered against the ceiling.
And when all the world came back
And the light crept up between the shutters
And you heard the sparrows in the gutters,
You had such a vision of the street
As the street hardly understands;
Sitting along the bed's edge, where
You curled the papers from your hair,

or clasped the yellow soles of feet
In the palms of both soiled hands.

IV

His soul stretched tight across the skies
That fade behind a city block,
Or trampled by insistent feet
At four and five and six o'clock;
And short square fingers stuffing pipes,
And evening newspapers, and eyes
Assured of certain certainties,
The conscience of a blackened street
Impatient to assume the world.

I am moved by fancies that are curled
Around these images, and cling:
The notion of some infinitely gentle
Infinitely suffering thing.

Wipe your hand across your mouth, and laugh;
The worlds revolve like ancient women
Gathering fuel in vacant lots.

T.S. ELIOT

1. Identify the following people:
   a) the "you" in I, III, and the last stanza
   b) the "he" in IV
   c) the "I" in the second last stanza of the poem.
   Do they differ from one another in their views of city life?
2. What is the "infinitely gentle/Infinitely suffering thing" of the second last stanza?
3. Why is the poem called "Preludes"? What does the title suggest?
4. Write your own image poem about your own town, city, or area.

Thaw

Sticky inside their winter suits
The Sunday children stare at pools
In pavement and black ice where roots
Of sky in moodier sky dissolve.

An empty coach train runs along
The thin and sooty river flats

And stick and straw and random stones
Steam faintly when its steam departs.

Lime-water and licorice light
Wander the tumbled street. A few
Sparrows gather. A dog barks out
Under the dogless pale pale blue.

Move your tongue along a slat
Of a raspberry box from last year's crate.
Smell a saucepantilt of water
On the coal-ash in your grate.

Think how the Black Death made men dance,
And from the silt of centuries
The proof is now scraped bare that once
Troy fell and Pompey scorched and froze.

A boy alone out in the court
Whacks with his hockey-stick, and whacks
In the wet, and the pigeons flutter, and rise,
And settle back.

MARGARET AVISON

1. Why does the author insert one stanza of historical references in the middle of a poem which is mostly present-tense description?
2. How does the author employ vocabulary to create the mood of a thaw without describing it directly?
3. Choose your two favorite images from this poem. Explain why you think they are successful and how they affect the poem as a whole.

Toronto the Golden-Vaulted City

I'm in a rich cold city,
Toronto the golden-vaulted,
runnelled and hollowed,
British born, steeped by cliffs,
axed by watercourses,
its warehouses pure Ontario,
its lake like Michigan,
and all its warm bungalows
lighted with midwinter's
scarcity of snow.

STOP

Alas poor York;
the howling wind outside
shakes the grey plateau,
stalks the gothic arches
in the dark moist marketplace,
follows under the overpass,
pursues like Caligari
in subway alleys
where the white-tiled breath
of unearthly cold
foretastes the sooty grave.

Dragon-tall is my adversary;
from arctic cold he rises,
but I am murdered, bloodless
in the untenanted subdivision
among the broken bricks
and chickenwire debris
I'm dry as last year's berries
under the frozen hedge.

The moundbuilders are dead
in my native province,
the grain elevators
are locked on the lakehead,
and the vaulted city blazes
like a many-pronged golden
pitchfork stabbing the clouds
for light.

MIRIAM WADDINGTON

1. What pun and allusions are used in stanza 2 of the poem? What do they add to the description of Toronto?
2. How does Waddington feel about Toronto? Quote three images to support your opinion.
3. Who are the "moundbuilders" of stanza 4?
4. Does the poem present a favorable view of Toronto? Discuss.
5. Do you live in Toronto? Have you ever lived in or visited the city? Write down your impressions of Toronto, agreeing or disagreeing with the poet's views.

Fall Days

These are large days
        on the prairie
Each buffalo breath
dwarfed
hides in gusty winds
Skyscrapers
disappear in the fields
        they sink
through the crested grass
as slowly as elevators
The days
swallow all measurements
        even themselves
they are so large

E.F. DYCK

1. What impressions of the prairie does the poem create in the reader? Quote words and images that create these feelings.
2. How do spacing and line division affect the reader?
3. Write down five more images and words you associate with fall days on the Canadian prairie.
4. Do seasons and different landscapes affect people's feelings or moods? Discuss.
5. Using images, write a two paragraph description of any city or place in Canada. Read your description to the class and see if they can guess what your subject is.

The Spell of the Yukon

I wanted the gold, and I sought it;
  I scrabbled and mucked like a slave.
Was it famine or scurvy—I fought it,
  I hurled my youth into the grave.
I wanted the gold and I got it—
  Came out with a fortune last fall,—
Yet somehow life's not what I thought it,
  And somehow the gold isn't all.

No! There's the land. (Have you seen it?)
It's the cussedest land that I know,
From the big, dizzy mountains that screen it,
To the deep, deathlike valleys below.
Some say God was tired when He made it;
Some say it's a fine land to shun;
Maybe: but there's some as would trade
For no land on earth—and I'm one.

You come to get rich (damned good reason),
You feel like an exile at first;
You hate it like hell for a season,
And then you are worse than the worst.
It grips you like some kinds of sinning;
It twists you from foe to a friend;
It seems it's been since the beginning;
It seems it will be to the end.

I've stood in some mighty-mouthed hollow
That's plumb-full of hush to the brim;
I've watched the big, husky sun wallow
In crimson and gold, and grow dim,
Till the moon set the pearly peaks gleaming,
And the stars tumbled out, neck and crop;
And I've thought that I surely was dreaming,
With the peace o' the world piled on top.

The summer—no sweeter was ever;
The sunshiny woods all athrill;
The greyling aleap in the river,
The bighorn asleep in the hill.
The strong life that never knows harness;
The wilds where the caribou call;
The freshness, the freedom, the farness—
O God! how I'm stuck on it all.

The winter! the brightness that blinds you,
The white land locked tight as a drum,
The cold fear that follows and finds you,
The silence that bludgeons you dumb.
The snows that are older than history,
The woods where the weird shadows slant;
The stillness, the moonlight, the mystery,
I've bade 'em good-bye—but I can't.

There's a land where the mountains are nameless,
And the rivers all run God knows where;

There are lives that are erring and aimless,
And deaths that just hang by a hair;
There are hardships that nobody reckons;
There are valleys unpeopled and still;
There's a land—oh, it beckons and beckons,
And I want to go back—and I will.

They're making my money diminish;
I'm sick of the taste of champagne.
Thank God! when I'm skinned to a finish
I'll pike to the Yukon again.
I'll fight—and you bet it's no sham-fight;
It's hell!—but I've been there before;
And it's better than this by a damsite—
So me for the Yukon once more.

There's gold, and it's haunting and haunting,
It's luring me on as of old;
Yet it isn't the gold that I'm wanting
So much as just finding the gold.
It's the great, big, broad land 'way up yonder,
It's the forests where silence has lease;
It's the beauty that thrills me with wonder,
It's the stillness that fills me with peace.

ROBERT SERVICE

1. As a class, do a choral reading of the poem.
2. Why did the speaker come to the Yukon?
3. a) What were the speaker's original feelings about the Yukon?
   b) How and why did these feelings change?
   c) What are his final impressions of the place?
4. "The Yukon is a land of many contrasts."
   Discuss with references to stanzas 2, 4, 5, 6, and 7.
5. Referring to the speaker's attitude toward gold and the land, describe his character.

Sign (found poem)

Welcome
to Snowdrift
184 Indians
191 dogs
no cats

STEPHEN HUME

1. Where do you suppose the author found this poem? What is appealing about it?
2. Study the words and phrases in your environment over the day and locate two found poems. They may be from any source—signs, announcements, junk mail, etc.—and should consist of phrases or sentences you want to draw attention to.
3. Using bold-face words from magazines or newspapers, compose a short intriguing poem.

Island Estate at St. Andrew's

Approaching the house
along the old carriage road
that leads from the tidal bar
you expect to be greeted at the door
by some monstrous hunchbacked caretaker

you expect naturally
to be led by candlelight
into the dark interior
where the house itself
like that of Usher
will drive you mad
or to your death
long before daylight comes again

you feel
that since you are here at all
your fate is sealed
like a coffin
and forevermore you will be
one insignificant mention
in a story no one will believe

but as you walk
stepping carefully up the steps
to the main entrance
there is no one to meet you
the house is locked tight
the grass threatens the path
to the garden gate
and the only sound
is that of the seagulls
swirling high in the sky
overhead

from there on the top step
standing in deep shadow
your back turned
to the great dark door
observe what perfect patterns
the bright whitecapped waves make
as they glisten silver in the sunlight
all the way to the thin horizon
and beyond

AL PITTMAN

1. What do the "hunchbacked caretaker" image, the allusion to Edgar Allan Poe's "The Fall of the House of Usher," and the coffin image add to the mood of the poem and the reader's impressions of Island Estate?
2. What is ironic about the speaker's first impressions about Island Estate?
3. Do some research on Island Estate at St. Andrew's. Where is it? What is it like?
4. Tell your impressions of an eerie, intriguing house or place you once visited.

Low Tide On Grand Pré

The sun goes down, and over all
  These barren reaches by the tide
Such unelusive glories fall,
  I almost dream they yet will bide
  Until the coming of the tide.

And yet I know that not for us,
  By any ecstasy of dream,
He lingers to keep luminous
  A little while the grievous stream,
  Which frets, uncomforted of dream—

A grievous stream, that to and fro
  Athrough the fields of Acadie
Goes wandering, as if to know
  Why one beloved face should be
  So long from home and Acadie.

Was it a year or lives ago
  We took the grasses in our hands,

And caught the summer flying low
  Over the waving meadow lands,
  And held it there between our hands?

The while the river at our feet—
  A drowsy inland meadow stream—
At set of sun and after-heat
  Made running gold, and in the gleam
  We freed our birch upon the stream.

There down along the elms at dusk
  We lifted dripping blade to drift,
Through twilight scented fine like musk,
  Where night and gloom awhile uplift,
  Nor sunder soul and soul adrift.

And that we took into our hands
  Spirit of life or subtler thing—
Breathed on us there, and loosed the bands
  Of death, and taught us, whispering,
  The secret of some wonder-thing.

Then all your face grew light, and seemed
  To hold the shadow of the sun;
The evening faltered, and I deemed
  That time was ripe, and years had done
  Their wheeling underneath the sun.

So all desire and all regret,
  And fear and memory, were naught;
One to remember or forget
  The keen delight our hands had caught;
  Morrow and yesterday were naught.

The night has fallen, and the tide . . .
  Now and again comes drifting home,
Across these aching barrens wide,
  A sigh like driven wind or foam:
  In grief the flood is bursting home.

BLISS CARMAN

1. Working in small groups, discuss the following questions and be prepared to report back to the class.
   a) What is the poet dreaming of in stanza 1?
   b) Who is the "He" of stanza 2?
   c) Who is the "beloved face" of stanza 3?

d) To what does the poet refer in stanza 4?
e) What is the "birch" in stanza 5?
f) What is the significance of the last two lines of stanza 6?
g) What is "The secret of some wonder-thing" in stanza 7?
h) What does the speaker say about time in stanza 8?
i) Explain why "Morrow and yesterday were naught" in stanza 9?
j) On the basis of stanza 10, what would you say has happened?

2. a) What is the significance of the poem's title?
   b) What role does water play in the poem?
3. Trace the changing moods of the speaker through the poem.
4. How is this poem similar to Edgar Allan Poe's "Annabel Lee" (p. 51)?
5. Write a short story with a tragic conclusion based on the events of stanzas 4-9. Write the story from the point of view of the speaker in the first person.

Dover Beach

The sea is calm tonight,
The tide is full, the moon lies fair
Upon the straits;—on the French coast the light
Gleams and is gone; the cliffs of England stand,
Glimmering and vast, out in the tranquil bay.
Come to the window, sweet is the night-air!
Only, from the long line of spray
Where the sea meets the moon-blanched land,
Listen! you hear the grating roar
Of pebbles which the waves draw back, and fling,
At their return, up the high strand,
Begin, and cease, and then again begin,
With tremulous cadence slow, and bring
The eternal note of sadness in.

Sophocles long ago
Heard it on the Aegean, and it brought
Into his mind the turbid ebb and flow
Of human misery; we
Find also in the sound a thought,
Hearing it by this distant northern sea.

The Sea of Faith
Was once, too, at the full, and round earth's shore

Lay like the folds of a bright girdle furled.
But now I only hear
Its melancholy, long, withdrawing roar,
Retreating, to the breath
Of the night-wind, down the vast edges drear
And naked shingles of the world.

Ah, love, let us be true
To one another! for the world, which seems
To lie before us like a land of dreams,
So various, so beautiful, so new,
Hath really neither joy, nor love, nor light,
Nor certitude, nor peace, nor help for pain;
And we are here as on a darkling plain
Swept with confused alarms of struggle and flight,
Where ignorant armies clash by night.

MATTHEW ARNOLD

1. a) What feelings and moods do you get as you read this poem?
   b) Which images, lines, and stanzas suggest tranquility? Chaos?
2. What is "the eternal note of sadness"?
3. What associations and allusions does Arnold make with Dover Beach?
4. There is a conflict in this poem between the "land of dreams" and the "darkling plain."
   a) How are each of these described?
   b) What do each of these stand for?
5. Comment on the effectiveness of the wording of lines 32-34 as a turning point.
6. Is Arnold an optimist or pessimist? Defend your views with references to the poem.

LANDSCAPES AND LOCALES

1. Write a one page paper telling which place mentioned in any of the poems you'd like to or not like to visit and why.
2. Name three places anywhere in the world you'd like to visit. Provide a rationale for your choices.
3. Compose a brochure designed to be a teenager's guide to

another town or city of your choice. Illustrate with drawings or photographs.

4. Write a script spoofing C.B.C.'s *Cities* series, using different locales in a town or city of your choice.
5. If you have slides of your travels to other places, prepare a talk illustrated with slides and do a presentation for the class telling interesting things about the place(s) you have visited.
6. Invite a person from another country to your class. Have him or her tell a little about daily life and culture in that country.

Moods

Hunter's Lament

GOOSE
GOOSE
GOOSE
W-H-Y F-L-Y S-O H-I-G-H ? GOOSE
GOOSE
GOOSE
GOOSE

EDWARD JOHN

1. This is a concrete poem. How does it work on a visual level?
2. What is the hunter lamenting?
3. What makes the poem humorous?
4. Choose a hobby or sporting activity you have participated in and write a concrete poem sharing a lament (e.g., Bowler's Lament, Tennis Player's Lament, Stamp Collector's Lament).

Bright Morning

The baby's hairbrush, blue handle
soft silver bristles
rests in the window
on a box of bullets
The fine print reads
"308 cal. soft nosed
180 grams" in this bilingual land
"Balle a extrémité emoussée"

I shoot that rifle
makes a helluva noise
that leaves the silence terrified
But can't drown out a railroad
or a mother's cry

I love the mountains

From the window
they are silver maned
posed, resolute
Wind combs them

I brush the baby's hair
he loves the red label
on a jar of nivea cream

SID MARTY

1. "Bright Morning" makes a comment by contrasting two patterns of imagery. What are these patterns?
2. What do the railroad and the mother's cry represent within the scene being described?
3. What statement or observation does the poem make through its imagery?

The Freshly Cut Grass

comes in on the children's shoes.
    The house is laughing.

DOROTHY CAMERON SMITH

1. Describe the mood of this poem.
2. Identify the poem type; give reasons for your choice.

Rain Song

The rain a river upended

the flowers plain pink or
cream striped with mauve
laundry left on the line

the outdoor cafe
deserted
except for the tables like lost cattle

a bird flies out of the corner of the eye
making the world
give a little shiver
making everything jump
one inch irretrievably
to the left

and in the green igloos of summer leaves
all the birds are keeping mum

ROO BORSON

1. How heavy is the rain? Which image communicates that?
2. Why does the author describe the flowers and the laundry in the same stanza?
3. What might the author's purpose be in comparing the tables to lost cattle? Is the simile appropriate? Comment.
4. The fourth stanza draws the reader's eyes directly into the scene being described. Why is the bird's movement significant? Is the description effective? Explain.
5. What sound in the scene is not described? What absent sound is pointed out? Why?
6. List all the common phrases we use to describe a heavy rainfall. Find a fresh description and use it to start a poem describing a rainstorm you recall.

Midnight

From where I sit, I see the stars,
  And down the chilly floor
The moon between the frozen bars
  Is glimmering dim and hoar.

Without in many a peakèd mound
  The glinting snowdrifts lie;
There is no voice or living sound;
  The embers slowly die.

Yet some wild thing is in mine ear;
  I hold my breath and hark:
Out of the depth I seem to hear
  A crying in the dark:

No sound of man or wife or child,
  No sound of beast that groans,
Or of the wind that whistles wild,
  Or of the tree that moans:

I know not what it is I hear;
  I bend my head and hark;
I cannot drive it from mine ear,
  That crying in the dark.

ARCHIBALD LAMPMAN

1. a) What is the "wild thing" in the speaker's ear?
   b) What is the "crying in the dark"?
2. a) Why do you think Lampman wrote this poem?
   b) Have you ever had an experience like the one described by the poem? Tell the class about it, especially recalling how you felt.
3. a) Why is this a lyric poem?
   b) How might the poet have justified his use of four line rhyming stanzas?
4. a) Quote one example of parallel line structure.
   b) Explain the effectiveness of this device.

The Skater

My glad feet shod with the glittering steel
I was the god of the winged heel.

The hills in the far white sky were lost;
The world lay still in the wide white frost;

And the woods hung hushed in their long white dream
By the ghostly, glimmering, ice-blue stream.

Here was a pathway, smooth like glass,
Where I and the wandering wind might pass

To the far-off palaces, drifted deep,
Where Winter's retinue rests in sleep.

I followed the lure, I fled like a bird,
Till the startled hollows awoke and heard

A spinning whisper, a sibilant twang,
As the stroke of the steel on the tense ice rang;

And the wandering wind was left behind
As faster, faster I followed my mind;

Till the blood sang high in my eager brain,
And the joy of my flight was almost pain.

Then I stayed the rush of my eager speed
And silently went as a drifting seed,—

Slowly, furtively, till my eyes
Grew big with the awe of a dim surmise,

And the hair of my neck began to creep
At hearing the wilderness talk in sleep.

Shapes in the fir-gloom drifted near.
In the deep of my heart I heard my fear.

And I turned and fled, like a soul pursued,
From the white, inviolate solitude.

CHARLES G.D. ROBERTS

1. a) Of the five main types of poetry studied in Chapter 4, which would you say "The Skater" was?
   b) Defend your decision.
   c) Find another poem in Chapter 8 which is a blend of the main poetry types, state what they are, and defend your opinion.
2. What meanings, associations, and effects are created by the following words: "retinue," "sibilant twang," "furtively," "awe," "dim surmise," "inviolate solitude"?

3. Find three similes and comment on their effectiveness in accomplishing the author's purpose.
4. In five prose paragraphs, describe a similar experience you had in which you were "spooked." Use images and figures of speech to clarify how you felt.
5. How is this poem similar to Archibald Lampman's "Midnight" (p. 222)?

The Stickhandler

Not like the solid defenceman
who, stymied by forecheckers,
can only dump the puck
out to center ice;
or the faithful leftwinger
who diligently patrols his wing
doing what is required of him
& scoring his share of goals . . .

The phenom steals the puck
in his own zone
& skates around his net
deftly evading his check
fakes a pass
& loops across the blueline
(back & forth goes the puck
at the end of his stick
as if magnetized by willpower,
obedient & sure).
Now he is at center, gathering
speed,
      dodges
the tricky rightwinger
trying to cut him off
stickhandles
round the backward-skating referee
& hair flying, 30 miles per hour,
splits the defence.

Nothing protests.
Even the laws of probability
hold their breath
as the stickhandler makes his final deke
& faking a slapshot

backhands the puck
past the wide-eyed goalie
who stands there frozen,
more like an accomplice
than an opponent.

DAVID SOLWAY

1. Quote lines and images that reveal the phenom's ability and skills as a hockey player.
2. a) What are the "laws of probability" mentioned in stanza 3?
   b) Why do they "hold their breath"?
3. How is the goalie more "like an accomplice/than an opponent"?
4. Would this poem have been better if it rhymed? Explain.
5. Write a brief persuasive essay about the hockey player you feel is the best in the N.H.L.

Jump Shot

Lithe, quicker than the ball itself;
Spinning through the blocking forearms,
Hands like stars, spread to suspend
The ball from five, and only five,
Magic fingerprints.

The rebound resounding down the pole
And into asphalt, pounded hard by sneakers
Raggedier than the missing-tooth grimaces.
Grimaces. No smiles here. Concentration.
Movement. The calculation.
The arch-back leap. And off the rim again.
Once in ten the satisfying swoosh.

And no time wasted to enjoy it.
Grasp that globe and keep it dribbling:
Elbows were meant for eyesockets;
Work it up higher than hands,
Higher than the grab of gravity.

Working, each man for himself,
Yet deftly, deftly weaving in the pattern.

RICHARD PECK

1. Define the words "lithe," "grimaces," and "deftly" and explain what contribution they make to the poem.
2. What are the "five magic fingerprints"?
3. Explain the following line: "Elbows were meant for eye-sockets."
4. Find a simile in the poem and discuss what its purpose is.
5. Write a poem about another sport which gives the reader a similar sense of what it is like to play this sport.

400-Meter Free Style

The gun full swing the swimmer catapults and cracks
s
i
x
feet away onto that perfect glass he catches at
a
n
d
throws behind him scoop after scoop cunningly moving
t
h
e
water back to move him forward. Thrift is his wonderful
s
e
c
ret; he has schooled out all extravagance. No muscle
r
i
p
ples without compensation wrist cock to heel snap to
h
i
s
mobile mouth that siphons in the air that nurtures
h
i
m
at half an inch above the sea level so to speak.

```
    T
  h
    e
    astonishing whites of the soles of his feet rise
                                                   a
                                                     n
                                                   d
    salute us on the turns. He flips, converts, and is gone
    a
  l
    l
    in one. We watch him for signs. His arms are steady at
                                                   t
                                                     h
                                                   e
    catch, his cadent feet tick in the stretch, they know
    t
  h
    e
    lesson well. Lungs know, too; he does not list for
                                                   a
                                                     i
                                                   r
    he drives along on little sips carefully expended
    b
  u
    t
    that plum red heart pumps hard cries hurt how soon
                                                   i
                                                     t
                                                   s
    near one more and makes its final surge TIME: 4:25:9
```

MAXINE W. KUMIN

1. a) What is interesting about the form of this concrete poem?
   b) What do you feel the author was trying to do?
   c) Does she succeed in fulfilling her purpose? Comment.
2. Write your own concrete poem about another type of competitive swimming (e.g. diving) or about another sport (golf, boxing, demolition derbies).

MOODS

1. Compare and contrast what the last three poems in this unit have to say about competitive sports.
2. Write a letter to the author of the mood poem you enjoyed most, telling what you liked about his/her work.
3. Comment on nineteenth century British poet William Wordsworth's statement that "poetry is the spontaneous overflow of powerful feelings."
4. Write an appropriate poem to fit the mood of a favorite instrumental piece. Include the record or tape with your poem.
5. Discuss the effective use of form in any two unit poems.
6. Put together a slide presentation or a video to accompany any song lyric in this text.

Journeys and Flights

Puff (The Magic Dragon)

Puff the magic dragon lived by the sea
And frolicked in the autumn mist in a land called Honah Lee,
Little Jackie Paper loved that rascal, Puff,
And brought him strings and sealing wax and other fancy stuff.

Chorus:
Oh! Puff the magic dragon lived by the sea
And frolicked in the autumn mist in a land called Honah Lee.

Together they would travel on a boat with billowed sail,
Jackie kept a lookout perched on Puff's gigantic tail.
Noble kings and princes would bow whene'er they came,
Pirate ships would lower their flags when Puff roared out his name.

Chorus

A dragon lives forever but not so little boys.
Painted wings and giant's rings make way for other toys.

One gray night it happened, Jackie Paper came no more,
And Puff that mighty dragon, he ceased his fearless roar.

His head was bent in sorrow, green scales fell like rain.
Puff no longer went to play along the cherry lane.
Without his lifelong friend, Puff could not be brave.
So Puff, that mighty dragon, sadly slipped into his cave.

Chorus

PETER YARROW AND LEONARD LIPTON

1. What kind of picture is presented in the first two stanzas?
2. What did Jackie Paper gain from his relationship with Puff?
3. Why did Jackie stop coming to visit Puff?
4. What does the song suggest we leave behind when we enter adulthood?
5. This song has been popular for many years. What makes it appealing to so many people?
6. Compose an additional stanza that tells what happened after the dragon slipped into his cave. As near as possible, keep the same rhyme and rhythm pattern established by the preceding stanzas.
7. Role play a conversation that Jackie might have had with Puff. Follow this by improvising a conversation between Jackie and his parents as he tries to explain about Puff.

What Do I Remember of the Evacuation?

What do I remember of the evacuation?
I remember my father telling Tim and me
About the mountains and the train
And the excitement of going on a trip.
What do I remember of the evacuation?
I remember my mother weeping
A blanket around me and my
Pretending to fall asleep so she would be happy
Though I was so excited I couldn't sleep
(I hear there were people herded
Into the Hastings Park like cattle.
Families were made to move in two hours
Abandoning everything, leaving pets
And possessions at gun point.

I hear families were broken up
Men were forced to work. I heard
It whispered late at night
That there was suffering) and
I missed my dolls.
What do I remember of the evacuation?
I remember Miss Foster and Miss Tucker
Who still live in Vancouver
And who did what they could
And loved the children and who gave me
A puzzle to play with on the train.
And I remember the mountains and I was
Six years old and I swear I saw a giant
Gulliver of Gulliver's Travels scanning the horizon
And when I told my mother she believed it too
And I remember how careful my parents were
Not to bruise us with bitterness
And I remember the puzzle of Lorraine Life
Who said "Don't insult me" when I
Proudly wrote my name in Japanese
And Tim flew the Union Jack
When the war was over but Lorraine
And her friends spat on us anyway
And I prayed to God who loves
All the children in his sight
That I might be white.

JOY KOGAWA

1. What evacuation is the writer describing?
2. What do we learn about the speaker from her memories?
3. What emotions does the speaker remember feeling?
4. What method of development does the writer use? Is it effective? Comment.
5. Evaluate the poem's ending. Does it strengthen the poem? Explain.
6. Rewrite the poem as a personal letter the speaker might have written to a niece or nephew who wanted to know what the evacuation was like.
7. Write a letter that the speaker's mother or father might have written to a member of Parliament after having been evacuated.

A note on the public transportation system

It's not hard to begin
a conversation with the person
who happens to be seated
nearest you, especially when she's been
reading with apparent interest
a book that's one of your
favourites and can't find
her matches.
The difficulty is
once you've spoken you can never
go back to being comfortable
with silence,
even if you learn
you've nothing to say
and would rather not
listen.
You can stop talking
but you can't forget
the broken wires
dangling there between you.
You'll smile
almost guiltily
when your glances
accidentally bump
against each other.
It may get so bad
that one of you will have to
pretend to fall asleep.

ALDEN NOWLAN

1. Why does the speaker want to begin a conversation with the person next to him? What are two excuses he gives?
2. Why is it difficult to go back to silence after having talked to a stranger?
3. What do the images of "the broken wires" and the glances that accidentally "bump" emphasize? Are they effective? Why?
4. Working with a partner, improvise an impromptu conversation that two strangers might have on a bus or in a waiting room.
5. Using dialogue form, write out a conversation you remember having with a stranger. Describe the setting and give your impressions of the other person.

Hitch-Hiking

that spring
I remember
how the cold nightwind
knifing the prairie
somewhere south
of north battleford
poisoned me.

each hour added
another spoon of hate
to my marrow
as I became more
violent—cursing
every truckdriver
that passed me.

i know that
if the world
had been a single brick
about that time,
one karate blow
propelled by the helium
of my hate
would have cracked it
in half.

and then a truck stopped—
that very moment
i could have become
a downright bootlicker.

i could have curled
the dust
on that man's boots
into a nightingale
which might have flown
away with the first
puff of air
as his foot tramped
the gas pedal to the floor.

ANDREW SUKNASKI

1. What were the speaker's feelings before he obtained a ride? Which words or images communicate those feelings best?

2. What were his feelings after he obtained a ride?
3. What is the purpose of the nightingale image in the last stanza? Is it effective?
4. Why does the author use a capitalized "I" in the first half of the poem but a small "i" in the second half?
5. Comment on the effectiveness of the figurative language used in the first three stanzas. How are the images linked?
6. Working in small groups, prepare and present a conversation that might have taken place between the hitch-hiker and the driver who gave him a ride.
7. Extend the scene in the poem a little further and assume that the speaker has settled in for the night at a town a distance from his destination. Adopt the point of view of the speaker and write a letter home to give them some news.

On the Move

The blue jay scuffling in the bushes follows
Some hidden purpose, and the gust of birds
That spurts across the field, the wheeling swallows,
Have nested in the trees and undergrowth.
Seeking their instinct, or their poise, or both.
One moves with an uncertain violence
Under the dust thrown by a baffled sense
Or the dull thunder of approximate words.

On motorcycles, up the road, they come:
Small, black, as flies hanging in heat, the Boys,
Until the distance throws them forth, their hum
Bulges to thunder held by calf and thigh.
In goggles, donned impersonality,
In gleaming jackets trophied with the dust,
They strap in doubt—by hiding it, robust—
And almost hear a meaning in their noise.

Exact conclusion of their hardiness
Has no shape yet, but from known whereabouts
They ride, direction where the tires press.
They scare a flight of birds across the field;
Much that is natural, to the will must yield.
Men manufacture both machine and soul,
And use what they imperfectly control
To dare a future from the taken routes.

It is a part solution, after all.
One is not necessarily discord
On earth; or damned because, half animal,
One lacks direct instinct, because one wakes
Afloat on movement that divides and breaks.
One joins the movement in a valueless world,
Choosing it, till, both hurler and the hurled,
One moves as well, always toward, toward.

A minute holds them, who have come to go:
The self-defined, astride the created will
They burst away; the towns they travel through
Are home for neither bird nor holiness,
For birds and saints complete their purposes.
At worst, one is in motion; and at best,
Reaching no absolute, in which to rest,
One is always nearer by not keeping still.

THOM GUNN

1. Why does the poet begin by describing the movement of birds? How does he eventually link the birds and the motorcyclists? What do they have in common?
2. What movement is there in stanza two? What senses are affected most by the approach of the motorcyclists?
3. What does the speaker think of the motorcyclists?
4. Is the speaker a pessimist or an optimist? How does he view life?
5. What is one moving "toward, toward" (stanza four)?
6. Design and illustrate a wall poster intended to cheer up people who wonder about the meaning of life.
7. Role play a conversation between the poem's speaker and two or three bikers.
8. Improvise a talk show with two or three motorcyclists as guests.

A Horse with No Name

On the first part of the journey
I was looking at all the life
There were plants and birds and rocks and things
There was sand and hills and rings
The first thing I met was a fly with a buzz
And the sky with no clouds

The heat was hot and the ground was dry
But the air was full of sound

I've been through the desert on a horse with no name
It felt good to be out of the rain
In the desert you can remember your name
'Cause there ain't no one for to give you no pain
La, la. . . .

After two days in the desert sun
My skin began to turn red
After three days in the desert fun
I was looking at a river bed
And the story it told of a river that flowed
Made me sad to think it was dead

You see I've been through the desert on a horse
with no name
It felt good to be out of the rain
In the desert you can remember your name
'Cause there ain't no one for to give you no pain
La, la. . . .

After nine days I let the horse run free
'Cause the desert had turned to sea
There were plants and birds and rocks and things
There was sand and hills and rings
The ocean is a desert with its life underground
And a perfect disguise above
Under the cities lies a heart made of ground
But the humans will give no love

You see I've been through the desert on a horse
with no name
It felt good to be out of the rain
In the desert you can remember your name
'Cause there ain't no one for to give you no pain
La, la. . . .

DEWEY BUNNELL

1. Various readers have seen different messages in this song. Study the stanzas carefully and decide if they can be seen as commenting on:
   a) the world before and after a nuclear war;
   b) an individual's feelings of alienation from society;

c) the journey from childhood to adulthood;
d) the problem of pollution as a threat to our future.

2. You have considered four possible interpretations. Can you think of any other explanations of this song's content?
3. Which of the interpretations that you explored is the best one? Why?
4. Write a poem in which you describe three stages of a journey. You may wish to write about an actual trip or about another sort of journey, such as the first years of school, gaining skills in a sport, or changing tastes in music or reading.
5. Imagine that this song was inspired by a dream. Write a dream diary entry the author might have written upon awakening just after the dream was over.

Don Quixote

Through the woodland, through the valley
Comes a horseman wild and free.
Tilting at the windmills passing,
Who can the brave young horseman be?

He is wild but he is mellow.
He is strong but he is weak.
He is cruel but he is gentle.
He is wise but he is weak.

Reaching for his saddlebag,
He takes a battered book into his hand.
Standing like a prophet bold,
He shouts across the ocean to the shore
'Til he can shout no more.

"I have come o'er moor and mountain
Like the hawk upon the wing.
I was once a shining knight
Who was the guardian of a king.

I have searched the whole world over
Looking for a place to sleep.
I have seen the strong survive
And I have seen the lean grow weak.

See the children of the earth
Who wake to find the table bare.
See the gentry in the country
Riding off to take the air."

Reaching for his saddlebag,
He takes a rusty sword into his hand.
Then striking up a knightly pose,
He shouts across the ocean to the shore
'Til he can shout no more.

"See the jailer with his key
Who locks away all trace of sin.
See the judge upon the bench
Who tries the case as best he can.

See the wise and wicked ones
Who feed upon life's sacred fire.
See the soldier with his gun
Who must be dead to be admired.

See the man who tips the needle.
See the man who buys and sells.
See the man who puts the collar
On the ones who dare not tell.

See the drunkard in the tavern,
Stemming gold to make ends meet.
See the youth in ghetto black,
Condemned to life upon the street."

Reaching for his saddlebag,
He takes a tarnished cross into his hand.
Standing like a preacher now,
He shouts across the ocean to the shore.

Then in a blaze of tangled hooves,
He gallops off across the dusty plain
In vain to search again
Where no one will hear.

Through the woodland, through the valley
Comes a horseman wild and free.
Tilting at the windmills passing,
Who can the brave young horseman be?

He is wild but he is mellow.
He is strong but he is weak.
He is cruel but he is gentle.
He is wise but he is meek.

GORDON LIGHTFOOT

1. a) Who was Don Quixote?
   b) Why do you think that Lightfoot chose to write about this famous literary character?
2. a) How does the author portray Don Quixote in the song lyrics?
   b) What do the images of the following stanzas (3, 7, 12) add to the portrayal of this figure?
3. a) What views of our society are presented in this selection?
   b) Is there any implied social criticism?
4. a) What do you think Don Quixote is searching for?
   b) What do you think he is shouting?
   c) Why does no one hear?
5. Draw a picture to illustrate one of the scenes described in the poem.
6. If you are familiar with other songs by Lightfoot and enjoy his work, name his best song lyric and give reasons for your selection.

Jazz Solo

Let music pierce the night
The clarinet has spoken
And the drums
The trombone had its moments
Piano keys rang out
Hold your breath, melody
It's time for trumpet talk:

Listen—let it carry you
Over and away
Fierce and golden
Into the endless, nameless night
As you soar with it
Beyond the city
So high above:

A meteor of melody
To light the sky
Dazzle it with
Total incandescence

Northern Lights of sound
Shifting elusively
Faster than vision
Brighter than fire

Clear and mysterious
Like midnight touching dawn

Listen till melody
Bursts into echo
And silence shouts
Into memory

Oh, yes, you heard it
And you were it
And it was you

And the end
Was only the beginning . . .

R. GLENN MARTIN

1. What experience is the speaker describing?
2. What words or images help to convey the intensity of the experience?
3. What common thread links the imagery in stanzas two, three, and four?
4. Deep enjoyment of music, art, dance, or reading is difficult to describe. To some people, it is a "magic moment"—a transcending of self. Has this poet succeeded in capturing the experience? Comment.
5. Listen to your favorite music and jot down phrases that describe how it sounds and how it makes you feel. Organize the phrases, add to them, and revise them until you have produced a free verse poem that captures the experience of listening to your favorite music.

Crash

Emergency Landing

city like dropped stars
dazzled, the engines forget,
powerless, we fall

Ambulances

like vultures below,
and it is we who circle,
broken-winged above.

LEONA GOM

1. Aside from the 5-7-5 syllable/line structure, what patterns in content or subject matter are revealed by these haiku?
2. Do some research on the haiku. Bring in some examples of the haiku written by Japanese and translated into English. How and why do these haiku differ from the ones in your textbook?

JOURNEYS AND FLIGHTS

1. The poems in this unit deal with several types of journeys: into adulthood, across land, into progress, and out of life. Can you think of other journeys we make? Write a poem in which you describe one of the journeys you identified.
2. Which poem in this unit did you most enjoy? Why?
3. Compare the attitude toward life in "Hitch-Hiking" with that in "On the Move".
4. Write a poem from the point of view of Jackie, Puff ("The Magic Dragon"), the truck driver ("Hitch-Hiking"), or a biker ("On the Move").
5. A journey we all make is through time. To examine how you use time, try the following: draw up a schedule for tomorrow, showing what you expect to be doing from when you get up to when you go to sleep. After going through the day, sit down and examine the schedule. In a paragraph or two, give your thoughts about what you expected to do as compared to what you did.
6. If you have been on a long journey and have photographs or slides of it, prepare and present a talk to the class. Aim at interesting them in taking the same trip.
7. The journey is a frequent motif in literature. How many works can you name that involve journeys? Why is the journey such a popular motif for literary works?

Visions

AUGUST

Saturday **27**

They are setting
up new rules—

a smaller particle
was discovered.

CARL FERNBACH-FLARSHEIM

1. Account for the source of this poem.
2. Do you like this selection? Why or why not?
3. Compose a similar found poem in note form as a result of an actual telephone conversation with a friend.
4. What does found poetry teach us about the nature of poetry in general?

Wired for Sound

I like small speakers, I like tall speakers,
If they've music, they're wired for sound.

Walkin' about with a head full of music,
Cassette in my pocket and I'm gonna use it—stereo—
Out in the street you know—oh, oh . . .
Into the car, go to work and I'm cruisin',
I never think that I'll blow all my fuses,
Traffic flows into the breakfast show—oh, oh . . .

Power from the needle to the plastic,
A.M.-F.M., I feel so ecstatic now.
It's music I've found
And I'm wired for sound.

I was small boy who don't like his toys,
I could not wait to get wired for sound.

I met a girl and she told me she loved me,
I said, "You love me, but love means you must like what I like.
My music is dynamite—oh, oh . . ."
She said, "I'm not a girl you put on at a standby,
I am a girl who demands that her love is amplified.
Switch into overdrive."—oh, oh . . .

Power from the needle to the plastic,
A.M.-F.M., I feel so ecstatic now.
It's music I've found
And I'm wired for sound.

ALAN TARNEY AND B.A. ROBERTSON

1. Find examples of the following in this song lyric: rhyme, rhythm, chorus, and parallel structure.
2. What is meant by the following audio equipment expressions: "plastic," "A.M.," "F.M.," "standby," "amplified," "overdrive," and "wired for sound?"

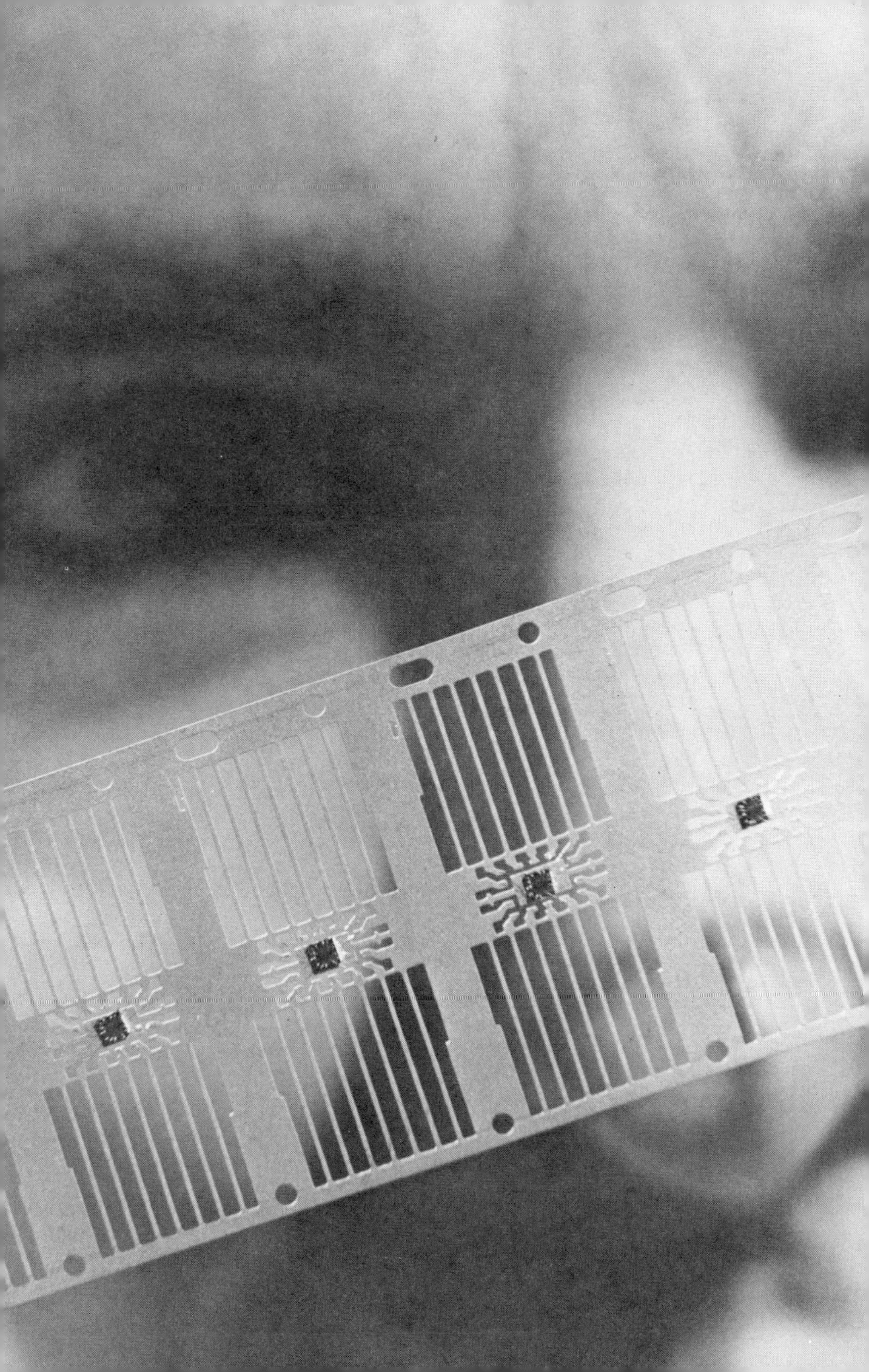

3. Find two examples of puns and explain the humor.
4. By its nature, rock and roll music breaks various musical and language conventions. a) Find one example of informal language usage and another example of poor grammar. b) Discuss what these two examples add to the overall impact of the lyrics on the listener.
5. a) What evidence is there that the speaker is obsessed with music?
   b) What evidence is there that he is a chauvinist?
   c) What evidence is there that his girl won't be pushed around by him?
6. Write down the lyrics for your favorite song. Tell why you enjoy the words and/or why you consider the lyrics to be poetry.

Klaxon

All day cars mooed and shrieked,
Hollered and bellowed and wept
Upon the road.
They slid by with bits of fur attached,
Fox-tails and rabbit-legs,
The skulls and horns of deer,
Cars with yellow spectacles
Or motorcycle monocle,
Cars whose gold eyes burnt
With too-rich battery,
Murderous cars and manslaughter cars,
Chariots from whose foreheads leapt
Silver women of ardent bosom.
Ownerless, passengerless, driverless,
They came to anyone
And with headlights full of tears
Begged for a master,
For someone to drive them
For the familiar chauffeur.
Limousines covered with pink slime
Of children's blood
Turned into the open fields
And fell over into ditches,
The wheels kicking helplessly.
Taxis begged trees to step inside,
Automobiles begged of posts

The whereabouts of their mother.
But no one wished to own them anymore.
Everyone wished to walk.

JAMES REANEY

1. What might have prompted the poet to write about cars as he did?
2. Comment on the meanings of the following images:
   a) "All day cars mooed and shrieked"
   b) "Cars with yellow spectacles/Or motorcycle monocle"
   c) "Taxis begged trees to step inside".
3. Why is the poem called "Klaxon"?
4. Make a collage to express your responses to this poem.
5. Contact the local police department for information about motor vehicle accidents in your area. Report your findings to the class, stating whether or not Reaney's poem is relevant to your area.

The Memory of a Poem

Out of the air I draw the memory of a bird.
Out of the earth I draw the memory of a tree.
From the memory of the bird
and the memory of the tree
I make the memory of a poem
that weighs lighter than air
and floats away without wind.

MICHAEL BULLOCK

1. According to the speaker, what is a poem?
2. What quality of poetry does "The Memory of a Poem" emphasize?
3. Within the poem, the word "memory" is repeated five times. What would be the poet's purpose in doing so? Is the repetition effective? Comment.
4. Of the poems in Chapter 1 of this book, which do you think is the most memorable? Why?

More Intricate

More intricate
than ferns,
the keys of being.

Before this writing
you stood opaque.

My poem and
now this
suddenness of seeing.

MILTON ACORN

1. What motivated the author to write this poem?
2. What has the author gained from writing it?
3. According to Acorn, what is one benefit of writing poetry?

A Kite Is a Victim

A kite is a victim you are sure of.
You love it because it pulls
gentle enough to call you master,
strong enough to call you fool;
because it lives
like a desperate trained falcon
in the high sweet air,
and you can always haul it down
to tame it in your drawer.

A kite is a fish you have already caught
in a pool where no fish come,
so you play him carefully and long,
and hope he won't give up,
or the wind die down.

A kite is the last poem you've written,
so you give it to the wind,
but you don't let it go
until someone finds you
something else to do.

A kite is a contract of glory
that must be made with the sun,
so you make friends with the field

the river and the wind,
then you pray the whole cold night before,
under the travelling cordless moon,
to make you worthy and lyric and pure.

LEONARD COHEN

1. a) What similes and metaphors are used by Cohen to describe the kite?
   b) How are each of these appropriate?
2. Comment on whether or not the poet's use of "you" is a successful device.
3. Imitating Cohen's style, write a two or three stanza poem on another simple, but "liberating" object, such as a frisbee or a book.

T-Bar

Relentless, black on white, the cable runs
through metal arches up the mountainside
At intervals giant pickaxes are hung
on long hydraulic springs. The skiers ride
propped by the axehead, twin automatons
supported by its handle, one each side.

In twos they move slow motion up the steep
incision in the mountain. Climb. Climb.
Somnambulists, bolt upright in their sleep
their phantom poles swung lazily behind,
while to the right, the empty T-bars keep
in mute descent, slow monstrous jigging time.

Captive the skiers now and innocent,
wards of eternity, each pair alone.
They mount the easy vertical ascent,
pass through successive arches, bride and groom,
as through successive naves, are newly wed
participants in some recurring dream.

So do they move forever. Clocks are broken.
In zones of silence they grow tall and slow,
inanimate dreamers, mild and gentle-spoken,
blood brothers of the haemophilic snow
until the summit breaks and they awaken
imagos from the stricture of the tow.

Jerked from her chrysalis the sleeping bride
suffers too sudden freedom like a pain.
The dreaming bridegroom severed from her side
singles her out, the old wound aches again.
Uncertain, lost, upon a wintry height
these two not separate yet no longer one.

But clocks begin to peck and sing. The slow
extended minute like a rubber band
snaps back to nothing and the skiers go
quickly articulate, while far behind
etching the sky-line, obdurate and slow
the spastic T-bars pivot and descend.

P.K. PAGE

1. What is being described in stanza 1?
2. What metaphors does the author use to describe the skiers? How are the metaphors connected? Are they effective? Explain.
3. The ride up the T-bar is unreal, like a vision. How does the author emphasize the specialness of that moment?
4. Explain the paradox in line 30.
5. Examine the poem for references to time. How does the movement of time change in the poem? Why are the references to time important?
6. Some circumstances cause us to lose our sense of reality temporarily, to feel that something is "unreal". Think of such a circumstance (e.g., while shopping, at a party, working while tired, eating in the school cafeteria, taking your driver's test, etc.) and write down any images that come to mind. Use these images to create a poem that captures the "unreality" of the situation.

Circle of Steel

Rows of lights in a circle of steel
Where you place your bets on a great big wheel,
High windows flickerin' down through the snow,
A time you know.
Sights and sounds of the people goin' 'round,
Everybody's in step with the season.

A child is born to a welfare case

Where the rats run around like they own the place.
The room is chilly, the building is old.
That's how it goes.
A doctor's found on his welfare rounds,
And he comes and he leaves on the double.

"Deck the Halls" was the song they played
In the flat next door where they shout all day.
She tips her gin bottle back 'til it's gone,
The child is strong.
A week, a day, they will take it away
For they know about all her bad habits.

Christmas dawns and the snow lets up
And the sun hits the handle of her heirloom cup.
She hides her face in her hands for awhile,
Says, "Look here, child.
Your father's pride was his means to provide
And he's servin' three years for that reason."

Rows of lights in a circle of steel
Where you place your bets on a great big wheel,
High windows flickerin' down through the snow,
A time you know.
Sights and sounds of the people goin' 'round,
Everybody's in step with the season.

GORDON LIGHTFOOT

1. a) What is the setting established in stanza 1?
   b) Would the poem have worked as well with a different setting?
2. a) What is the situation of the main characters of the poem?
   b) What circumstances caused or contributed to their situation?
3. What is the significance of the reference to the "heirloom cup"?
4. Why does the poem end with the first stanza repeated?

The Chimney Sweeper

When my mother died I was very young,
And my father sold me while yet my tongue
Could scarcely cry " 'weep! 'weep! 'weep! 'weep!"
So your chimneys I sweep, and in soot I sleep.

There's little Tom Dacre, who cried when his head,
That curled like a lamb's back, was shaved; so I said,
"Hush, Tom! never mind it, for, when your head's bare,
You know that the soot cannot spoil your white hair."

And so he was quiet, and that very night,
As Tom was asleeping, he had such a sight!
That thousands of sweepers, Dick, Joe, Ned, and Jack,
Were all of them locked up in coffins of black.

And by came an Angel who had a bright key,
And he opened the coffins and set them all free;
Then down a green plain leaping, laughing, they run,
And wash in a river, and shine in the sun

Then naked and white, all their bags left behind,
They rise upon clouds and sport in the wind;
And the Angel told Tom if he'd be a good boy,
He'd have God for his father, and never want joy.

And so Tom awoke, and we rose in the dark,
And got with our bags and our brushes to work.
Though the morning was cold, Tom was happy and warm;
So if all do their duty they need not fear harm.

WILLIAM BLAKE

1. a) What is the subject of this poem?
   b) What is the theme of this poem?
2. a) Find three images that support the poem's subject and theme. Discuss their effectiveness.
   b) Find three interesting uses of sound (eg. rhyme, alliteration) that support the poem's subject and theme. Discuss their effectiveness.
3. Discuss the impact the following changes would have on the sound and image effectiveness of the poem:
   line 3–changing "weep" to "sweep"
   4–changing "soot" to "ashes"
   6–eliminating the simile
   8–changing "white" to "blond"
   9–changing "that very" to "one"
   11–changing "thousands" to "many"; changing "Ned" to "Johnny"
   13–eliminating "bright"; changing line to read "And an angel came by who had a key,"

15–changing "leaping" to "jumping"
16–changing "shine" to "smile"
21–changing "rose" to "got up"
23–changing "cold" to "damp"
24–changing "all" to "all chimney sweeps"

Wondering Where the Lions Are

Sun's up, uh huh, looks okay
the world survives into another day
and I'm thinking about eternity
some kind of ecstasy got a hold on me.

I had another dream about lions at the door
they weren't half as frightening as they were before
but I'm thinking about eternity
some kind of ecstasy got a hold on me.

Walls, windows, trees, waves coming through
you be in me and I'll be in you
together in eternity
some kind of ecstasy got a hold on me.

Up among the firs where it smells so sweet
or down in the valley where the river used to be
I got my mind on eternity
some kind of ecstasy got a hold on me.

And I'm wondering where the lions are ...
I'm wondering where the lions are ...

Huge orange flying boat rises off a lake
thousand year-old petroglyphs doing a double-take
pointing a finger at eternity
I'm sitting in the middle of this ecstasy.

Young men marching, helmets shining in the sun
polished and precise like the brain behind the gun
(should be) they got me thinking about eternity
some kind of ecstasy got a hold on me.

And I'm wondering where the lions are ...
I'm wondering where the lions are ...

Freighters on the nod on the surface of the bay
one of these days we're going to sail away
going to sail into eternity
some kind of ecstasy got a hold on me.

And I'm wondering where the lions are . . .
I'm wondering where the lions are . . .

BRUCE COCKBURN

1. What emotion is the speaker expressing through this lyric?
2. Examine the imagery. How does it help to communicate the speaker's feelings?
3. What does the speaker mean by "eternity"? What has caused him to think about it?
4. What do the lions symbolize?
5. How does the speaker feel about his own mood? Does he think it will last? Explain.
6. Think of your favorite setting and compose a poem that describes it vividly for the reader. Try to capture what it is about the spot that makes it so special.
7. Using the basic idea of this poem, prepare a collage or a slide presentation that juxtaposes peaceful moments with apprehensive feelings.

VISIONS

1. What do the visions in "A Kite Is a Victim" and "T-Bar" have in common?
2. If "Klaxon" were read with music in the background, what type of music would be most effective? Why? What type of music would be best behind "T-Bar"? Why?
3. Consider the poems in this unit. How might the world be changed if human beings lost the ability to envision, to dream?
4. Create your own visions as you listen to an instrumental song. Let the music suggest pictures or images for you. After you have listened to the music, jot down a brief description of the images and listen once more. Adjust or extend the images until you feel they reflect the full movement of the music. Take the images you have described and convert them into a script for a film that could be used with the music as its soundtrack.
5. Working in small groups, prepare and tape a children's radio program focusing on fairy tales.
6. What similar feelings are expressed in "Wondering Where the Lions Are" and "Jazz Solo"?
7. Discuss the poetic visions presented by "Memory of a Poem," "More Intricate" and "A Kite Is a Victim."

As I See It

Standing on Tiptoe

Standing on tiptoe ever since my youth
  Striving to grasp the future just above,
I hold at length the only future—Truth,
  And Truth is Love.

I feel as one who being awhile confined
  Sees drop to dust about him all his bars:—
The clay grows less, and, leaving it, the mind
  Dwells with the stars

GEORGE FREDERICK CAMERON

1. What is the author conveying through the image of standing on tiptoe? Is it effective? Why?
2. In what way can Truth be considered to be a person's future?
3. What does the author mean by "Truth is Love"?
4. What feeling is being expressed in the last stanza? What has given the speaker that feeling?
5. Many people have searched for the meaning of life, and many have different opinions as to what is meaningful. Write a personal essay giving your thoughts on what makes life worth living.
6. Write a poem addressed to the graduating class for this year. Offer the graduate's thoughts about finding a direction in life.

The Gambler

On a warm summer's evenin' on a train bound for nowhere,
I met up with a gambler; we were both too tired to sleep.
So we took turns a-starin' out the window at the darkness
'Til boredom overtook us, and he began to speak.

He said, "Son, I've made a life out of readin' people's faces,
And knowin' what their cards were by the way they held their
  eyes.
So if you don't mind my sayin', I can see you're out of aces.
For a taste of your whiskey, I'll give you some advice."

So I handed him my bottle and he drank down my last
swallow.
Then he bummed a cigarette and asked me for a light.
And the night got deathly quiet, and his face lost all
expression.
He said, "If you're gonna play the game, boy, you gotta learn to
play it right.

You got to know when to hold 'em, know when to fold 'em,
Know when to walk away, and know when to run.
You never count your money when you're sittin' at the table.
There'll be time enough for countin' when the dealin's done.

Every gambler knows that the secret to survivin'
Is knowin' what to throw away and knowin' what to keep;
'Cause every hand's a winner and every hand's a loser,
And the best that you can hope for is to die in your sleep."

And when he'd finished speakin', he turned back toward the
window,
Crushed out his cigarette and faded off to sleep.
And somewhere in the darkness, the gambler, he broke even,
But in his final words I found an ace that I could keep.

"You got to know when to hold 'em, know when to fold 'em,
Know when to walk away and know when to run.
You never count your money when you're sittin' at the table,
There'll be time enough for countin' when the dealin's done."

DON SCHLITZ

1. a) What is the game mentioned in stanza 3?
   b) Interpret the various card terms mentioned.
2. This is an example of a *dramatic poem*. Explain what you think is meant by the term and how "The Gambler" illustrates the main features of dramatic poetry.
3. In one or two paragraphs, analyze life in terms of another game, pastime or hobby.
4. Tell about an experience in which someone, a stranger perhaps, changed your views on life.
5. Act out and/or videotape your own original interpretation of "The Gambler." (You may wish to use Kenny Rogers' recording for accompaniment.)

Advice to the Young

1
Keep bees and
grow asparagus,
watch the tides
and listen to the
wind instead of
the politicians
make up your own
stories and believe
them if you want to
live the good life.

2
All rituals
are instincts
never fully
trust them but
study to im-
prove biology
with reason.

3
Digging trenches
for asparagus
is good for the
muscles and
waiting for the
plants to settle
teaches patience
to those who are
usually in too
much of a hurry.

4
There is morality
in bee-keeping
it teaches how
not to be afraid
of the bee swarm
it teaches how
not to be afraid of
finding new places
and building in them
all over again.

MIRIAM WADDINGTON

1. What can be learned from growing asparagus? From keeping bees? If we are able to learn such valuable things from those two acts, what does that suggest about living close to nature?
2. According to the speaker, what value is there in watching the tides and listening to the wind instead of the politicians?
3. Why must people make up their own stories and believe them in order to live the good life?
4. What does the speaker mean by "rituals"? Why should we never fully trust them?
5. What, ultimately, is the advice being given in this poem? Is it good advice? Explain.
6. A magazine for senior citizens is asking for poetry submissions. Compose a poem called "Advice to the Elderly" or "Advice to Seniors".
7. Compose a concrete or free verse poem called "The Good Life". Print the poem on a large sheet and illustrate it with a collage or magazine pictures or with original artwork.

Trees

I think that I shall never see
A poem lovely as a tree.

A tree whose hungry mouth is pressed
Against the earth's sweet flowing breast;

A tree that looks to God all day,
And lifts her leafy arms to pray;

A tree that may in summer wear
A nest of robins in her hair;

Upon whose bosom snow has lain;
Who intimately lives with rain.

Poems are made by fools like me,
But only God can make a tree.

JOYCE KILMER

Song of the Open Road

I think that I shall never see
A billboard lovely as a tree.

Indeed, unless the billboards fall
I'll never see a tree at all.

OGDEN NASH

1. "Trees" draws a comparison between poetry and trees. According to Kilmer, in what way is a tree more beautiful than a poem?
2. What does the closing couplet have to say about art and nature?
3. In "Song of the Open Road", Nash draws a comparison between billboards and trees. In what way is his comparison similar to Kilmer's?
4. What comment does Nash make through his poem? How is his comment similar to Kilmer's?
5. Compose your own parody of Kilmer's poem. Begin with the same opening line and substitute your own noun for "poem" (and for "tree", if you wish).

Paper Matches

My aunts washed dishes while the uncles
squirted each other on the lawn with
garden hoses. Why are we in here,
I said, and they are out there,
That's the way it is,
said Aunt Hetty, the shrivelled-up one.

I have the rages that small animals have,
being small, being animal.
Written on me was a message,
'At Your Service' like a book of
paper matches. One by one we were
taken out and struck,
We come bearing supper,
our heads on fire.

PAULETTE JILES

1. What did Aunt Hetty mean by her statement, "That's the way it is"?
2. What is the speaker emphasizing by describing herself as a "small animal"?

3. How does the speaker see the role of women in relation to men? How does she feel about it?
4. Is the comparison of women's roles to paper matches effective? Explain.
5. Script or improvise a dialogue between the poem's speaker and one of the uncles.
6. In small groups, discuss and report back to the class your views on this question: what does it mean for any individual, man or woman, to be liberated?

Let No Charitable Hope

Now let no charitable hope
Confuse my mind with images
Of eagle and of antelope;
I am in nature none of these.

I was, being human, born alone:
I am, being woman, hard beset;
I live by squeezing from a stone
The little nourishment I get.

In masks outrageous and austere
The years go by in single file:
But none has merited my fear,
And none has quite escaped my smile.

ELINOR WYLIE

1. How does the speaker see herself?
2. What is the speaker's attitude toward life?
3. What are the images of the eagle and the antelope intended to symbolize?
4. Explain the double meaning in the phrase "in single file".
5. Is the speaker a happy person? Comment.
6. The poem refers to two animals as symbols for types of character. What animal would you liken your own character to? Write a poem in which you explain the similarities.

New Year's Day, 1978

If I had thought forty years ago
when I asked myself where I would be

twenty—thirty—forty years from then—

If someone had told me then,
"On New Year's Day of 1978
you'll be sitting alone in a highrise apartment
in Saskatoon, Saskatchewan
writing a poem to yourself,"
how disappointed would I have been?

A fifteen-year-old romantic,
a brainy silly goose in love for the first time of many,
full of high ideals, religion, bad poetry, incurable shyness:
it's easy to laugh at myself as I was then
if I don't envy myself.

Fame, I thought.
Love, I thought.
Sons and daughters.
A big house with an orchard behind it.
Athens. Troy.
Heaven at the end, where I would meet my friends and
relatives
miraculously young again.

I drink coffee, watch the smoke wreaths
rise above clustered branches,
imagine the delicate tracery
of hoarfrost on red berries.

I have lived all my life in rented rooms;
my loves have been temporary;
my best friends are dead;
I have no children.
I have yet to visit Troy (Where is it?)
My great book is still to be written.
I believe in God
only intermittently.
I live (like everyone else)
in fear of the destruction
of my country and my world.

Yet I would not change
these forty years,
would not omit depressions, wars, conflict,
death, pain,
or this solitude in which I drink coffee.

Smoke rises. The river flows under the ice.
There is a new blossom on my geranium.

A friend writes she is having a baby in July.
Next week I am giving a party.

Ten years from now
I may write my great book.
My lover may marry me
for my old-age pension.

In heaven I shall be a ballet dancer
creating perfect patterns
without words.

ELIZABETH BREWSTER

1. What circumstances prompted the speaker to evaluate her life?
2. What did the speaker originally want from life? How much of it has she accomplished? How does she feel about it?
3. How does the speaker feel about the future? What is her concept of heaven? In what way is the vision appropriate for her?
4. Select one stanza and examine it in detail. What does it reveal? How does it add to the poem?
5. Working in small groups, discuss the following: what do most people want from life? What changes our wants?
6. Write a letter addressed to yourself, to be opened on New Year's day in twenty years' time.

Mending Wall

Something there is that doesn't love a wall,
That sends the frozen-ground-swell under it,
And spills the upper boulders in the sun;
And makes gaps even two can pass abreast.
The work of hunters is another thing:
I have come after them and made repair
Where they have left not one stone on a stone,
But they would have the rabbit out of hiding,
To please the yelping dogs. The gaps I mean.
No one has seen them made or heard them made,
But at spring mending-time we find them there.
I let my neighbour know beyond the hill.
And on a day we meet to walk the line
And set the wall between us once again.,
We keep the wall between us as we go.

To each the boulders that have fallen to each.
And some are loaves and some so nearly balls
We have to use a spell to make them balance:
'Stay where you are until our backs are turned!'
We wear our fingers rough with handling them.
Oh, just another kind of out-door game,
One on a side. It comes to little more:
There where it is we do not need the wall:
He is all pine and I am apple orchard.
My apple trees will never get across
And eat the cones under his pines, I tell him.
He only says, 'Good fences make good neighbours.'
Spring is the mischief in me, and I wonder
If I could put a notion in his head:
'*Why* do they make good neighbours? Isn't it
Where there are cows? But here there are no cows.
Before I built a wall I'd ask to know
What I was walling in or walling out,
And to whom I was like to give offence.
Something there is that doesn't love a wall,
That wants it down.' I could say 'Elves' to him,
But it's not elves exactly, and I'd rather
He said it for himself. I see him there
Bringing a stone grasped firmly by the top
In each hand, like an old-stone savage armed.
He moves in darkness as it seems to me,
Not of woods only and the shade of trees.
He will not go behind his father's saying.
And he likes having thought of it so well
He says again, 'Good fences make good neighbours.'

ROBERT FROST

1. What is meant by "something there is that doesn't love a wall" (lines 1 and 35)? Why did Frost repeat the line?
2. What is the speaker's attitude toward the wall? What mood is he in as he and his neighbor repair the wall?
3. How does the neighbor feel about the wall? What can we surmise about the neighbor's personality?
4. Is it true that "good fences make good neighbors"?
5. What other sorts of walls do people build around themselves? Can the wall in the poem be viewed as a symbol? Discuss.

6. Improvise a dialogue in which one neighbor who has been annoyed by overly-frequent visits from another neighbor explains the value of good fences.
7. Working in small groups, write and present a skit that illustrates one way in which people put barriers between themselves and others.
8. What is it that doesn't love a wall? Write and record a children's story that explains how walls come to be damaged.

In praise of the great bull walrus

I wouldn't like to be one
of the walrus people
for the rest of my life
but I wish I could spend
one sunny afternoon
lying on the rocks with them.
I suspect it would be similar
to drinking beer in a tavern
that caters to longshoremen
and won't admit women.
We'd exchange no
cosmic secrets. I'd merely say,
"How yuh doin' you big old walrus?"
and the nearest of
the walrus people
would answer,
"Me? I'm doin' great.
How yuh doin' yourself,
you big old human being, you?"
How good it is to share
the earth with such creatures
and how unthinkable it would have been
to have missed all this
by not being born:
a happy thought, that,
for not being born is
the only tragedy
that we can imagine
but need never fear.

ALDEN NOWLAN

1. How does the poet's informal tone affect the impact of the last four lines?
2. Is this a well written poem? Defend your answer with quotations from the poem.
3. Write your own poem entitled "In praise of the great bull walrus" dealing with a different aspect of the animal's relation to man.

AS I SEE IT

1. Would the speakers of "The Gambler" and "Advice to the Young" likely get along, considering their individual views? Comment.
2. In your view, which poem presents the best philosophy, insight, or comment? Defend your choice by explaining the poem's value.
3. In what way could the message in "Mending Wall" apply to "Paper Matches" and "Let No Charitable Hope"?
4. Experience in life teaches everyone some principles by which to live. Identify one or two of these "rules" for life that you believe in and present them in a poem entitled "As I See It".
5. Write a script in which you present a conversation between the speakers in:
   A. "Let No Charitable Hope" and "Mending Wall".
   B. "Advice to the Young" and "Paper Matches".
6. Which of the unit poems has a(n)
   a) tongue-in-cheek tone,
   b) bitter tone,
   c) resigned tone
   d) ambiguous tone,
   e) conversational tone,
   f) hopeful tone,
   g) satirical tone?

Love and Separation

The Passionate Shepherd to His Love

Come live with me, and be my love,
And we will all the pleasures prove,
That valleys, groves, hills, and fields,
Woods, or steepy mountain yields.

And we will sit upon the rocks,
Seeing the shepherds feed their flocks,
By shallow rivers, to whose falls
Melodious birds sing madrigals.

And I will make thee beds of roses,
And a thousand fragrant posies,
A cap of flowers, and a kirtle
Embroider'd all with leaves of myrtle;

A gown made of the finest wool,
Which from our pretty lambs we pull,
Fair-lined slippers for the cold,
With buckles of the purest gold;

A belt of straw and ivy buds,
With coral clasps and amber studs,
And if these pleasures may thee move,
Come live with me, and be my love.

The shepherds' swains shall dance and sing
For thy delight each May morning.
If these delights thy mind may move,
Come live with me and be my love.

CHRISTOPHER MARLOWE

1. a) To whom is the poem addressed?
   b) What is the aim of the speaker?
2. This poem is an *idyll*. What characteristics of the idyll does the poem have?
3. What view of love is presented by this poem?
4. Imagine and write the reply from the point of view of a woman's rights activist.

Crossing to Brentwood on the Mill Bay Ferry —November 4, 1975

Now, for the moment, everything is promised.
It is a calm bright day.
Not even any mist over the trees,
nor ice in the slippery roots.
No sense of urgency.

We are crossing the water.
I hold your hand needing
only that. The bare sea is simple enough
and the clean sky that no longer seems
lonely. Birds circle the boat
full of their good messages.

Last night snow fell on the
mountains. I woke up
shivering and afraid.
I needed to know everything about you.
Suddenly I needed to know
more than what there was.

Today, for the moment, everything is forgotten.
I hold your warm hand as if it were something
I had just found wanting to be held and
you smile back. Later when we talk
ours will be other voices.
Now, crossing the water,
I am certain there is only us.

SUSAN MUSGRAVE

1. Is this poem optimistic or pessimistic? Defend your answer with quotations from the poem.
2. What is the relationship between the environment and the speaker's mood and thoughts?
3. Why do you think Musgrave divided the poem into four stanzas? How are these stanzas units?
4. Why did the poet "frame" the poem with two sentences beginning with the word *now*?

love is more thicker than forget

love is more thicker than forget
more thinner than recall
more seldom than a wave is wet
more frequent than to fail

it is most mad and moonly
and less it shall unbe
than all the sea which only
is deeper than the sea

love is less always than to win
less never than alive
less bigger than the least begin
less littler than forgive

it is most sane and sunly
and more it cannot die
than all the sky which only
is higher than the sky

e.e. cummings

1. Working in groups, paraphrase what cummings is saying in each stanza.
2. Would you describe this love poem's tone as positive? Comment.
3. What conventions of poetry-writing does this poem break?
4. Think of three more lines to describe love and write them down, imitating cummings' style (e.g., "love is more closer than friendship").

Such is the power of the lover's sonnet

Tons of force trapped in a handsome bonnet,
compacted by the dreaming bullet's skin
and aching for the liberation of the pin;
such is the power of the lover's sonnet.
I say, release it. Make it fly towards
the hidden targets of this woman's heart.
Carve on the bullet; leave it marked
with runes and crosses, magic words.
What can be lost? At worst you'll miss,
draw curious glances, even scorn

that such a passion should be flown
amid the brassy leavings of spent verse.
Or you might strike and see her colours dip:
Love hits the hardest fired from the hip.

STEPHEN HUME

1. What is the poem about?
2. a) What is the central metaphor of the poem?
   b) To what do the following words refer: "bonnet," "pin," "leavings"?
   c) Is the metaphor a suitable one for describing the subject?
3. What are a) "runes" and b) "spent verse"?
4. What does the poem mean by its last line?
5. If you would like a challenge, try writing your own sonnet about love.

We Are Two Flowers

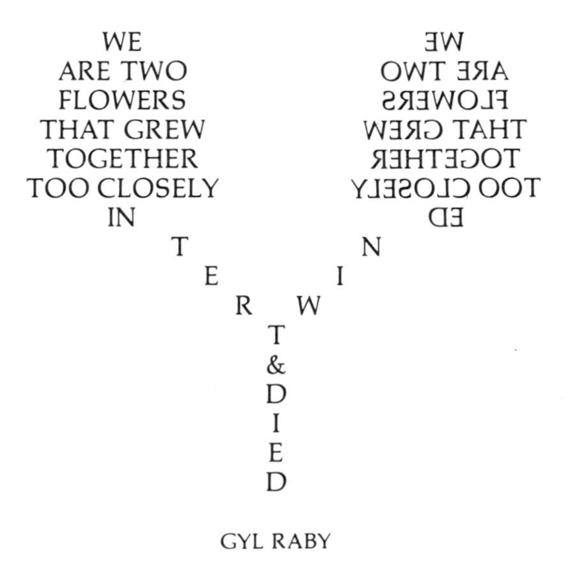

GYL RABY

1. What type of poem is this?
2. What metaphor is used to describe this relationship?

3. What puns are contained in the word "intertwined"? How do they support meanings expressed by the poem?
4. Write your own concrete poem about love.

Like Two Slant Trees

"Lean on me," he said
loving her weakness

And she leaned hard
adoring his strength

Like two slant trees
they grew together

their roots the wrong way
for standing alone

FRED COGSWELL

1. How are the lovers like two slant trees?
2. Using the phrase beginning "Like two ______," construct your own short poem to describe any past, present, or imagined relationship in your life.

The Fisherman's Wife

When I am alone,
The wind in the pine-trees
Is like the shuffling of waves
Upon the wooden sides of a boat.

AMY LOWELL

1. Discuss the effectiveness of this poem's simile.
2. Using similes, write a description of how you feel when you are alone or lonely.

Carol

I was a lover of turkey and holly
But my true love was the Christmas tree.

We hung our hearts from a green green bough
And merry swung the mistletoe.

He decked the tree with a silver apple
And a golden pear,
A partridge and a cockle shell
And a fair maiden.

No rose can tell the fumes of myrrh
That filled the forest of our day
Till fruit and shell and maid fell down
And the partridge flew away.

Now I swing from a brittle twig
For the green bough of my true love hid
A laily worm. Around my neck
The hangman ties the holly.

ANNE WILKINSON

1. Discuss your understanding of the poem, explaining the various images and symbols.
2. Discuss the relationships between stanzas 2 and 3, and 1 and 4.
3. Why do you think the poem is called "Carol"? Can you think of a more appropriate, less personalized title?
4. What view of love is presented in the poem?
5. Does love change in all relationships after a period of time, or do you agree with Shakespeare's sentiments in "Let Me Not to the Marriage of True Minds" (p. 128) that true love is fixed and never changes? Discuss.
6. Script a scene between the speaker and a counsellor.

Amelia

I was driving across the burning desert
When I spotted six jet planes
Leaving six white vapor trails across the bleak terrain
It was the hexagram of the heavens
It was the strings of my guitar
Amelia, it was just a false alarm

The drone of flying engines
Is a song so wild and blue

It scrambles time and seasons if it gets through to you
Then your life becomes a travelogue
Of picture post card charms
Amelia, it was just a false alarm.

People will tell you where they've gone
They'll tell you where to go
But 'til you get there yourself you never really know
Where some have found their paradise
Others just come to harm
Amelia, it was just a false alarm

I wish that he was here tonight
It's so hard to obey
His sad request of me to kindly stay away
So this is how I hide the hurt
As the road leads cursed and charmed
I tell Amelia, it was just a false alarm.

A ghost of aviation
She was swallowed by the sky
Or by the sea, like me she had a dream to fly
Like Icarus ascending
On beautiful foolish arms
Amelia, it was just a false alarm

Maybe I've never really loved
I guess that is the truth
I've spent my whole life in clouds at icy altitudes
And looking down on everything
I crashed into his arms
Amelia, it was just a false alarm.

I pulled into the Cactus Tree Motel
To shower off the dust
And I slept on the strange pillows of my wanderlust
I dreamed of 747's
Over geometric farms
Dreams, Amelia, dreams and false alarms.

JONI MITCHELL

1. Who is the Amelia to whom the speaker refers? What do the speaker and Amelia have in common?
2. What action is taking place on the literal level?

3. What is the speaker thinking about? What emotions is she feeling?
4. This song contains several figurative devices. Identify those listed below and explain what each adds to the lyric:
   a) "It was the hexagram of the heavens
      It was the strings of my guitar" (ll.4-5)
   b) "The drone of flying engines
      Is a song so wild and blue" (ll.7-8)
   c) "Then your life becomes a travelogue
      Of picture post card charms" (ll.10-11)
   d) "As the road leads cursed and charmed" (l.23)
   e) "Like Icarus ascending" (l.28)
   f) "I've spent my whole life in clouds at icy altitudes" (l.33)
5. Compare the attitude of the speaker in "Amelia" with that of the speaker in "Carol". How does each react to a broken relationship?
6. According to the speaker, her love requested that she "kindly stay away". Write a monologue presenting the actual words you think her love might have used in breaking off their relationship.
7. The speaker describes what she thought was true love as being a false alarm. Assume that a friend asks you how to tell true love from a false alarm. What would you reply?

LOVE AND SEPARATION

1. Compare and contrast the views of love presented in any two of these poems.
2. Referring to any of the poems, give your own definition of *love*.
3. Photocopy your favorite love poem not in this unit. Attach a write-up explaining why you like this selection.
4. Write two paragraphs about aspects of love which you feel are missing in the poems of this section.
5. Working in small groups, tape record any love poem in the text using suitable sound effects and background music.
6. Pick one of the love poems in this unit or from elsewhere in the text and present a close reading of the poem to your class.

Aging and Death

She Remembers

She stares out the windowpane
Watching the day begin
She loves how the colors change with the dawn
Everyday . . . everyday
She watches everyday slip away
Dreaming of yesterday . . . yesterday

Chorus:
She remembers what a beautiful woman she was
And the man that she loved
In the silence after
All the tears and laughter and time
She knows life has not passed her by

Music and photographs
They keep her company
She loves walking down the path to the sea
Everyday . . . everyday
She goes there everyday, everyday
See how she fades away . . . fades away

She stares out the windowpane
Watching the night fall
She loves how the colors change with the dusk
Everyday . . . everyday
She watches everyday slip away
Dreaming of yesterday . . . yesterday

SHARI ULRICH

1. What does this song lyric have to say about old age?
2. Does the woman in the poem have any regrets?
3. Is there a change in mood between the first and third stanzas?
4. a) What are some different ways that people respond to old age?
   b) How do you think you will feel about your own old age?
   c) What reactions do you have to Peter Townshend's statement in The Who's "My Generation": "I hope I die before I get old"?
5. Using flashbacks, write a short story of a day in the life of this woman.

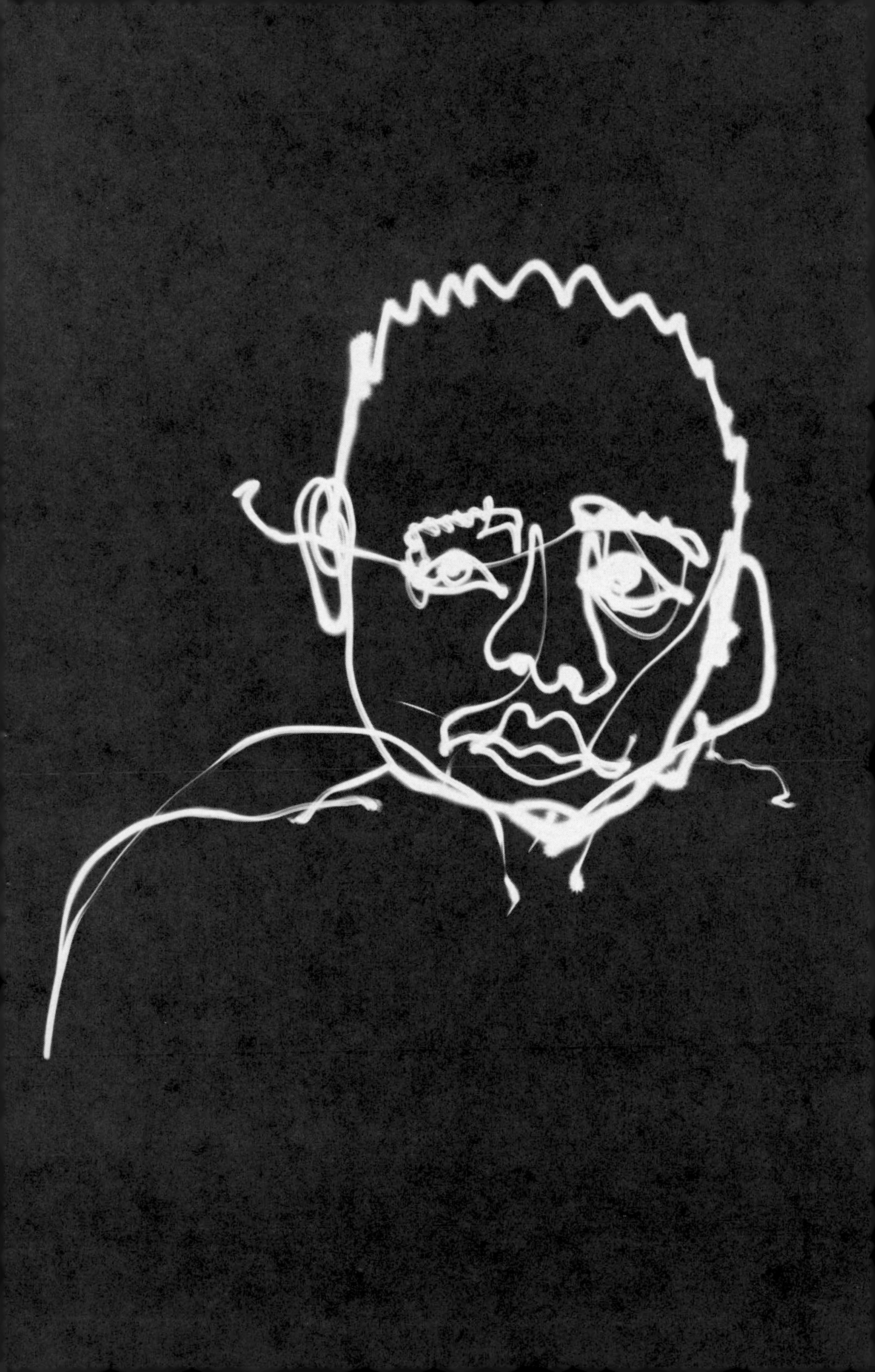

Museum Piece

Today I have the foreboding
That I shall not live
Much longer.

I may laugh at
That statement
When I'm ninety,

But at least it has
Diabetes
Going for it.

The conviction
Makes me want to
Share everything I know,

Everything I've thought,
Seen, felt, loved,
With all who survive me.

I feel as though
I'm an immense museum
Loaded with wonders

Not of my making
But given to me
By countless benefactors

—Memories, perspectives,
Eye-witness knowledge,
Painfully-learned wisdom.

If I could load out,
In boxes, what's been
Entrusted to me

And donate it
Far and wide
To the world's other museums

A treasure would be saved
—And the rest of me
Couldn't matter less.

R. GLENN MARTIN

1. What does the speaker mean by stanza 3?
2. What is the "conviction"?

3. a) What is the central metaphor of the poem?
   b) Is it an appropriate one for old age?
4. Who are the "benefactors"?
5. What is the "treasure"?
6. Discuss the meaning of the last two lines.
7. What fears does the poem express?
8. Assume that you too are a "museum piece." Write a one or two page summary of "everything you know."

Treasures on earth

Put on pajamas. Go outdoors
and join the joggers. Do not eat
butter or eggs. Beware of drink.
Avoid extremes of cold or heat.
Abjure tobacco. Watch for lumps.
Get enough rest. Control your fears.
And, barring accidents, you ought
to live for years and years and years.

That is what the doctors told her.
The lady did as she was told.
In return for her exertions.
she knows the joys of being old.
Installed in Sunset Manor House,
she now partakes of such delights
as crosswords, paint-by-number kits
and semi-monthly Bingo nights.

ALDEN NOWLAN

1. a) What advice about old age and life are given in this poem?
   b) What is the tone of this advice?
   c) How can you tell?
2. What is the significance of the poem's title?
3. Put together a pamphlet of advice designed to prepare pre-teenagers for the teenage years. If you have a younger brother, sister, or cousin, you may wish to address/dedicate the pamphlet to him or her.
4. What sorts of things make life worthwhile? Discuss.
5. Tape record an interview with a senior citizen from your community. Have a sample list of questions you plan to ask

okayed by your teacher before you do the interview. Play your tape for the class and tell what you learned from the experience.

Overheard at a Taxpayers' Meeting

Mr. Alderman it's about the old people's home there
they're getting out all the time
something will have to be done about it
it's not nice

They sneak out the back way and prowl around the grounds
and as soon as a person opens the gate
the ambulance maybe or a delivery van or the lads from the
funeral home
they're off you can't stop them they're quick they're artful
that's all they have to think about getting away
they sit together in the corners and scheme
when they're supposed to be drinking their cocoa
the moment the head nurse gets a headache and goes to lie
down
that's it they swarm out the windows
it's like an anthill
stepstools tables kitchenchairs benches
ropes too I wouldn't wonder
I bet they use ropes
there's no keeping them back

I was talking last night to the guard at the school crossing
he was in shock
a covey of grannies in slippers and mohair shawls
bald as the back of your hand
took over his crossing they wouldn't wait for his flag
staggering and wheezing all over the highway
traffic was backed up half way to West Hill
it's not right

The nurses are run ragged
of course they're understaffed who isn't understaffed
if they guard one exit the old devils slip out the other
old men improperly dressed on the public streets
flashing striped cotton pyjamas at innocent kids
well maybe a jersey
you have to call the fire department and the St. Vincent
de Paul
to get some clothes on them

it isn't a thing respectable people want to see
a lot of old people like that
it's not decent

It's getting so people don't know what to expect
you can't keep them out of the garden
I daren't look in the shrubbery
for fear that a drove of escaped senior citizens
will have up and died on me overnight
and who pays to clear them away just tell me that
while here we are trying to upgrade the neighbourhood
well it's disheartening

I came home lateish the other evening
humming the goodbye theme from Wayne and Shuster
it had been a long day I was looking foward to that
martini
there was an old person in the kitchen
munching at the fridge
chicken or brisket or Ken-l-ration
it's all one to them with their energetic old gums
what they can't chew they mumble
well I had to send for the cops I mean to say
took them an hour to get here
and there was I with an old person in the house
it's not what we have a right to expect
why do we pay taxes

If you leave a downstairs window open only a bare crack
they're in like a shot
dragging their old soft bones in over the sill
trailing canes and crutches
we find them clustered squatting around the TV
watching reruns of *Queen for a Day* and *This Is Your Life*
muttering incomprehensible curses

We tell the kids not to go near the place
to tell the truth we don't like it either
feeling those gummy eyes on your back
and gate creaks behind you
and you hear a grunting and a tapping of sticks
why can't they build a big wall with spikes
they could bar the windows
it wasn't to have them scattering all over Metro
their families paid good money to put them away
in Sunset Acres.

FRANCIS SPARSHOTT

1. a) Who is the speaker? What kind of person is he?
   b) To whom is he speaking?
   c) What are his main concerns about the old people's home?
2. a) Find three examples of hyperboles in the poem.
   b) What do these tell you about the speaker's character?
3. Find three views of old people in the poem. Discuss whether or not these views describe stereotypes.
4. Would the poem have been more effective if it had been written in four line stanzas? in sonnet form? Discuss.
5. In the poem, the speaker says "We tell the kids not to go near the place". Does our society discourage mixing between the old and the young? From what you have observed, answer the question.
6. Write the alderman's answer to the speaker in dramatic monologue, assuming one of the following:
   a) the alderman is seventy years old,
   b) the alderman is middle-aged and in the process of "putting away" his parents in Sunset Acres, or
   c) the alderman is seeking re-election.

Do not go gentle into that good night

Do not go gentle into that good night,
Old age should burn and rave at close of day;
Rage, rage against the dying of the light.

Though wise men at their end know dark is right,
Because their words had forked no lightning they
Do not go gentle into that good night.

Good men, the last wave by, crying how bright
Their frail deeds might have danced in a green bay,
Rage, rage against the dying of the light.

Wild men who caught and sang the sun in flight,
And learn, too late, they grieved it on its way,
Do not go gentle into that good night.

Grave men, near death, who see with blinding sight
Blind eyes could blaze like meteors and be gay,
Rage, rage against the dying of the light.

And you, my father, there on the sad height,
Curse, bless, me now with your fierce tears, I pray.

Do not go gentle into that good night.
Rage, rage against the dying of the light.

DYLAN THOMAS

1. a) What is the poem about?
   b) Why do you think Thomas wrote the poem?
   c) Why do you think this modern poem is now a classic?
2. Explain what sort of people are described in stanzas 2, 3, 4, and 5. How do they view death?
3. Comment on the sound devices used by the poet. How do they reinforce meaning and mood?
4. Present your own views on death in a personal essay. You may wish to mention some of the points of view expressed in this poem.
5. How does Thomas's view of death compare/contrast with those presented in any of the following poems: "Terry" (p. 5), "To an Athlete Dying Young" (p. 285), "Annabel Lee" (p. 51), "View of a Pig" (p. 178), and "The Gambler" (p. 255)?

Because I could not stop for Death

Because I could not stop for Death,
He kindly stopped for me;
The carriage held but just ourselves
And Immortality.

We slowly drove; he knew no haste,
And I had put away
My labor and my leisure too,
For his civility.

We passed the school, where children strove,
At recess, in the ring,
We passed the fields of gazing grain;
We passed the setting sun.

Or rather, he passed us;
The dews drew quivering and chill;
For only gossamer, my gown;
My tippet, only tulle.

We paused before a house that seemed
A swelling of the ground;

The roof was scarcely visible,
The cornice, in the ground.

Since then, 'tis centuries and yet
Feels shorter than the day
I first surmised the horses' heads
Were toward eternity.

EMILY DICKINSON

1. a) Using a dictionary, define the following words according to their contexts:
   "civility," "gossamer," "tippet," "tulle," "cornice," and "surmised."
   b) What do these words add to the meanings and moods of the poem?
2. a) How is the figure of Death personified?
   b) What words support this portrayal of death?
3. a) What views of death are presented by the poem?
   b) Would you consider Dickinson to be an optimist or a pessimist in outlook?
   c) How do her views on death relate to your own? Discuss.
4. Discuss what you think Dickinson was attempting to show the reader in stanzas 3, 5, and 6.

"Out, Out—"

The buzz-saw snarled and rattled in the yard
And made dust and dropped stove-length sticks of wood,
Sweet-scented stuff when the breeze drew across it.
And from there those that lifted eyes could count
Five mountain ranges one behind the other
Under the sunset far into Vermont.
And the saw snarled and rattled, snarled and rattled,
As it ran light, or had to bear a load.
And nothing happened: day was all but done.
Call it a day, I wish they might have said
To please the boy by giving him the half hour
That a boy counts so much when saved from work.
His sister stood beside them in her apron
To tell them "Supper." At the word, the saw,
As if to prove saws knew what supper meant,
Leaped out at the boy's hand, or seemed to leap—

He must have given the hand. However it was,
Neither refused the meeting. But the hand!
The boy's first outcry was a rueful laugh,
As he swung toward them holding up the hand
Half in appeal, but half as if to keep
The life from spilling. Then the boy saw all—
Since he was old enough to know, big boy
Doing a man's work, though a child at heart—
He saw all spoiled. "Don't let them cut my hand off—.
The doctor, when he comes. Don't let him sister!"
So. But the hand was gone already.
The doctor put him in the dark of ether.
He lay and puffed his lips out with his breath.
And then—the watcher at his pulse took fright.
No one believed. They listened at his heart.
Little—less—nothing!—and that ended it.
No more to build on there. And they, since they
Were not the one dead, turned to their affairs.

ROBERT FROST

1. Why does Frost begin the poem with several lines of lyrical description?
2. Why does he use the word "So" as a sentence in line 27? What effect does it have on a) the pace and rhythm of the poem, and b) the mood?
3. Compare this poem with "Departmental" on page 69. Is the subject matter similar? How are the different moods of the two poems achieved?

Death, Be Not Proud

Death, be not proud, though some have called thee
Mighty and dreadful, for thou art not so;
For those whom thou think'st thou dost overthrow
Die not, poor Death, nor yet canst thou kill me.
From rest and sleep, which but thy pictures be,
Much pleasure, then from thee much more must flow,
And soonest our best men with thee do go,
Rest of their bones, and soul's delivery.
Thou art slave to fate, chance, kings, and desperate men,
And dost with poison, war, and sickness dwell,

And poppy or charms can make us sleep as well,
And better than thy stroke; why swell'st thou then?
One short sleep past, we wake eternally,
And death shall be no more; Death, thou shalt die.

JOHN DONNE

1. According to Donne, why should death not be proud?
2. In what sense is death a "slave"?
3. a) What is the recurring metaphor used to describe death?
   b) Is this metaphor appropriate? Discuss.
4. Describe the tone of the last two lines.
5. Of the personification poems on death, a) Which of the two do you like better? Why? b) Which of the two do you consider to be a better poem? Why? c) Discuss whether there is any point in asking questions 5a) and 5b) separately.
6. In one or two paragraphs, describe life and/or death using different metaphors from Donne or Dickinson.

To an Athlete Dying Young

The time you won your town the race
We chaired you through the market-place;
Man and boy stood cheering by,
And home we brought you shoulder-high.

To-day the road all runners come,
Shoulder-high we bring you home,
And set you at your threshold down,
Townsman of a stiller town.

Smart lad, to slip betimes away
From fields where glory does not stay
And early though the laurel grows
It withers quicker than the rose.

Eyes the shady night has shut
Cannot see the record cut,
And silence sounds no worse than cheers
After earth has stopped the ears:

Now you will not swell the rout
Of lads that wore their honours out,
Runners whom renown outran
And the name died before the man.

So set, before its echoes fade,
The fleet foot on the sill of shade,
And hold to the low lintel up
The still-defended challenge-cup.

And round that early-laurelled head
Will flock to gaze the strengthless dead,
And find unwithered on its curls
The garland briefer than a girl's.

A.E. HOUSMAN

1. In your own words, tell what each stanza is about.
2. What does the laurel represent?
3. How do the rhymes of the poem support its message or theme?
4. Discuss the relevance of the line, "And the name died before the man" as it applies to modern-day athletes and heroes.
5. Imagine the athlete's life and death. Write the news story which might have appeared in the sports pages of his town's newspaper.

Elegy for a Nature Poet

It was in October, a favorite season,
He went for his last walk. The covered bridge,
Most natural of all the works of reason,
Received him, let him go. Along the hedge

He rattled his stick; observed the blackening bushes
In his familiar field; thought he espied
Late meadow larks; considered picking rushes
For a dry arrangement; returned home, and died

Of a catarrh caught in the autumn rains
And let go on uncared for. He was too rapt
In contemplation to recall that brains
Like his should not be kept too long uncapped

In the wet and cold weather. While we mourned,
We thought of his imprudence, and how Nature,
Whom he'd done so much for, had finally turned
Against her creature.

His gift was daily his delight, he peeled
The landscape back to show it was a story;

Any old bird or burning bush revealed
At his hands just another allegory.

Nothing too great, nothing too trivial
For him; from mountain range or humble vermin
He could extract the hidden parable—
If need be, crack the stone to get the sermon.

And now, poor man, he's gone. Without his name
The field reverts to wilderness again,
The rocks are silent, woods don't seem the same;
Demoralized small birds will fly insane.

Rude Nature, whom he loved to idealize
And would have wed, pretends she never heard
His voice at all, as, taken by surprise
At last, he goes to her without a word.

HOWARD NEMEROV

1. Check the definition for *elegy* given by your glossary. Why might Nemerov have written an elegy for a nature poet?
2. What omens foreshadowed the poet's death?
3. What was the cause of the poet's death?
4. What irony was noted by the poet's friends?
5. What were the accomplishments of the poet?
6. What effects will the poet's absence have on nature?
7. Does the last stanza end positively? Explain.

AGING AND DEATH

1. "Poets often regard old age and death, not with fear or suspicion, but with wit, humor, and insight."
   Discuss this statement with reference to three or more poems in this unit.
2. Write a persuasive essay on the advantages and benefits of being an elderly person in society today.
3. What might you say to a 13-year old contemplating suicide to convince him or her that life is truly worth living?
4. Identify the poems in this unit that you strongly empathized with. Tell what you liked or agreed with in these poems.
5. Write an elegy for a recently deceased famous person whom you admired.

Hope and Despair

Reading the Brothers Grimm to Jenny

Jenny, your mind commands
kingdoms of black and white:
you shoulder the crow on your left,
the snowbird on your right;
for you the cinders part
and let the lentils through,
and noise falls into place
as screech or sweet roo-coo,
while in my own, real, world
gray foxes and gray wolves
bargain eye to eye,
and the amazing dove
takes shelter under the wing
of the raven to keep dry.

Knowing that you must climb,
one day, the ancient tower
where disenchantment binds
the curls of innocence,
that you must live with power
and honor circumstance,
that choice is what comes true—
oh, Jenny, pure in heart,
why do I lie to you?

Why do I read you tales
in which birds speak the truth
and pity cures the blind,
and beauty reaches deep
to prove a royal mind?
Death is a small mistake
there, where the kiss revives;
Jenny, we make just dreams
out of our unjust lives.

Still, when your truthful eyes,
your keen, attentive stare,
endow the vacuous slut
with royalty, when you match
her soul to her shimmering hair,

what can she do but rise
to your imagined throne?
And what can I, but see
beyond the world that is,
when, faithful, you insist
I have the golden key—
and learn from you once more
the terror and the bliss,
the world as it might be?

LISEL MUELLER

1. What images of good and evil are there in stanza one? What does the color gray symbolize?
2. According to the speaker, what picture of the world is presented by fairy tales?
3. How does the speaker see the real world? Is she an optimist, a pessimist, or simply a realist? Explain.
4. Why is the speaker concerned about reading fairy tales to Jenny? Is the concern legitimate? Comment.
5. How does the speaker resolve her concern? What could adults stand to learn from children?
6. Role play a dialogue between Jenny and her parents as they try to caution her about fairy tales.
7. Your local paper has printed an editorial insisting that all fairy tale books should be removed from the libraries and schools in your area, claiming that such stories are harmful to children. Write a letter to the editor agreeing or disagreeing with his views.
8. With the class sitting in a circle, have someone begin a fairy tale by saying, "Once upon a time. . . ." Each person in turn should add one or two sentences to the story, until it has gone all the way around the circle. The last person has the "happily ever after" job. After your class has composed a story, discuss it for its similarities to patterns in other fairy tales.
9. Working in small groups, compose a trivia test based on popularly-known fairy tales. Administer it to the class and see who scores the highest.

Dreams

Hold fast to dreams
For if dreams die
Life is a broken-winged bird
That cannot fly.

Hold fast to dreams
For when dreams go
Life is a barren field
Frozen with snow.

LANGSTON HUGHES

1. a) What metaphors are used to describe life?
   b) Do these comparisons strike you as being clever and original or stale and hackneyed? Explain.
   c) Compose your own original metaphor about life.
2. Do you agree with the poet's views of life?
3. Compare the thoughts and philosophy of "Dreams" with those in "A Kite Is a Victim," (p. 248)?
4. Script the dialogue for an imaginary discussion involving Cohen ("A Kite Is a Victim") and Hughes ("Dreams"). Have them talk about what each writer was attempting to do, and how their poems compare and contrast to one another.

Picketing Supermarkets

Because all this food is grown in the store
do not take the leaflet.
Cabbages, broccoli and tomatoes
are raised at night in the aisles.
Milk is brewed in the rear storage areas.
Beef produced in vats in the basement.
Do not take the leaflet.
Peanut butter and soft drinks
are made fresh each morning by store employees.
Our oranges and grapes
are so fine and round
that when held up to the lights they cast no shadow.
Do not take the leaflet.

And should you take one
do not believe it.

This chain of stores has no connection
with anyone growing food someplace else.
How could we have an effect on local farmers?
Do not believe it.

The sound here is Muzak, for your enjoyment.
It is not the sound of children crying.
There *is* a lady offering samples
to mark Canada Cheese Month.
There is no dark-skinned man with black hair beside her
wanting to show you the inside of a coffin.
You would not have to look if there was.
And there are no Nicaraguan heroes
in any way connected with the bananas.

Pay no attention to these people.
The manager is a citizen.
All this food is grown in the store.

TOM WAYMAN

1. a) What is the situation of the poem?
   b) Who are "these people" in the last stanza?
   c) Who is the "you" of the poem?
   d) What information is probably contained in the leaflet?
2. Quote three examples of irony, explaining what is ironical about each example.
3. "All a poet can do is warn."
   - Wilfred Owen

   Is this statement an accurate description of why Wayman wrote the poem?
4. Comment on how sentence structure and tone make this a successful social commentary.
5. Interview a grocery store manager in your area to find out the following information:
   a) where the various food he stocks comes from,
   b) how much is locally produced,
   c) why some non-local, non-provincial, and non-Canadian brands are stocked,
   d) what natural, political, or labor problems have created problems in stocking certain foods.

   Report your findings to the class in the style of a T.V. news reporter.

6. Role-play an on-the-spot-interview with the characters of the poem. You will need to fill the following parts: the picketers, customers, store manager, store employees, and T.V. reporter. If you wish to add a realistic dimension videotape the interview in a spontaneous way.
7. Shelley once said that "Poets are the unacknowledged legislators of the world." What do you think he meant? How does this statement apply to "Picketing Supermarkets" and "Circle of Steel," (p.250)?

The Lifeguard

In a stable of boats I lie still,
From all sleeping children hidden.
The leap of a fish from its shadow
Makes the whole lake instantly tremble.
With my foot on the water, I feel
The moon outside

Take on the utmost of its power.
I rise and go out through the boats.
I set my broad sole upon silver,
On the skin of the sky, on the moonlight,
Stepping outward from earth onto water.
In quest of the miracle

This village of children believed
That I could perform as I dived
For one who had sunk from my sight.
I saw his cropped haircut go under.
I leapt, and my steep body flashed
Once, in the sun.

Dark drew all the light from my eyes.
Like a man who explores his death
By the pull of his slow-moving shoulders,
I hung head down in the cold,
Wide-eyed, contained, and alone
Among the weeds,

And my fingertips turned into stone
From clutching immovable blackness.
Time after time I leapt upward
Exploding in breath, and fell back
From the change in the children's faces
At my defeat.

Beneath them, I swam to the boathouse
With only my life in my arms
To wait for the lake to shine back
At the risen moon with such power
That my steps on the light of the ripples
Might be sustained.

Beneath me is nothing but brightness
Like the ghost of a snow field in summer.
As I move toward the center of the lake,
Which is also the center of the moon,
I am thinking of how I may be
The savior of one

Who has already died in my care.
The dark trees fade from around me.
The moon's dust hovers together.
I call softly out, and the child's
Voice answers through blinding water.
Patiently, slowly,

He rises, dilating to break
The surface of stone with his forehead.
He is one I do not remember
Having ever seen in his life.
The ground that I stand on is trembling
Upon his smile.

I wash the black mud from my hands.
On a light given off by the grave,
I kneel in the quick of the moon
At the heart of a distant forest
And hold in my arms a child
Of water, water, water.

JAMES DICKEY

1. Give your impressions of the situation of the poem.
2. How does the poet involve the reader in the poem's action?
3. What images suggest the frustration and horror of the speaker?
4. If you were able to meet the lifeguard, what might you say to him?
5. Write the spontaneous, random thoughts of one of the children as he or she witnesses the scene.
6. a) Tell about a similar situation in which you felt completely helpless or witnessed a death.

b) Describe your feelings and those of others involved.
c) Do you feel the same way now?

7. Read James Dickey's article on poetry on p. 323.

The Diver

The bridge like a Roman fort
held the river and the beach
held our vision steady through waving heat
held us all while the solitary figure
struggled up the arch
his knees braced against the rivets
Below someone shook out his towel
while others bet upon his chance
At the summit of the span he rose
his arms outstretched
flung a cross against the sun
and the whole world hung beneath him
our eyes nailing him to the sky
Suspension for an instant and forever
A slow plunge toward the water
and he came down from above
dropping beneath the surface like a stone
The river circling away
grew silent as held breath
                    still as death
Then from unknown depths
his head broke the water
shook out a crown of sunlit spray
brought release   new life
thrilling in our chests

ROBERT CURRIE

1. What similes make the setting and action of the poem more intense and vivid?
2. What impressions are conveyed to the reader by the following lines?
   a) "others bet upon his chance"
   b) "our eyes nailing him to the sky"
   c) "... brought release   new life/thrilling in our chests"?
3. Tell about the closest brush you ever had with death, explaining how you avoided it.

4. Compose a brochure for junior high students on the subject of peer pressure dares.
5. For an interesting analysis of this poem, read the student essay on p. 330.

There Will Come Soft Rains

War Time

There will come soft rains and the smell of the ground,
And swallows circling with their shimmering sound;

And frogs in the pools singing at night,
And wild plum-trees in tremulous white.

Robins will wear their feathery fire
Whistling their whims on a low-fence-wire;

And not one will know of the war, not one
Will care at last when it is done.

Not one would mind, neither bird nor tree,
If mankind perished utterly;

And Spring herself, when she woke at dawn
Would scarcely know that we were gone.

SARA TEASDALE

1. What prediction is the speaker making?
2. According to the speaker, how will nature react to war?
3. What does the poem reveal about the speaker's attitude toward humanity? What is implied about the relationship between man and nature?
4. Explain how the sound, imagery, and structure of the poem help to convey the theme.
5. Many movies and works of literature have depicted the end of the human race. How many such works can you name? What was the cause of the ultimate disaster in each? Which works left the viewer or reader with hope for a better world? Now that you have considered the views of others about the future of humanity, you might ask yourself how you feel. Would you call yourself an optimist or a pessimist? Why?
6. The poem uses effective imagery to describe the beauties of nature. Reflect for a moment on what you think is one of the

more beautiful scenes in nature; you might choose a setting such as a lake or beach, or you might focus on a more specific, single item, such as a tree covered with frost or a host of sparrows feeding in your garden. Use vivid, fresh imagery to capture the scene for the reader.

7. Read the short story "There Will Come Soft Rains", by Ray Bradbury (available in *Prose For Discussion*, Gage, 1980), and discuss the following questions:
   a) Is the message in the poem identical to the one in the story? Comment.
   b) In what way does the inclusion of the poem strengthen Bradbury's story?
   c) What qualities does the poem have that the story lacks? In the same way, what does the story have that is missing from the poem? Why might a writer choose to express a thought as a poem rather than illustrate it in the form of a story?

When You Gonna Wake Up?

God don't make
Promises He don't keep
You got some big dreams, baby
But in order to dream you still gotta be asleep

chorus:
When you gonna wake up
When you gonna wake up
When you gonna wake up
And strengthen the things that remain?

Counterfeit philosophies
Have polluted all of your thoughts
Karl Marx's got you by the throat
And Henry Kissinger's got you tied up into knots

You got innocent men in jail
Your insane asylums are filled
You got unrighteous doctors
Dealin' drugs that'll never cure your ills

You got men who can't control their peace
Women who can't control their tongues
The rich seduce the poor
And the old are seduced by the young

Adulterers and judges
And pornography in the schools
You got gangsters in power
And lawbreakers makin' rules

Spiritual advisors
And gurus to guide your every move
Instant inner peace
In every step you take's got to be approved

Do you ever wonder
Just what God requires
You think He's just an errand boy
To satisfy your wandering desires

You can't take it with you
And you know it's too worthless to be sold
They tell you time is money
As if your life was worth its weight in gold

There's a man on the cross
And He be crucified for you
Believe in His power
That's about all you got to do

BOB DYLAN

1. How does the speaker view the world?
2. What does the speaker mean by "... in order to dream you still gotta be asleep"? Does that line contradict the chorus? Explain.
3. According to the speaker, how do some people view God?
4. What is the speaker's solution to all the troubles and false values he describes? What does the lyric reveal about the character of the speaker?
5. How would you describe the language used in this song? Do the cliche expressions weaken the song? Comment.
6. How does the vision of humanity in this selection differ from that in "There Will Come Soft Rains"?
7. Many of this song's examples are typical of the news stories we sometimes hear or read. Clip several headlines from a newspaper you receive, cut each word free, and arrange several on a page to form a poster poem.

On His Blindness

When I consider how my light is spent,
Ere half my days in this dark world and wide,
And that one talent which is death to hide,
Lodged with me useless, though my soul more bent
To serve therewith my Maker, and present
My true account, lest he returning chide,
"Doth God exact day-labor, light denied?"
I fondly ask. But Patience, to prevent
That murmur, soon replies, "God doth not need
Either man's work or his own gifts. Who best
Bear his mild yoke, they serve him best. His state
Is kingly; thousands at his bidding speed,
And post o'er land and ocean without rest;
They also serve who only stand and wait."

JOHN MILTON

1. Look up the parable of the talents in the Bible (Matthew XXV 14-30). Why does Milton allude to this story in relation to his own situation?
2. How would the effect of the poem be changed if Milton had written "They also serve who only *sit* and wait"?
3. What is Milton's attitude towards his blindness? What is his attitude towards God?
4. Do you agree with the sentiment of the last line? Give reasons.

At the Long Sault: May, 1660

Under the day-long sun there is life and mirth
    In the working earth,
And the wonderful moon shines bright
    Through the soft spring night,
The innocent flowers in the limitless woods are springing
    Far and away
    With the sound and the perfume of May,
And ever up from the south the happy birds are winging,
    The waters glitter and leap and play
    While the gray hawk soars.

But far in an open glade of the forest set
    Where the rapid plunges and roars,

Is a ruined fort with a name that men forget,—
A shelterless pen
With its broken palisade,
Behind it, musket in hand,
Beyond message or aid
In this savage heart of the wild,
Mere youngsters, grown in a moment to men,
Grim and alert and arrayed,
The comrades of Daulac stand.
Ever before them, night and day,
The rush and skulk and cry
Of foes, not men but devils, panting for prey;
Behind them the sleepless dream
Of the little frail-walled town, far away by the
plunging stream.
Of maiden and matron and child,
With ruin and murder impending, and none but they
To beat back the gathering horror
Deal death while they may,
And then die.

Day and night they have watched while the little plain
Grew dark with the rush of the foe, but their host
Broke ever and melted away, with no boast
But to number their slain;
And now as the days renew
Hunger and thirst and care
Were they never so stout, so true,
Press at their hearts; but none
Falters or shrinks or utters a coward word,
Though each setting sun
Brings from the pitiless wild new hands to the Iroquois
horde,
And only to them despair.

Silent, white-faced, again and again
Charged and hemmed round by furious hands,
Each for a moment faces them all and stands
In his little desperate ring; like a tired bull moose
Whom scores of sleepless wolves, a ravening pack,
Have chased all night, all day
Through the snow-laden woods, like famine let loose;
And he turns at last in his track
Against a wall of rock and stands at bay;
Round him with terrible sinews and teeth of steel
They charge and recharge; but with many a furious plunge
and wheel

Hither and thither over the trampled snow,
He tosses them bleeding and torn;
Till, driven, and ever to and fro
Harried, wounded, and weary grown,
His mighty strength gives way
And all together they fasten upon him and drag him down.

So Daulac turned him anew
With a ringing cry to his men
In the little raging forest glen,
And his terrible sword in the twilight whistled and slew.
And all his comrades stood
With their backs to the pales, and fought
Till their strength was done;
The thews that were only mortal flagged and broke
Each struck his last wild stroke,
And they fell one by one,
And the world that had seemed so good
Passed like a dream and was naught.

And then the great night came
With the triumph-songs of the foe and the flame
Of the camp-fires.
Out of the dark the soft wind woke,
The song of the rapid rose alway
And came to the spot where the comrades lay,
Beyond help or care,
With none but the red men round them
To gnash their teeth and stare.

All night by the foot of the mountain
  The little town lieth at rest,
The sentries are peacefully pacing;
  And neither from East nor from West

Is there rumor of death or of danger;
  None dreameth tonight in his bed
That ruin was near and the heroes
  That met it and stemmed it are dead.

But afar in the ring of the forest,
  Where the air is so tender with May
And the waters are wild in the moonlight
  They lie in their silence of clay.

The numberless stars out of heaven
  Look down with a pitiful glance;

And the lilies asleep in the forest
Are closed like the lilies of France.

ARCHIBALD LAMPMAN

Note: This poem is about an unsung Canadian hero, Adam Daulac (Dollard), who, with a small volunteer group of Frenchmen, fought a much larger contingent of Iroquois at the Long Sault rapids in order to save the neighboring town of Hochelaga (early Montreal) from attack. Although they were deserted by their Indian allies (who then joined the Iroquois) and then ultimately killed and tortured, Daulac and his men's hearty resistance may have caused the Iroquois to reconsider attacking the town.

1. What is the purpose of the first stanza?
2. a) What is the dream of the second stanza?
   b) What is the reality of the second stanza?
   c) What is the purpose of the contrast between the dream and the reality?
3. Referring to stanzas 2-3, discuss the problems experienced by Daulac and his men.
4. Referring to stanzas 2, 3, 4, and 6, discuss the stereotyped depiction of the Iroquois.
5. Discuss the appropriateness of the simile in stanza 4.
6. a) Why does the poem switch to four line stanzas after stanza 6?
   b) What points does Lampman effectively make in the last four stanzas?
   c) What images and symbols develop these points?
7. Write a brief five paragraph essay analyzing the significance of the references to dreams and dreaming in this poem.
8. For an analysis of this poem, see the student essay on p. 318.

The Mary Ellen Carter

She went down last October in a pouring driving rain,
The skipper, he'd been drinking, and the mate, he felt no pain.
Too close to Three Mile Rock and she was dealt her mortal blow
And the Mary Ellen Carter settled low.
There was just us five aboard her when she finally was awash.

We'd worked like hell to save her, all heedless of the cost
And the groan she gave as she went down, it caused us to
proclaim
That the Mary Ellen Carter would rise again.

Well, the owners wrote her off; not a nickel would they spend.
"She gave twenty years of service, boys, then met her sorry
end.
"But insurance paid the loss to us, so let her rest below",
Then they laughed at us and said we had to go.
But we talked of her all winter, some days around the clock,
For she's worth a quarter million, alfoat and at the dock.
And with every jar that hit the bar we swore we would remain
And make the Mary Ellen Carter rise again.

Chorus
Rise again, rise again, that her name not be lost
To the knowledge of men.
All those who loved her best and were with her til the end
Will make the Mary Ellen Carter rise again.

All spring, now, we've been with her on a barge lent by a
friend.
Three dives a day in a hard hat suit and twice I've had the
bends—
Thank God it's only sixty feet and the currents here are slow
Or I'd never have the strength to go below.
But we've patched her rents, stopped her vents, dogged hatch
and porthole down,
Put cables to her, 'fore and aft and girded her around.
Tomorrow, noon, we hit the air and then take up the strain
And watch the Mary Ellen Carter rise again.

Chorus
For we couldn't leave her there, you see, to crumble into
scale—
She'd saved our lives so many times, living through the gale
And the laughing, drunken rats who left her to a sorry grave
They won't be laughing in another day. . . .
And you, to whom adversity has dealt the final blow
With smiling bastards lying to you everywhere you go,
Turn to, and put out all your strength of arm and heart and
brain
And, like the Mary Ellen Carter rise again!

Rise again, rise again—though your heart be broken
And life about to end.

No matter what you've lost, be it a home, a love, a friend—
Like the Mary Ellen Carter, rise again.

STAN ROGERS

1. What caused the sinking of the "Mary Ellen Carter"?
2. Why did the crew proclaim that the ship would rise again?
3. How did the owners feel about the sunken ship? How did the crew feel about it? What is the reason for the difference in attitude?
4. Why was the crew so determined to raise the ship?
5. What moral does the author draw from the fate of the "Mary Ellen Carter"?
6. What personal qualities were displayed by the men who raised the ship?
7. Improvise a dialogue between the members of the crew as they try to convince the owners to raise the ship.
8. Write the news story or tape the radio broadcast that reported on the sinking of the "Mary Ellen Carter".

HOPE AND DESPAIR

1. English Romantic poet Samuel Taylor Coleridge said "No man was ever a great poet, without at the same time being a profound philosopher." Discuss with reference to three poems in this unit.
2. Write a personal essay on the topic "Hope and Despair: Our World Today." You may wish to quote from some of the unit poems.
3. Debate the resolution: "Be it resolved that writing poetry is a hopeful activity."
4. Do a close reading of any poem in the text. Use the student essay on "The Diver" (p. 330) as a reference.
5. Using any three social criticism poems in the text a) tell what aspects of society are being criticized, and b) explain what solutions are suggested to remedy these ills.
6. Four poems in this unit touch on religion, which is a recurring topic in the history of poetry. Put together a short collection (five poems) of religious verse drawn from a variety of sources. If you wish, the collection could be composed of poems similar to "The Diver," in which religious allusions or symbols are used. Write a preface for your collection.

Appendix I

Answering Test and Essay Questions about Poetry

You have read, listened to, talked and written about poetry, and you have composed it. In exchanging views and in experiencing the writing of poetry, you will have gained some insights into it, found several enjoyable poems, and increased your skills as a reader. Because the study of poetry is a part of your course work, your appreciation of it and your skills as a reader will be evaluated through either tests or essays on poetry, or both. It is the aim of this section to give you some practical guidelines for answering test and essay questions about poetry; in other words, it is intended to provide you with some practical strategies you might follow in order to improve your marks.

Whether you are answering a test or an essay question, the first step is to gain an understanding of the poem, and the second is to know clearly what the question is asking.

The preceding chapters, particularly Chapter 7 ("Becoming a Critical Reader"), have discussed many points about poetry, revealing that reading to understand its basic meaning is only part of reading. Test and essay questions ask the reader to go further and read critically. This might involve anything from analyzing a poem in its entirety to evaluating the effect of a particular feature (e.g., imagery, tone, form) on the poem's meaning.

Whatever the task required by a question, it is necessary to read the poem through once to gain an impression of its content. If the poem is relatively straight-forward, you might turn to the question and reread the poem in light of it. If the poem is more complex, as is often the case for tests and essays, you will have to rely on a dictionary and your reading skills to arrive at an understanding of the poem's basic meaning.

The greatest barriers to understanding a poem are these: new vocabulary, unfamiliar allusions, and abstract or complicated wording. If a dictionary and other reference books are available, the first two difficulties can be solved easily. The third difficulty can be overcome by careful reading, in which you pay particular attention to punctuation marks and transitional words. For example, if there is no punctuation at the end of a line of poetry, then you should not stop when you reach that point; read on and link that line to the one that follows. Such a reading will help you to hook up thoughts that belong together and will make the meaning of the poem clear.

If no dictionary is available to help you overcome the first two barriers, you must rely on two basic reading skills to discover the meaning of new vocabulary and unfamiliar allusions.

The first reading skill uses context clues to determine meaning. This means studying the line, sentence, or poem as a whole to see if there are any clues to the meaning of the word or allusion. In "Klaxon", a poem from Chapter 8 (p. 246), we read of:

Cars with yellow spectacles
Or motorcycle monocles,
Cars whose gold eyes burnt
With too-rich battery . . .

If you did not know what "monocle" meant, you might decipher its meaning from its context. The poem seems to be emphasizing vision through the words "spectacles" and "eyes". You know that spectacles are glasses, that motorcycles have one headlight, and, knowing that the prefix "mono" means "one", you might correctly conclude that a monocle is a single glass lens and that the reference is to the single headlight of a motorcycle. For a second example, let's look at another poem from Chapter 8—"The Bull Calf" (p. 179). The poet, Irving Layton, uses the following allusion:

He was too young for all that pride.
I thought of the deposed Richard II.

From the context, the reader might assume that Richard II was a proud king, which was, in fact, the case. A deeper understanding of who Richard II was would not be necessary for understanding the poem.

The second reading skill, breaking down a word into its parts (prefix, root word, suffix) to determine its meaning, can help you understand new vocabulary. Breaking down a new word allows you to piece together its total meaning by considering the meaning of its parts. For example, in his poem "The Lonely Land" (p. 76), A.J.M. Smith uses the word "dissonance". If we divide the word into its parts, dis-son-ance, we can identify the word's meaning from the prefix of root word alone. The prefix "dis-" means "differently", and in the root word we can recognize "sonar" or "sonic", meaning "sound". Putting these parts together, we see that "dissonance" means "different sounds".

What patterns should you pay attention to? Repetition of key words or phrases will give a poem structure and, often, will emphasize the poem's main idea. Images, as well, frequently form a pattern that helps to establish the poem's meaning and to unify its various parts. If we return once more to A.J.M. Smith's poem, "The Lonely Land", a careful reading reveals two patterns that are worth paying attention to. Smith repeats some key words: the pine trees are referred to in the first and third stanzas, the words "stagger and fall" are repeated in stanza two, and, most important, the words "beauty" and "strength" are repeated in the final stanza. A quick check of the imagery reveals that most of Smith's descriptive words are harsh, strong, or violent (e.g., "jagged", "sharp", "snap", "Passionate", "cry", "wind-battered", and "broken", among others). These two observations help the reader to see immediately what A.J.M. Smith is emphasizing through his poem.

Finally, you are left with the task of identifying any other information that is essential for understanding the poem fully. This may require checking the poem's form to determine if knowing the type of poem (e.g., whether it is a sonnet, a ballad, free verse, blank verse, etc.) will provide more information that will assist in interpreting it. It is helpful, for example, when reading a Shakespearean sonnet, to know that the first quatrain will introduce a concern, the second and third quatrains will restate the concern, and the final couplet will resolve or summarize the concern. The reader should also identify the poem's specific purpose and theme. Vocalizing the purpose and theme in a single, clear thought helps a reader to put the entire poem into perspective and understand the function of each part. Recognizing, for example, that a poem's purpose is to satirize, to express awe, or to lament, tells a reader why the poet chose specific words and images and arranged them as he did. In other words, recognizing the purpose of a poem enables you to understand more deeply the poem's structure and theme. A clear statement of the poem's theme gives the reader the same advantages.

Once you are confident that you have understood the poem's basic meaning, the next step is to study the test or essay question to determine what is being asked. A brief look at test and essay questions, along with some model answers, might be helpful in identifying some cautions and strategies.

SHORT ANSWER ITEMS

Short answer items on an examination generally fall into one of two categories: questions (beginning with the familiar what, who, why, which, how, etc.) and tasks (beginning with words such as explain, describe, compare, discuss, analyze, etc.). Both types of items test the student's understanding of the poem's meaning and the poet's style.

When answering questions you should begin by studying the poem until you have a good grasp of its meaning. Following that, it is a matter of reading the question carefully to determine what it is asking. Once the question is understood, the next step is to reread the poem and make notes as you proceed. These notes should help you to organize your thoughts and identify examples before beginning to write out the answer. Often, students lose marks because they include too little or too much in an answer; such flaws are caused by a failure to prepare properly before beginning to write. We will say more about organizing an answer and using supporting evidence after we have looked at the second type of short answer item.

Often lengthier and more difficult to answer than questions, task items require careful planning and thought. In addition to clearly identifying the task to be done, students should study carefully the focus of the task. Knowing what aspect of the poem is to be considered—whether it be theme, language, form, or the meaning of a single line—saves time and establishes a purpose for rereading the poem. This allows you to focus your own thoughts and select appropriate details in preparing an answer.

In responding to short answer items, three principles are worth keeping in mind. First, the process of making notes in order to gather thoughts and organize an answer is very important. Notes help to organize initial impressions and establish a sense of direction. Such an approach saves marks that might otherwise be lost on vague, wandering answers.

Second, answers should be well-phrased. Despite the pressure of an examination, students ought to take time to consider such matters as sentence completeness, spelling, and punctuation. A common mistake is to answer a question with a sentence fragment, as many people do in everyday speech.

The third principle to keep in mind is to provide sufficient supporting evidence or illustrations for argument points or observations. Quote words and phrases or refer to specific lines in the poem in order to convince the reader that your answer is valid and based on a careful, rational reading of the poem. Remember to comment on any quotation or references you include. The quotation itself is not enough; it must be clear to your reader what you are trying to illustrate through your use of it.

MULTIPLE-CHOICE QUESTIONS

In addition to short answer items, multiple-choice questions are used frequently on quizzes, major tests, and entrance examinations. This type of question (for students who have not encountered it) usually consists of a question or a statement which has to be completed. Four alternatives are offered as possible answers to the question or completions of the statement. The student has to choose the correct alternative. This type of question poses its own special difficulties. Some advice on preparing for and writing such tests should help you to improve your performance on multiple-choice examinations.

Unless a test has a deliberately narrowed focus, most multiple-choice questions will test a student's skills in interpreting a poem's meaning. This type of examination can be particularly frustrating if none of the possible answers fit with your interpretation of the poem. Such a problem might be avoided if the reading strategies at the start of this chapter and those recommended in Chapter 7 are followed. If there are still no answers that fit your interpretation of the poem, another important strategy is made available by the nature of this testing format. You can read ahead through all the questions and their alternatives to identify a pattern of answers – and there will be one – that offers another logical, consistent interpretation of the poem.

Other reading strategies can be applied to multiple-choice questions to eliminate the problem of there seeming to be more than one correct answer to a question:

1. Reread the question carefully. Test makers attempt, as much as possible, to make their wording precise and clear. If, for example, the question asks what a particular line or image implies, then you must look for something that is implied rather than explicitly stated.
2. Take single lines or images in context. When the question gives a line reference and asks for the meaning of the line or an image within it, the student should consider them in terms of the entire poem.
3. Read all alternatives before choosing one as the answer. An alternative that sounds right might be weak when compared to another possible answer.
4. Remember levels of generality. Occasionally, one alternative will be better than another because it encompasses a whole topic, rather than focussing on only one part or aspect of it.
5. Use the process of elimination. When the correct answer is not apparent immediately, begin by eliminating one or two alternatives from consideration. This will narrow the possibilities and help to identify the correct answer.
6. Make a note of the questions you are uncertain of. When you are forced to guess an answer, note the number. If you finish early, go back and check the guesses first.
7. Keep an eye on the time. It may not be worthwhile to linger too long on an especially difficult question. Instead, note the number and return to it when you are confident of your remaining time.

ANSWERING ESSAY QUESTIONS ABOUT POETRY

The ultimate test of a student's ability to present a detailed analysis of a poem will come with the assignment of an essay. While essays on poetry sometimes focus on one aspect of a poem - how an author uses imagery or sound to establish tone, for instance - they more often require a student to analyze or explicate a complete poem. The section that follows examines the steps in preparing an essay on a poem and aims at helping students develop their ideas, organize their material, draft the essay, and revise it effectively.

GETTING STARTED

The first task, of course, is to understand the poem. The reading strategies suggested at the start of this chapter might be helpful. With a dictionary and library resources available, the subtler levels of meaning can be identified and studied in preparation for writing.

The second task is to understand what the question is asking. If it asks for an explication or an analysis, you should explain what the poem means. If it focuses on one aspect of the poem, such as its use of sound or imagery, you are usually expected to consider that one aspect in terms of its impact on the whole poem. Whatever type of essay you are asked for, the following questions may help you gather your thoughts about the poem.

GETTING AT THE POEM'S MEANING AND TECHNIQUE

Ask yourself the following questions that apply to your essay topic. Make notes as you go and you will find it easier to organize your thoughts for your first draft.

A. The poem's basic content
    1. What is the context of the poem? Identify the speaker(s) and any background information that would help explain the poem's basic message.
    2. How are the thoughts organized?
    3. Does the poet contrast any ideas? Does he juxtapose any for effect?
    4. What feelings does the speaker reveal? How are the feelings communicated?
    5. What meaning does the poem have on the literal level?

B. The poem's figurative level
    1. Does the poet use any emotionally-charged words? What effect do they have?
    2. What images stand out? How do the images help to convey the poem's main idea?
    3. Are any of the images used as symbols? What do they represent?
    4. Are any of the actions described in the poem intended to be viewed as symbolic? What do they represent?
    5. Is the poem limited to a specific situation or does it comment on life in general? What comment does it make?
    6. What is the significance of the poem's thoughts or theme?

C. The poem's main purpose
    1. Is the poem mostly concerned with communicating thoughts?
    2. Does the poem tell a story or present a dramatic situation? Does it amuse or entertain? Does it succeed?
    3. Is the poem an explanation or exploration of feelings?

4. Does it aim at persuading the reader to believe something? What?
5. Does the poem attempt to shock the reader into a realization? Is it effective?
6. Is the poem commenting on a problem in our society? What is it saying?

D. The poem's tone
1. What feelings is the speaker expressing?
2. What words or images convey those feelings best? Why?
3. Are there any sounds in the poem that help to communicate the speaker's attitude? Which? How do they help?
4. Does the poem's rhythm relate to the feelings being expressed? How? What is the effect?
5. Have the details of the poem been especially selected to convey the speaker's attitude? How have they been limited? Is it effective?

E. The poem's use of words, sounds, and rhythm
1. Which words are repeated? Why?
2. Have any words been isolated or given special emphasis? What effect was the poet trying to achieve?
3. What use does the poet make of imagery? What patterns link the images together?
4. Does the author give special emphasis to any single image? Which one? Why?
5. Are there any symbols in the poem? Where? What do they mean?
6. How do the images and symbols help to establish the poem's meaning?
7. What use does the poet make of sounds? How do the sounds in the poem add to its meaning?
8. How would you describe the poem's rhythm? Does the rhythm slow down, speed up, or change at any point? Why?

F. The poem's structure
1. What type of poem is this? Why did the poet choose this type?
2. What pattern of rhyme did the poet use? How does the pattern of rhymes add to the impact of the poem?
3. Are the lines of the poem arranged in a special pattern? What purpose did the poet have in choosing that pattern?
4. Does the poem have a consistent meter? What type is it?

How many feet are in each line?
5. What rhyme scheme, if any, did the poet use?

This exercise will enable you to organize your thoughts and gather some preliminary notes on your subject. If the assignment requires you to include some of the critics' views as well, this is the point at which library research should be done. Unless the assignment specifically asks you to give only your own thoughts, you will find research helpful even if it is not required.

Commentary on your subject will be listed at the library in several ways. Here are some possibilities:

1. Under the author's name in the author or the subject index.
2. Under the poem's title - if it is a major work - in the subject index.
3. In a collection listed according to the period in which the poet wrote. For example, comments on a sonnet by Shakespeare might be found in a book on Elizabethan writing.
4. In a collection listed according to the nationality of the author. For instance, comments on a poem by Alden Nowlan might be found in a collection of essays on Canadian poetry.
5. In the *Reader's Guide to Periodical Literature*, if the criticism is an article from a magazine. This is an important source, especially for finding material on current writers.

As you read through the critics' comments, take care to note all the biographical information for each book or article as you go. This will assist you in creating your footnotes and bibliography, and will allow you to locate the book quickly should you need it again. Check with your teacher regarding the format you should use for footnotes and bibliographies.

Any critical comments that might be useful are probably handiest if they are quoted on cards with the source listed at the bottom. When you are ready to write, the cards can be shuffled and arranged in their order of use. Irrelevant quotations can be removed easily.

GETTING ORGANIZED TO WRITE

Now that you have collected your own thoughts along with those of the critics, the next step is to organize the materials in preparation for writing. Before determining which pattern of organization to use, you must give careful thought to the essay's specific purpose. In other words, before you can select and arrange the specific details, you must know what main idea you are trying to get across to your reader. As a check to see if your understanding of the essay's purpose is clear, try stating the main thought in a single sentence. For example, a student analyzing Frost's "Mending Wall" might write: "In 'Mending Wall', Frost reveals that people build literal or figurative walls to maintain mutual goodwill and community peace."

This single statement should appear in the introductory paragraph, and can help to organize and control your essay's content. If you see your interpretation as a view to be explained to the reader, then a pattern of organization might emerge naturally as you reread the material with your interpretation in mind. Following are two common organizational patterns for essays presenting an explication of a central statement.

PATTERN ONE:

Introductory paragraph: begins with a general introduction of the topic and moves to a specific statement of the essay's main thought or purpose.

↓

Examination and explanation of the poem's first major segment (may be one stanza, one quatrain, the first three lines - whatever is a natural division of thought).

↓

Examination and explanation of the poem's second major segment. Included here should be some comment on how the author develops the thoughts and patterns established in the first segment.

↓

The pattern of discussing each remaining segment, one per paragraph, should be continued until the entire poem has been dealt with. Care should be taken to keep the focus on the interpretation you stated in the introductory paragraph.

↓

The second-last paragraph, sometimes combined with the concluding paragraph, would consider the poem as a whole, pointing out any further meaning the poem takes on when considered in its entirety.

The concluding paragraph would restate, in fresh words, the general interpretation you are presenting and might comment on the significance or effectiveness of the poem as a whole. The pattern of thought here is from the specific to the general.

PATTERN TWO:

Introductory paragraph: begins with a general introduction of the topic and moves to a specific statement of the essay's main thought or purpose.

↓

A brief explanation of the poem's literal level. This might include initial responses to the poem or identification of essential information about it (such as the speaker, audience, or context).

↓

In the following paragraphs, an explanation of the poem's figurative level should be given. Paragraph divisions should be made with each shift of focus as discussion moves from the first to the last major thought. It is helpful to remember that the figurative level involves interpreting the poem's meaning, while the literal level is a simple statement of the poem's basic content.

↓

Analysis of the poem will lead to an understanding of the poem's organizing principle or theme. The second-last paragraph (which may be combined with the concluding paragraph), should consider the poem as a whole and point out its theme or deeper meaning.

↓

The concluding paragraph would restate, in fresh words, the general interpretation you are presenting and might comment on the significance or effectiveness of the poem as a whole. The pattern of thought here is from the specific to the general.

The above patterns are just that: patterns that might be used. They can be altered or adjusted to suit a particular poem or to make room for comments that must be included but are not accounted for in these patterns. Like any plan, these patterns should be a means for organizing your ideas so that they flow logically and smoothly, rather than functioning as restrictive structures that inhibit your creativity. Just remember to check back occasionally to see if you are accomplishing what you set out to do: explain to your reader your interpretation of the poem's meaning.

DRAFTING YOUR ESSAY

Once you have a pattern or plan in mind and have slotted your material into the various parts of the essay outline, you are ready to start writing. The following points might help you to present your views more effectively.

1. The introductory paragraph
   Many introductions to literary essays have three parts: a general statement that sets up the topic, a statement or two that serve to focus the topic, and a statement that presents your specific view on the topic. This three-part pattern can be used if you wish.

   If you are inspired and have a special angle in mind, you might want to structure your own introduction. If you do so, it is helpful to remember that good writing gets to the point quickly and presents it clearly.
2. Using quotations from critics
   Unless your main point is to present and evaluate a critic's interpretation of a poem, quotations from critics should be used sparingly to support or elaborate your own views. They should not dominate the essay or present the case for you.
3. Using quotations or references to the poem
   In order to help your reader see what you mean when you comment on the poem, show the reader where in the poem examples can be seen to illustrate or support your statement. This is done easily by making references to specific lines or stanzas, by quoting words or entire lines, or by paraphrasing the poem's thoughts. Quote only enough examples to strengthen your essay, though. Over-use of quotations will clutter an essay, give an impression of disunity, and suggest a lack of conviction in the student's mind.

4. Integrating quotations into the essay
   Your teacher will explain the conventions regarding the placement of shorter and longer quotations. Take care that the following steps are followed when using quotations: introduce the quotation, present it, and then explain its meaning or significance in terms of your essay's focus. Quotations that are not explained or commented on make no real contribution to an essay.
5. The concluding paragraph
   The conclusion is often a problem because there are several ways to end a paper. It is helpful to keep in mind in mind the two functions of a concluding paragraph: 1) to summarize the main thoughts of the essay (in fresh words), and 2) to generalize about the significance of those thoughts.

Two common errors in concluding paragraphs are worth mentioning here. Stuck for something further to say about the poem's significance, some writers resort to a comment about the author's ability, such as: "This poem is an excellent example of Shakespeare's power as a writer. His plays and poems are an invaluable part of our literary heritage." While the comment might be accurate, it has no place in an essay that is focussing on the poem rather than on the author's skills. In other words, such comments are almost always off-topic.

The second common error is made by students who shift from formal to informal style by making a personal statement in the conclusion. Here are two examples.

A. "This essay presents my own interpretation of the poem. I hope my thoughts are clear and convincing because I did my best."
B. "Now that I have analyzed the poem, I can say honestly that I do not like it."

Personal comments pinned onto the end of an essay are particularly disturbing because they break the tone of the essay and leave the reader remembering the comment more than the essay's main point.

REVISING AND EDITING

Once you have completed the first draft of the essay, you are ready to revise. The goal of revision is to make your writing as clear and effective as you can. This will involve working with both the content and the form of your writing. The suggestions that follow will assist you at this stage.

1. Reread your essay to check for organization.
   - Is your main idea made clear at the start?
   - Do the ideas follow each other logically and clearly?
   - Is there any material that should be omitted?
   - Should any paragraphs be divided further into additional paragraphs?
   - Are your introduction and conclusion clear and purposeful?
   - Have you used transitional devices to link your paragraphs for smoother reading?
2. Reread your essay to assess its content.
   - Have you stated your topic near the start?
   - Do your thoughts cover the topic thoroughly?
   - Have you made effective use of quotations?
   - Do any points require further explanation or examples?
   - Is each part of the essay clearly on topic?
   - Is the content clear and interesting?
3. Reread your essay to revise for style.
   - Have you used clear, precise words?
   - Are your sentences varied and interesting?
   - If you are writing formally, have you avoided use of the first person?
   - Have you avoided using slang or informal expressions?
   - Can any sentence be improved by eliminating unnecessary words?
4. Reread your essay for grammar, punctuation, and spelling problems.
   - When checking sentences, you might find it helpful to start with the last sentence and work your way forward to the first. That would allow you to consider each sentence separately, with no intrusion from what comes before or after.
   - Have you made effective use of the comma?
   - Where did you use the apostrophe? Is it correct? Should any other words have an apostrophe added? Did you use any formal contractions that should be eliminated?
   - Could any sentences be improved with the addition or deletion of punctuation?
   - Are you uncertain of how any word should be spelled? Check the spelling of any word that causes you to hesitate and wonder about its spelling. To double-check, you might have

someone go over your essay and underline any words that should be looked up.

- Have you shifted verb tenses in any part of the essay? To be certain you have not, scan the essay quickly and identify the verb tense in each paragraph.
- To discover and correct any other grammar problems, you might try reading the essay aloud or into a tape recorder, if you have one. Wording problems will show themselves and give you a chance to correct them before handing the paper in.

Revising and editing an essay is hard work, but it pays off to be thorough. If you are not confident that you have caught every error or wrinkle in your writing, you might find a partner in your class, exchange rough copies, and read each other's. Comments in pencil along the margins can be used to record any questions or concerns you have about the content and form. If you do not have the opportunity to exchange papers with someone in class, someone out of school is always an alternative.

You have been through a considerable amount of work to arrive at this point. You studied the poem and the topic, brainstormed ideas, researched, planned, wrote, revised, and revised again. You should have in hand an essay that requires only one more step before it is done: typing or writing the final copy. This step is the most satisfying because you can proceed knowing you have done your best to produce a good, effective essay. One final caution: do not forget to proof-read the final copy.

EXERCISE

Study the poem "At the Long Sault: May, 1660", by Archibald Lampman, found on page 298 of this text. Read the essay that follows it only after you feel you understand the poem. Written by a high school student, this essay has several characteristics worth considering. The questions that follow will provide some guidance for a discussion of it.

STOUT-HEARTED MEN

by Kerry Cameron

Early in the spring of 1660, the commander of the French garrison at Ville Marie (Montreal), Adam Dollard des Ormeaux (Daulac), received information that two tribes of Iroquois were converging to attack the three main settlements in New France – Montreal, Three Rivers, and Quebec – to drive the French from Canada forever. Daulac believed that if these Iroquois were allowed to come together, the colonists would not be able to defend themselves. He devised a plan in which a small band of men, consisting of himself and sixteen other young Frenchmen, along with a group of friendly Hurons and Algonquins, would ambush one group of Iroquois at a fort by the Long Sault Rapids. It was here, after the Hurons and Algonquins had deserted him, that Daulac and his companions fought for many days against ever-increasing odds, as more and more Iroquois arrived. Finally, the seventeen men were overwhelmed and all were killed. Their show of strength and courage ended the Iroquois plans to descend down the river and sack the French settlements.

Archibald Lampman, in his poem "At the Long Sault: May, 1660"[1], has chronicled an event in Canadian history comparable to such well-known heroic epics as Horatius' defense of Rome, Custer's last stand, the evacuation of Dunkirk and, of course, the Alamo. It is the story of Daulac and his companions, a band of resolute and fearless men, who were able to hold back overwhelming forces, thus saving the unsuspecting inhabitants of the little town of Montreal from being attacked. R.E. Rashley, in *Poetry in Canada*, pinpoints the theme in the following words:

> This . . . poem is concerned not with the heroics or drama of man's achievements but with the compassion for his fate. . . .[2]

In "At the Long Sault", Lampman has made the historical battle a vivid experience for the reader by his skillful use of figurative words and phrases. In the first stanza, he paints a joyful picture of spring. He speaks of "life and mirth", of flowers "springing", of "happy birds", and of waters that "leap and play". In the midst of all this beautiful spring-time gaiety, the second stanza shows the reader a grim setting where a small band of men have gathered to fight the advancing "hordes" of Iroquois. Lampman builds up the emotion of courage in the third stanza, which he contrasts with the despair of the little band as they realize that because of the odds they cannot win.

In the fourth stanza, Lampman parallels each individual of Daulac's band to a "tired bull moose" running from a "ravening pack" of wolves. Like the "harried, wounded, and weary grown" moose, each man strikes his "last wild stroke" and falls to his death. After this powerful metaphor, Lampman ends the poem with a lyric in anapaestic metre. The lyric soothes the spirit after the firm, deep sound of the preceding lines telling of the heroic end. The epigrammatic close reminds one of death, but also suggests rebirth. It is through this change of mood that Lampman stresses the endurance, heroism, and final death of both the moose and the men.

As in all of his poetry, Lampman uses the imagery of the wheel, or cycle, extensively to impress upon the reader the ambivalence of his thought. Pacey explains this imagery in the following passage:

> The wheel slowly turns, and as it turns light succeeds dark, heat cold, dry wet, and so on. These opposites are the spokes of the wheel: they have their place in an endless cycle which gives them each meaning and a final unity.[3]

Lampman uses this principle of balanced opposites throughout "At the Long Sault". A few examples would be these: the "day-long sun" and the "wonderful moon"; the "limitless woods" and "an open glade"; the "happy" birds "winging" and the "grey hawk soaring"; and the "rush of the foe" and "melted away". One of the major contrasts in this poem, of course, is that of the battle at the fort and the people asleep in the town, all-unsuspecting that at that very moment seventeen men were giving their lives for them.

The poet also uses the imagery of music, or onomatopoeia, to stress either the harmony of nature, or the disharmony of violence. At the beginning and very end of the poem, words such as "springing", "ringing", and "whistled" are used to show the loveliness of nature; while "soars", "plunges and roars", "panting", and "gnash" are used to emphasize the violence of the battle and the ferocity of the Indian warriors.

With these three writing devices, and his use of significant superlatives, Lampman shows his power in presenting men and their fate with dramatic intensity and a deep understanding.

"At the Long Sault" is considered by many to be Lampman's best work. The use of contrasts is effectively done and creates a unity of thought. More effective than the contrasts, however, is the metaphor of the moose, which creates a deep feeling of sympathy for the seventeen men who tried to hold back the hundreds of Iroquois. Lampman makes his poem very rich by painting pictures with colorful phrases and impelling adjectives. The poem is a masterpiece.

FOOTNOTES

[1]Lampman, Archibald, *At the Long Sault and Other New Poems* (Toronto: The Ryerson Press, 1943), pp. 1-4.
[2]Rashley, R.E., *Poetry in Canada – The First Three Steps* (Toronto: The Ryerson Press, 1958), p. 77.
[3]Pacey, Desmond, "A Reading of Lampman's 'Heat'", *Archibald Lampman*, ed. Michael Gnarowski (Toronto: The Ryerson Press, 1970), p. 184.

BIBLIOGRAPHY

Brown, E.K. *On Canadian Poetry*. Ottawa: The Tecumseh Press, 1973.

Brown, H. and J. *Canada in North America to 1800*. Vancouver: The Copp Clark Publishing Co., Ltd., 1960.

Gnarowski, Michael, editor. *Archibald Lampman*. Toronto: The Ryerson Press, 1970.

Lampman, Archibald. *At the Long Sault and Other New Poems*. Toronto: The Ryerson Press, 1943.

Pacey, Desmond. *Ten Canadian Poets*. Toronto: The Ryerson Press, 1958.

Rashley, R.E. *Poetry in Canada – The First Three Steps*. Toronto: The Ryerson Press, 1958.

QUESTIONS:

1. What is the main purpose of this essay?
2. Why did the writer begin with the poem's historical base?
3. What pattern of organization did the writer use in his essay?
4. Examine each paragraph in the main body. Has the writer made use of transitions? Point out two examples.
5. Did the writer make effective use of quotations from the critics? Comment.
6. Does the essay contain sufficient examples and specific references to support its main points?
7. Do you agree with the writer's views? Could any points be expanded? Comment.
8. Have any important points been omitted from the essay? Should any points have been left out? Explain.
9. Is the conclusion effective? Explain.

10. Comment on the essay's style. Are the sentences varied and interesting? Is the writing consistent in tone? Does the writer use words effectively? Give examples to support your observations.

Appendix II

Prose about Poetry

How to Enjoy Poetry

by James Dickey

What is poetry? And why has it been around so long? Many have suspected that it was invented as a school subject, because you have to take exams on it. But that is not what poetry is or why it is still around. That's not what it feels like, either. When you really feel it, a new part of you happens, or an old part is renewed, with surprise and delight at being what it is.

From the beginning, men have known that words and things, words and actions, words and feelings, go together, and that they can go together in thousands of different ways, according to who is using them. Some ways go shallow, and some go deep.

The first thing to understand about poetry is that it comes to you from outside you, in books or in words, but that for it to live, something from within you must come to it and meet it and complete it. Your response with your own mind and body and memory and emotions gives the poem its ability to work its magic; if you give to it, it will give to you, and give plenty.

When you read, don't let the poet write down to you; read up to him. Reach for him from your gut out, and the heart and muscles will come into it, too.

The sun is new every day, the ancient philosopher Heraclitus said. The sun of poetry is new every day, too, because it is seen in different ways by different people who have lived under it, lived with it, responded to it. Their lives are different from yours, but by means of the special spell that poetry brings to the *fact* of the sun – everybody's sun; yours, too – you can come into possession of many suns: as many as men and women have ever been able to imagine. Poetry makes possible the deepest kind of personal possession of the world.

The most beautiful constellation in the winter sky is Orion, which ancient poets thought looked like a hunter, up there, moving across heaven with his dog Sirius. What is this hunter made out of stars hunting for? What does he mean? Who owns him, if anybody? The poet Aldous Huxley felt that he did, and so, in Aldous Huxley's universe of personal emotion, he did.

> Up from among the emblems of the
>   wind into its heart of power,
> The Hunstman climbs, and all his
>   living stars
> Are bright, and all are mine.

The beginning of your true encounter with poetry should be simple. It should bypass all classrooms, all textbooks, courses, examinations, and libraries and go straight to the things that make your own existence exist: to your body and nerves and blood and muscles. Find your own way – a secret way that just maybe you don't know yet – to open yourself as wide as you can and as deep as you can to the moment, the *now* of your own existence and the endless mystery of it, and perhaps at the same time to one other thing that is not you, but is out there: a handful of gravel is a good place to start. So is an ice cube – what more mysterious and beautiful *interior* of something has there ever been?

As for me, I like the sun, the source of all living things, and on certain days very good-feeling, too. "Start with the sun," D.H. Lawrence said, "and everything will slowly, slowly happen." Good advice. And a lot *will* happen.

What is more fascinating than a rock, if you really feel it and *look* at it, or more interesting than a leaf?

> Horses, I mean; butterflies, whales;
> Mosses, and stars; and gravelly
> Rivers, and fruit.
>
> Oceans, I mean; black valleys; corn;
> Brambles, and cliffs; rock, dirt, dust, ice . . .

Go back and read this list – it is quite a list, Mark Van Doren's list! – item by item. Slowly. Let each of these things call up an image out of your own life.

Think and feel. What moss do you see? Which horse? What field of corn? What brambles are *your* brambles? Which river is most yours?

Part of the spell of poetry is in the rhythm of language, used by poets who understand how powerful a factor rhythm can be, how compelling and unforgettable. Almost anything put into rhythm and rhyme is more memorable than the same thing said in prose. Why this is, no one knows completely, though the answer is surely rooted far down in the biology by means of which we exist; in the circulation of the blood that goes forth from the heart and comes back, and in the repetition of breathing. Croesus was a rich Greek king, back in the sixth century before Christ, but this tombstone was not his:

> No Croesus lies in the grave you see;
> I was a poor laborer, and this suits me.

That is plain-spoken and definitive. You believe it, and the rhyme helps you believe it and keep it.

Writing poetry is a lot like a contest with yourself, and if you like sports and games and competitions of all kinds, you might like to try writing some. Why not?

The possibilities of rhyme are great. Some of the best fun is in making up your own limericks. There's no reason you can't invent limericks about anything that comes to your mind. No reason. Try it.

The problem is to find three words that rhyme and fit into a meaning. "There was a young man from . . ." *Where* was he from? What situation was he in? How can these things fit into the limerick form – a form everybody knows – so that the rhymes "pay off," and give that sense of completion and inevitability that is so deliciously memorable that nothing else is like it?

The more your encounter with poetry deepens, the more your experience of your own life will deepen, and you will begin to see things by means of words, and words by means of things.

You will come to understand the world as it interacts with words, as it can be re-created by words, by rhythms and by images.

You'll understand that this condition is one charged with vital possibilities. You will pick up meaning more quickly – and you will *create* meaning, too, for yourself and for others.

Connections between things will exist for you in ways that they never did before. They will shine with unexpectedness, wide-openness, and you will go toward them, on your own path. "Then . . ." as Dante says, ". . . Then will your feet be filled with good desire." You will know this is happening the first time you say, of

something you never would have noticed before, "Well, would you look at *that!* Who'd 'a thunk it?" (Pause, full of new light)
"*I* thunk it!"

Line Divisions in Free Verse Poetry*

Glen Kirkland

One of free verse poetry's best features - irregular line lengths - puzzles some readers and frustrates some writers. The critical question is this: what are the reasons for dividing a line in one specific place and not in any other place? An examination of some poems and excerpts will reveal that writers can have one or several reasons for dividing a line in a particular way.

At the most basic level, a writer may divide lines into sense units, usually clusters of words that contain sufficient thought to be sensible to the reader. Lines, then, tend to be clauses or phrases that can be read in an easy sweep of the eyes. Often, such lines end where the reader might draw a breath if reading aloud, or where a form of punctuation occurs or is implied. The following poem illustrates this:

Morning Mask

Framed in cold silver,
his morning mask is distant,
slack—even dead—
as he tugs tighter
the slim, austere
knot of boredom
and jackets himself
in the wooly warmth of
predictability.

The small boy
who buried treasures,
rescued prisoners of war,
and shot savage tigers
saves only his money now.

*All poems and excerpts in this essay were written by Glen Kirkland.

He sips the tedium of his days
like tepid tea, and—
surrounded by killing quiet—
fills his emptiness with words:

> "This may not be much,"
> he tells himself,
> "but at least I will have
> a comfortable death."

While some lines in "Morning Mask" were divided for special emphasis, which we will discuss later, most were divided into sense units for comfortable, clear reading. Two observations will make this even more apparent: first, the number of articles, prepositions, and conjunctions on the left margin of the poem indicates that several lines have been divided into grammatical units; second, the number of punctation marks on the right margin of the poem reveals that several lines have been divided where a reader might draw a breath or pause in reading.

In addition to dividing lines into sense units, writers of free verse may divide lines in order to give special emphasis to significant words or images, or to enhance the impact of the poem. For example, note the placement of the key words and the importance of the shorter lines in this poem:

Departure

leaving home
I stand with my dead
grandmother's suitcases in hand
coat slung carelessly over my shoulder
the car loaded down with
all my possessions
packed in boxes tied doubly
with string
(like a refugee from some
old movie)

my father coughs
shakes my hand
and offers me
a last-minute yellow screwdriver
with interchangeable heads

my mother kisses me
and says

as long as I have a sense of
humor
I will
survive

in the doorway now
I smile awkwardly and mutter
goodbye

my mother asks
again
have you
got
everything

yes
I say
I've got it
all

and
frightened suddenly
I want to paint my name
in huge red letters
on the ceilings and walls
of every room
carve my initials in
the coffee table
and leave a life-sized reproduction of myself
asleep upstairs

The placement of the key words and images in this poem reveal other reasons for dividing a line in a particular way. "Departure" is about relationships, and the words that identify the poem's characters tend to fall on the left margin (I . . . grandmother's . . . my father . . . my mother . . . I . . . I . . . my mother . . . I . . . I), where they receive emphasis in reading. Other words and images are emphasized by their isolation in a short line (leaving home . . . survive . . . goodbye . . . everything . . . all). If we examine those, we see that they underline the overwhelming impact of making a break from one's family.

The emotional significance of the moment is emphasized, too, by the shorter lines. The speaker is preparing to leave home for perhaps the rest of his life, and he realizes that as he lingers in the doorway. The shorter lines in the middle of the poem help to convey the inability of the characters to express adequately what they feel in such an emotional moment. The longer lines at the end read more rapidly, thereby conveying the rush of emotions that suddenly overtake the speaker. Clearly, then, the line divisions in a free verse poem can make an important contribution to the poem's impact.

The previously-mentioned reasons for dividing lines at a particular point addressed general practices that apply to several lines. Specific, individual lines might be divided at a point that brings out meaning that might otherwise be missed. For example, this excerpt describes a lonely old woman:

> Sitting in winter sunlight,
> surrounded by plants and family
> photos,
> frilly doilies and china dogs . . .

As we read the second line, we expect, for a brief moment, that she has family with her. As we read on and complete the next line, we realize she is surrounded by family photos. This reversal emphasizes more strongly the old woman's loneliness and her attempts to fend it off by surrounding herself with comforting objects. If "photos" had been left on the same line as "family", that effect would have been lost.

A second technique used to bring added meaning to specific lines within a poem is more typographical in nature. Occasionally, a writer can arrange lines to create a concrete, visual effect that helps to communicate the meaning of those individual lines. This excerpt illustrates that well:

. . . sometimes
    I feel like
                        old clothes
                        piled
                        in a corner

The arrangement of the last three lines suggests isolation and creates a visual image of the old clothes by piling the lines one on the other. While this device can add life to a poem, a caution should be noted. Overuse of this technique can make a poem tedious and "gimmicky".

These are but a few of the reasons a writer might give for

dividing a line at a specific point. Because free verse is such a flexible form, poets have been able to divide lines for more subtle effects. A line break may work to suggest a gesture or expression, such as a frown; it may mark a shift of emotions, surprise a reader, create irony, or simply manufacture a pun. There is no limit to the imaginative use of line divisions to add impact to a free verse poem.

An Analysis of "The Diver"*

Carmen Locke

The poem, "The Diver", by Robert Currie, is a symbolic poem written in free verse. On the first reading, it appears to be about a boy diving from a bridge while a group of his peers watch and wait for him to surface. On a deeper level, it is an analogy made to Christ, the crucifixion and the resurrection. Throughout the poem, there are many references to Christ's story.

The poem starts off by setting the scene and gives a brief description of the place:

> The bridge like a Roman fort
> held the river and the beach
> held our vision steady through the waving heat
> held us all . . .

Literally, this would suggest a river or stream, perhaps a swimming hole, where a gang of boys is diving on a hot day. Beyond the surface reading, the Roman fort in the first line can be seen as the walled city of Jerusalem and also as referring to the Roman influence in Christ's death. This section tells us the bridge is the focal point of the crowd and is the place where the boy is to dive from, as indicated in the next few lines:

> while the solitary figure
> struggled up the arch
> his knees braced against the rivets

*This student essay was written about Robert Currie's poem on p. 294.

Here the boy climbing up the bridge is a parallel to Jesus struggling up the hill, Golgotha. The climb up the arch can also be compared to His life, with its humble beginnings to His gradual rise as a religious leader and the building of his following.

The next two lines say:

> Below someone shook out his towel
> while others bet upon his chance

Literally, this means a peer of the boy is laying out his towel for him, while some of the other boys bet on his chance of making it. On the figurative level, it indicates someone is preparing His shroud, while the gamblers are the Roman soldiers betting on how long it will take Him to die.

The poem continues, making an analogy to the crucifixion:

> At the summit of the span he rose
> his arms outstretched
> flung a cross against the sun
> and the whole world hung beneath him
> our eyes nailing him to the sky

There is an obvious comparison here between the diver, who has reached the peak and is preparing to dive, and Jesus on the cross. The fourth line places His followers beneath Him and puts Him in both a physically and spiritually higher position. The line "our eyes nailing him" symbolizes the spikes driven through his hands and feet. The boys can be seen staring up at the diver, almost in awe of him.

The rest of the poem deals with the dive and resurfacing of the boy. The next four lines speak specifically of the actual dive:

> Suspension for an instant and forever
> A slow plunge toward the water
> and he came down from above
> dropping beneath the surface like a stone

The diving boy appears almost to move in slow motion. The slow plunge represents Jesus dying on the cross. He then dies, becoming as cold and lifeless as a rock.

The final section of the poem speaks of the boy resurfacing and is a parallel to the resurrection:

Then from unknown depths
his head broke the water
shook out a crown of sunlit spray
brought release   new life
thrilling in our chests

The resurfacing boy is compared to the reborn Christ. The "unknown depths" could be death, while the head breaking water is symbolic of his return to life. The "crown of sunlit spray" can be compared to the crown of thorns Jesus wore, or a halo. The final lines are suggestive of the idea of salvation through Christ. They suggest the idea of new life being "reborn" not only in this life but also in heaven.

This poem works for several reasons. Most importantly, it makes effective use of comparisons and is visually stimulating. It is possible to imagine the "waving heat" and the outline of a "solitary figure" against the sun. "Our eyes nailing him to the sky" and the "crown of sunlit spray", for instance, are very strong comparisons that greatly enhance the visual aspect and provide impact. The mind's eye can easily picture the scene described in the poem, and we can relate to the situation. On a different level, the poem is on well-known, widespread subjects – Christianity and Christ – and is, therefore, relevant to many people in Western society. Because the poem alludes, on a symbolic level, to the last part of Christ's life, it allows the reader to get a deeper meaning out of the poem and more enjoyment from reading it.

Appendix III

Glossary of Terms

Alliteration: the repetition of the same consonant or vowel sound at the start of words that are closely associated. For example, in "Leader of the Band", the speaker says, "I'm just a living legacy/To the leader of the band." (The "l" sound is repeated)

Allusion: a brief, undeveloped reference to a presumably familiar place, event, or figure from history, literature, mythology, or the Bible. In Irving Layton's poem "The Bull Calf", for example, the proud calf makes the speaker think of ". . . the deposed Richard II". The writer has assumed his readers will be familiar with Richard II, and, therefore, gave no added explanation. Allusion is one device for achieving compression in writing.

Ambiguity: an effect of richness and uncertainty produced by words or phrases that have two or more possible meanings. Ambiguity always leaves room for alternative reader reactions to multiple meanings of the same words.

Amphibraic: see meter

Anapestic: see meter

Apostrophe: a figure of speech consisting of words addressing an inanimate object, abstract idea, or deceased individual as though that object, idea, or person were alive; also, words addressing an absent person as though he were present. For example, in Shelley's "To a Skylark", the speaker addresses the skylark directly, beginning with the opening line, "Hail to thee, blithe Spirit!"

Assonance: the repetition of the same or similar vowel sounds within words in close proximity. In "Sampler", Robert Finch uses assonance strongly in the first two lines: "You dip the tips of your fingers in other lives/As in bowls of fragrant liquid. . . ."

Ballad: a fairly short, simple poem telling a story, often about a tragic event, popular legend, courageous act, or great love. Folk ballads are written to be sung (earlier ones were oral, anonymously written, and had several variations), while literary ballads are written to be read or recited. More generally, ballads tend to start near the action, use simple language, suggest antecedent action, contain dialogue, emphasize plot and character, use refrains and choruses, follow regular patterns, and make references to superstitions, dreams, and magic. Three examples of ballads in this text are "Lord Randal", "The Gambler", and "The Griesly Wife".

Blank Verse: a type of unrhymed poetry using five iambic feet. This form was popularized by Shakespeare and Milton. Frost's poem "Mending Wall" is an example of blank verse.

Cacophony: use of harsh, discordant, dissonant sounds for poetic effect. To suggest the noise of automobiles in his poem "Klaxon", Reaney uses cacophony, which is especially evident in the first two lines: "All day cars mooed and shrieked/Hollered and bellowed and wept. . . ."

Chorus: see refrain

Concrete Poem: a recent experimental form of poetry which is intended to combine visual and aural elements of art and music in poetic form. Concrete poems have a definite shape suggesting the poem's subject, and tend to play with letters, sounds, or words, using them in new, original ways. "Hunter's Lament" and "We Are Two Flowers" are two excellent examples of this type of poetic expression.

Connotation: the emotional associations implied or suggested by a word; these associations extend the meaning of a word beyond its dictionary meaning. Connotative words produce either highly personal impressions in individuals or general impressions, based on culture and shared by many.

Consonance: the repetition of the same consonant sound within words in close proximity. Ted Hughes, in his poem "View of a Pig", uses consonance in the line, "Such weight and thick pink bulk. . . ." (The "k" sound is repeated)

Couplet: two successive lines of rhyming verse having the same number of feet. Dryden's poem "Epitaph Intended for his Wife" is an example of a couplet that stands as a poem by itself. Other couplets that are a part of a poem can be seen in the closing lines of any Shakespearean sonnet.

Dactylic: see meter
Denotation: the precise, literal meaning or limited dictionary meaning of a word.
Diction: the choice and arrangement of words in a selection. Words in poetic writing are usually selected for their sound and meaning as well as the ideas and feelings they suggest. The diction in a poem depends on the subject, the poem type, the writer's purpose, and his style.
Dimeter: see meter
Dissonance: see cacophony
Dramatic Monologue: a poem written as a speech by a narrator addressing a silent audience. The poem, spoken aloud at a critical moment of conflict, suggests a situation and setting, and characterizes the narrator. Probably the best-known dramatic monologue is "My Last Duchess", by Robert Browning.

Elegy: a dignified poem expressing sorrow and, sometimes, praise for someone who is deceased.
End-rhyme: see rhyme
End-stopped Line: a line of poetry with a natural pause at the end.
Enjambement: see run-on line
Epic: a long narrative poem recounting the deeds of heroic figures from legends or history. Written in an elevated style, the epic typically focuses on a hero of national significance, deeds requiring great courage, supernatural forces intervening in the action, and many descriptive details. Among the best-known epics are *The Iliad* and *The Odyssey* by Homer, and *Beowulf*, from Old English.
Epigram: a short, witty poem or statement. Ogden Nash's poem "The Eel" is an example of an epigram.
Epitaph: a serious or humorous poem or statement on a gravestone commemorating the deceased. For an example, see Dryden's poem, "Epitaph Intended For His Wife".
Euphony: the pleasant, musical quality produced by agreeable sounds and images in a line of poetry. In "The Skater", Roberts' use of euphony to suggest the beauty of the setting is especially evident in the third

stanza: "And the words hung hushed in their long white dream/By the ghostly, glimmering, ice-blue stream."

Feminine Ending: an extra unstressed syllable at the end of a line of poetry that otherwise has a consistent metrical pattern. This ending is often found in blank verse, as in Frost's "Mending Wall": ". . . But they would have the rabbit out of hid*ing* . . ."
Feminine Rhyme: see rhyme
Figurative Language: language which contains figures of speech, many of which involve comparisons between unlike things. The figurative meaning of words used in a poem refers to the symbolic or suggested meanings conveyed by those words. These meanings and associations could not possibly be conveyed by the denotative or literal language.
Figures of Speech: language used in a deliberately unconventional, unliteral way in order to achieve a special effect – such as adding meaning, imagery, emphasis, or contrast. Figures of speech often add beauty, richness, and intensity to a poem. Some of the most commonly used figures of speech are the metaphor, simile, personification, hyperbole, metonymy, and synecdoche.
Foot: a basic unit of measurement for syllable groups in poetry. See meter for an explanation of different types of feet.
Free Verse: poetry which has no regular patterns of rhyme, meter or line length. Instead, it relies on natural speech rhythms. Freed from the traditional conventions associated with poetry, free verse allows the writer considerable flexibility. While there are many examples of free verse in this text, "This Is a Photograph of Me", by Margaret Atwood, provides an excellent example.

Haiku: a traditional form of Japanese poetry consisting of three lines and seventeen syllables (5-7-5). While haiku poems have many subtle characteristics, they usually present snapshot-like images of nature or everyday life, and reveal the emotions of the speaker or a brief, condensed philosophical view of life.
Hyperbole: a figure of speech which makes conscious use of exaggeration for emphasis, serious, or humorous effects. Stephen Hume, in "Such is the power of the lover's sonnet", begins with a hyperbole: "Tons of force trapped in a handsome bonnet. . . ." Through it, he emphasizes the impact of a

lover's sonnet.

Iamb: see meter

Iambic pentameter: see meter and blank verse

Idyll: see pastoral poem

Image: words or word groups that help the reader picture or sense what is being described. Images can be literal (when the description is to be taken for its denotative meaning) or figurative (consisting of such devices as metaphor, simile, personification, and symbol).

Imagery: the pattern of images in a single work.

Internal Rhyme: see rhyme

Irony: a general term describing a recognized discrepancy or incongruity in meaning. The most common types are verbal irony (the difference between what was said and what was intended), dramatic irony (the difference between what the audience knows and what a character believes to be true), and situational irony (the difference between expectation and fulfillment or what is and what would seem appropriate).

Light Verse: poetry whose prime purpose is to entertain or amuse. Because light verse includes such forms as parodies or satire, there may be a serious side or "bite" behind the poet's humor.

Limerick: a light verse form containing five mixed iambic and anapestic lines rhyming AABBA (first, second, and fifth lines in trimeter; third and fourth in dimeter). The first and last lines of limericks are often identical or slightly different in wording. Some examples of the limerick are found in Chapter 5.

Literal Language: refers to use of words in their usual, limited, most obvious, matter-of-fact sense. Literal meaning refers to the obvious, unexaggerated meaning of a word, line, or poem.

Lyric: a brief, music-like poem expressing strong emotions and thoughts. The term is sometimes used to describe the words of songs.

Masculine Ending: a stressed syllable at the end of a line of poetry. In Frost's poem "Mending Wall", we see an example of masculine ending when the speaker says, "My apple trees will never get across/And eat the cones under his pines, I tell *him*."

Masculine Rhyme: see rhyme

Meiosis: see understatement

Metaphor: a common figure of speech in which a direct comparison or identification is made between two unlike objects (without using "like" or "as").

Meter: a system for identifying and measuring the

rhythmic pattern of a poem according to its stressed and unstressed syllables. In order to identify the pattern of rhythm in a poem, the reader must scan one or two lines marking the stressed syllables, with a / and the unstressed syllables with a ∪. The reader should study the resulting pattern and divide each regular grouping with an oblique line. Here is an example from Wordsworth's "Daffodils":

"I wandered lonely as a cloud"

The pattern can be identified according to the type of rhythm: iambic (∪/), trochaic (/∪), anapestic (∪∪/), amphibraic (∪/∪), dactylic (/∪∪), spondaic (//), or pyrrhic (∪∪). Wordsworth's line, then, is in iambic meter.

In order to be more specific, the reader would go on to describe the number of feet in the scanned line (or number of times the same basic pattern occurs). The following terms are used to describe line lengths: monometer (one foot), dimeter (two feet), trimeter (three feet), tetrameter (four feet), pentameter (five feet), hexameter or alexandrine (six feet), heptameter (seven feet), and octameter (eight feet). Wordsworth's line is an example of iabmic tetrameter.

Metonymy: a figure of speech in which an object is described by its function or by a word closely associated with it. For example, we may say, "The law is at the door". In that case, we are substituting "law" for "policeman" because the policeman's function is to uphold the law. We may say, too, that "the kettle is boiling". We mean the water in the kettle is boiling, but it is more convenient to substitute the name of the object for its function.

Mood: the predominant atmosphere of a work. In poetry, mood is conveyed most forcefully through imagery and rhythm.

Moral: the lesson of a work of literature. The study of literature usually focuses on the extraction of a theme rather than a moral from a work. A moral reduces a passage to what it can teach its readers about how to live.

Narrative: a form of poetry that tells a story. In narrative poetry, the emphasis is on plot, external events, physical action. A well-known example of a narrative poem is "The Gambler", by Don Schlitz.

Octave: sometimes called an octet, this term refers to an eight-line poem or stanza, or the first eight lines of the Italian sonnet (see sonnet).

Ode: a longer lyric poem having a serious subject and dignified style, often addressed to some person, natural creature, or material object. For an example of an ode, see Percy Bysshe Shelley's poem "To a Skylark".

Onomatopoeia: the use of a word whose sound imitates, suggests, and reinforces its meaning (e.g., crash, roar, hum).

Overstatement: see hyperbole

Oxymoron: the deliberate side-by-side placement of words that seem contradictory in meaning. For example, the speaker in "Leader of the Band" describes his father as having "... a thundering, velvet hand."

Paradox: a statement which, on first reading, appears to be self-contradictory (saying two opposite things), but which, on closer examination, proves to be true. For example, in "T-Bar", by P.K. Page, a couple are described as "... not separate yet no longer one". Only after we have thought about it do we understand the line: the couple are no longer side-by-side physically, but their common experience has created a bond between them.

Paraphrase: the informative restatement of difficult lines of poetry in different words so as to clarify meaning or ideas. Although paraphrasing can help a reader overcome obscure or difficult lines or sentence structure, paraphrases in themselves are always unmemorable, commonplace renderings of translations of the original rich, intense, poetic language.

Pastoral: a brief poem that focuses on scenes from rural or pastoral life. It often contains descriptions of shepherds and idealized views of life. One example is "The Passionate Shepherd to his Love".

Personification: a figure of speech attributing human qualities to animals, inanimate objects, or abstract ideas. For example, in Sid Marty's poem "Bright Morning", the speaker fires a rifle which makes a noise "... that leaves the silence terrified."

Poem: a condensed, rhythmical composition with specially arranged lines, figurative language, and – sometimes – rhyme.

Poetry: a serious form of condensed, rhythmical writing which conveys intense emotional, intellectual, and spiritual experiences that cannot usually be expressed through other media. Poetry's related, less-significant form is verse.

Pun: a play on words. The pun has three forms: 1) a word with two different meanings; 2) similarity of meanings in two words that are homonyms; and 3) two words that are pronounced and spelled similarly but which have different meanings. For example, Williams' poem "This Is Just to Say" contains a pun on "just" – which can have two meanings, both applicable to the poem.

Pyrrhic: see meter

Quatrain: see stanza

Refrain (or Chorus): a phrase or sentence repeated at regular intervals in a poem or song. Refrains usually occur after each stanza.

Rhyme: the positioning of two or more words reasonably close together in order to emphasize a similarity or agreement in their sounds. A rhyme that occurs between the final words on two lines is called an end-rhyme, while a rhyme that occurs between two words within a single line is called internal rhyme. Other terms are available to describe types of rhyme. The [illegible]n masculine rhyme is used [illegible]scribe the rhyming of the [illegible]yllable in two lines [illegible]both syllables are stressed. Feminine rhyme describes the rhyming of the final two consecutive syllables in two lines when they follow a stressed-unstressed pattern. The term slant or imperfect rhyme is used to describe words in which the final consonants are identical but the preceding vowels differ (e.g., bought/fight). Finally, the term eye or sight rhyme is used to describe words that conclude with the same spelling but which do not rhyme (e.g., creak/break).

Rhyme Scheme: a labeling system used to describe the rhyming pattern in a poem. In it, the word at the end of the first line is labeled "A" and each word that rhymes with it at the end of subsequent lines is also labeled "A". The word at the end of the next unlabeled line is identified with a "B", and each word that rhymes with it is labeled "B" as well. The procedure is repeated until the pattern of rhyme in the whole poem is identified.

Rhythm: the pattern or recurrence of stressed and unstressed syllables (see meter).

Run-on Line: a line of poetry which continues into the next line with no designated stop or pause. A run-on line is sometimes called enjambement.

Satire: the use of wit, humor, or ridicule to criticize and provoke change. For example, "On Mona's Smile", by Winona Baker, pretends to explain a mystery that has intrigued the curious for many years: what Mona Lisa was smiling about. In her poem, Baker satirizes chauvinistic attitudes and points out the need for change.

Scansion: the analysis of a poem to determine its meter and the length of its lines (see meter). A full description of a poem's meter would include groupings of the lines according to the number of feet they contain, and classification of the stanzas according to the rhyme scheme and number of lines they contain.

Sestet: the last six lines of an Italian sonnet.

Simile: a figure of speech in which an indirect comparison between two dissimilar things is drawn using "like"or "as". In "like an eddy," Birney uses a simile that adds impact and meaning. By comparing his words to a water current, he reminds us of how powerful and dynamic poetry and language can be.

Sonnet: a lyrical poem consisting of fourteen lines in iambic pentameter with a complicated rhyme pattern. The structure of the thought and the rhyme scheme will vary depending upon the type of sonnet. The two most common types of sonnet are the Shakespearean and the Italian (or Petrarchan). A Shakespearean sonnet consists of three quatrains (ABAB CDCD EFEF) followed by a rhyming couplet (GG). Typically, the quatrains establish the theme, and the couplet closes the poem with a succinct conclusion or emphasis of the main point. The Italian sonnet consists of an octave (rhyming ABBA ABBA) and a sestet (rhyming CDE CDE). The subject, often a problem, question, or experience, is introduced in the octet. The sestet provides an answer or, at least, a commentary.

Speaker (or Persona): this term decribes the character who speaks to the reader or an imagined audience in the poem, especially in dramatic and narrative poems. In some cases, such as in most lyric poems, the speaker and the author are one and the same.

Spondaic: see meter

Stanza: lines which have been grouped together to form a unit within a poem. Stanzas are categorized according to the number of lines they contain. Most commonly used are the following: couplet (two lines); tercet or triplet (three lines); quatrain (four lines); sestet (six lines); rhyme royal (seven lines); octet, octave, or ottava rima (eight lines).

Style: the manner in which an author expresses his thoughts and feelings. In poetry, style is determined by imagery, rhythm, diction, patterns of sound, and arrangement of ideas and lines.

Symbol: an object, person, or action which has meaning or significance beyond itself. As a device, symbolism adds compression and complexity wherever it is used. Some symbols are generally known to the public; others depend on their context for their meaning.

Synecdoche: a figure of speech in which a part of something is used to represent the whole. In "Let Me Not to the Marriage of True Minds", Shakespeare uses a synecdoche to describe youth: "Love's not Time's fool, though rosy lips and cheeks/Within his bending sickle's compass come. . . ." "Rosy lips and cheeks" are used to describe the whole person.

Tercet: sometimes called triplet, this term refers to a three-line stanza on a single rhyme or the last half of an Italian sonnet's sestet.

Theme: the main idea of a work, usually stated indirectly. Theme should not be confused with moral (see moral).

Tone: the attitude of the author or speaker toward his subject and audience.

Trochaic: see meter

Understatement: sometimes called meiosis, understatement describes the deliberate restraining or downplaying of something as being less than it is. The effect is subtle and sometimes humorous.

Verse: can be used to mean a line or a group of lines within a poem, or a complete selection. Verse, when referring to a complete work, is usually thought of as being less significant, less figurative, and less intense than poetry (see poetry).

Indexes

I. INDEX OF AUTHORS

II. INDEX OF TITLES

Acknowledgements

The authors gratefully acknowledge the following educators, writers, and editors whose thinking had a significant impact on the approaches, directions, and contents of this text.

Northrop Frye
Florence McNeil
Martin O'Hara
David Perlman
Henry Petroski
Louise Rosenblatt
James Squire
Ronald Wallace
Norm Wood

Every effort has been made to obtain permission for copyright material used in this book, and to acknowledge all such indebtedness accurately. All errors and omissions called to our attention will be corrected in future printings.

Adolescence by P.K. Page. From CRY ARARAT! by P.K. Page. Used by permission of The Canadian Publishers, McClelland and Stewart Limited, Toronto.
Advice to the Young by Miriam Waddington. From DRIVING HOME by Miriam Waddington. © Oxford University Press Canada.
After the Ballad "Lord Randall, My Son" by Anne C. Wilkinson. Reprinted by permission of Alan O. Gibbons and Canada Permanent Trust Company—Executors.
Alligator Pie by Dennis Lee. Reprinted by permission of Macmillan of Canada, a Division of Gage Publishing Limited.
Amelia by Joni Mitchell. © 1976 CRAZY CROW MUSIC. Used by permission. All rights reserved.
Anthem for Doomed Youth from COLLECTED POEMS by Wilfred Owen published by Chatto & Windus. The Hogarth Press.
Ars Poetica by Archibald MacLeish from NEW AND COLLECTED POEMS by Archibald MacLeish. Copyright © 1976 by Archibald MacLeish. Reprinted by permission of Houghton Mifflin Company
Autumn morning wind by C.M. Buckaway. Reprinted by permission of Three Trees Press.

The Back Road Farm by Charles Bruce. From THE MULGRAVE ROAD by Charles Bruce. Reprinted by permission of Harry Bruce.

The Base Stealer by Robert Francis. Copyright © 1948 by Robert Francis. Reprinted from THE ORB WEAVER by permission of Wesleyan University Press.

Bear by Keith Gunderson. Reprinted from TO SEE A THING—RHYTHMS, TYPEGRAPHS, AND PROSE POEMS by Keith Gunderson, Nodin Press.

The Beautiful Tiger by Keith Gunderson. Reprinted from TO SEE A THING—RHYTHMS, TYPEGRAPHS, AND PROSE POEMS by Keith Gunderson, Nodin Press.

Because I could not stop for Death by Emily Dickinson. Reprinted by permission of the publishers and the Trustees of Amherst College from THE POEMS OF EMILY DICKINSON, edited by Thomas H. Johnson, Cambridge, Mass.: The Belknap Press of Harvard University Press, Copyright 1951, © 1955, 1979, 1983 by the President and Fellows of Harvard College.

Birches by Robert Frost. From THE POETRY OF ROBERT FROST edited by Edward Connery Lathem. Copyright 1916, 1930, © 1969 by Holt, Rinehart and Winston. Copyright 1944, © 1958 by Robert Frost. Copyright © 1967 by Lesley Frost Ballantine. Reprinted by permission of Holt, Rinehart and Winston, Publishers.

Birdsong by H. Volavková from I NEVER SAW ANOTHER BUTTERFLY—with permission of Dr. H. Volavková-Editor.

The Blue Heron. From THE LEATHER BOTTLE by Theodore Goodridge Roberts. Reprinted by permission of McGraw-Hill Ryerson Limited.

Both Sides Now by Joni Mitchell. © 1967 Siquomb Publishing Corp. Used by Permission. All rights reserved.

Bright Morning by Sid Marty. From HEADWATERS by Sid Marty. Used by permission of The Canadian Publishers, McClelland and Stewart Limited, Toronto.

The Bull Calf by Irving Layton. Used by permission of The Canadian Publishers, McClelland and Stewart Limited, Toronto.

The Bus by Leonard Cohen. From FLOWERS FOR HITLER by Leonard Cohen. Used by permission of The Canadian Publishers, McClelland and Stewart Limited, Toronto.

Canadian January Night by Alden Nowlan. From BETWEEN TEARS AND LAUGHTER by Alden Nowlan © 1971 Clarke, Irwin & Company. Used by permission of Clarke Irwin (1983) Inc.

Carol by Anne C. Wilkinson. Reprinted by permission of Alan O. Gibbons and Canada Permanent Trust Company—Executors.

Catalogue by Rosalie Moore. © 1940, 1968 The New Yorker

Magazine, Inc.
Child's Song by Murray McLauchlan. © Gulwing Music Limited. Taken from The True North Album ONLY THE SILENCE REMAINS.
CPR Window by George Bowering. From ROCKY MOUNTAIN FOOT by George Bowering. Used by permission of The Canadian Publishers, McClelland and Stewart Limited, Toronto.
Crash by Leona Gom. From THE SINGLETREE. Reprinted with the permission of Sono Nis Press.
crickets by Aram Saroyan from WORKS by Aram Saroyan. (Lines Press, New York, 1966). © Copyright 1966 by Aram Saroyan. Used with the permission of the author.
Cross by P.K. Page. Reprinted by permission of the author © 1974.
Crossing to Brentwood on the Mill Bay Ferry—November 4, 1975 by Susan Musgrave. From A MAN TO MARRY, A MAN TO BURY by Susan Musgrave. Used by permission of The Canadian Publishers, McClelland and Stewart Limited, Toronto.
The day dark with rain by Ann Atwood. From HAIKU-VISION: IN POETRY & PHOTOGRAPHY. Copyright © 1977 Ann Atwood. Reprinted with the permission of Charles Scribner's Sons.
Departmental by Robert Frost. From THE POETRY OF ROBERT FROST edited by Edward Connery Lathem. Copyright 1936 by Robert Frost. Copyright © 1964 by Lesley Frost Ballantine. Copyright © 1969 by Holt, Rinehart and Winston. Reprinted by permission of Holt, Rinehart and Winston, Publishers.
Diefenbay-ker by Alistair Grosart. From RENEGADE IN POWER by Peter Newman. Used by permission of The Canadian Publishers, McClelland and Stewart Limited, Toronto.
The Diver by Robert Currie is reprinted from DIVING INTO FIRE by permission of Oberon Press.
Do not go gentle into that good night from COLLECTED POEMS by Dylan Thomas. Publishers: JM Dent. Reprinted by permission.
Dreams. From THE DREAM KEEPER AND OTHER POEMS, by Langston Hughes. Copyright 1932 by Alfred A. Knopf, Inc. and renewed 1960 by Langston Hughes. Reprinted by permission of the publisher.
Dulce et Decorum Est from COLLECTED POEMS by Wilfred Owen published by Chatto & Windus. The Hogarth Press.
The Eel by Ogden Nash. From VERSES FROM 1929 ON. Used by permission of Little, Brown and Company.
Elegy for a Nature Poet by Howard Nemerov. From THE COLLECTED POEMS OF

HOWARD NEMEROV. The University of Chicago Press, 1977. Reprinted by permission of the author.

Fall Days by E.F. Dyck reprinted by permission of the author. From NUMBER ONE NORTHERN: POETRY FROM SASKATCHEWAN published by Coteau Books.

first draft of Anthem for Doomed Youth from COLLECTED POEMS by Wilfred Owen published by Chatto & Windus. The Hogarth Press.

The Fisherman's Wife from THE COMPLETE POETICAL WORKS OF AMY LOWELL. Copyright © 1955 by Houghton Mifflin Company. Reprinted by permission of Houghton Mifflin Company.

For Better Or For Worse by Lynn Johnston. Copyright, 1979, Universal Press Syndicate. Reprinted with permission. All rights reserved.

400-Meter Free Style by Maxine W. Kumin. From OUR GROUND TIME HERE WILL BE BRIEF by Maxine Kumin. Copyright © 1961 by Maxine Kumin. Reprinted by permission of Viking Penguin Inc.

The freshly cut grass (Haiku) by Dorothy Cameron Smith. By permission of the author.

Frosted by Carolyn D. Redl-Hlus. From EARTHBOUND, Borealis Press Ltd., 1978.

The Gambler by Don Schlitz. Copyright 1978. Writers Night Music.

Getting It On by Robert Currie. Reprinted from DIVING INTO FIRE by permission of Oberon Press.

A Glass of Beer by James Stephens. The Society of Authors on behalf of the copyright owner, Mrs. Iris Wise.

Graduation Evening by Elizabeth Brewster is reprinted from THE WAY HOME by permission of Oberon Press.

The Griesly Wife by John Manifold in his COLLECTED VERSE. University of Queensland Press 1978.

Herman by Jim Unger. Copyright, 1980, Universal Press Syndicate. Reprinted with permission. All rights reserved.

Hey Diddle Diddle by Paul Dehn. Reprinted by permission of Simon & Schuster, Inc. Copyright 1958, 1961 by Paul Dehn.

Hitch-Hiking by Andrew Suknaski. From STORMWARNING, editor: Al Purdy. Used by permission of the Canadian Publishers, McClelland and Stewart Limited, Toronto.

Houdini by Ken Norris. From THE PERFECT ACCIDENT. Montreal: Vehicule Press, 1978.

Housewife by Susan Fromberg Schaeffer. Reprinted by permission of Russell & Volkening, Inc. as agents for the author. Copyright © 1974 by Susan Fromberg Schaeffer.

Hunter's Lament by Edward John. Reprinted by permission of Douglas & McIntyre Ltd., publishers.
In praise of the great bull walrus from I'M A STRANGER HERE MYSELF, by Alden Nowlan. © 1974. Used by permission of Irwin Publishing, Inc.
Inside the River by James Dickey. Copyright © 1960, 1961 by James Dickey. Reprinted from DROWNING WITH OTHERS by permission of Wesleyan University Press.
Island Estate at St. Andrew's by Al Pittman. Printed by permission of Breakwater. Copyright © Al Pittman 1975.
Is My Team Ploughing? by A.E. Housman. The Society of Authors as the literary representative of the Estate of A.E. Housman, and Jonathan Cape Ltd., publishers of A.E. Housman's COLLECTED POEMS.
Jazz Solo by R. Glenn Martin. By permission of the author.
Jump Shot by Richard Peck. By permission of the author.
King of Pain from the album "Synchronicity". Words and Music by Sting. Magnetic/Regatta/Illegal Songs, Inc. © 1983 A & M Records, Inc. All Rights Reserved.
A Kite is a Victim by Leonard Cohen. From SELECTED POEMS 1956-58 by Leonard Cohen. Used by permission of The Canadian Publishers, McClelland and Stewart Limited, Toronto.
Klaxon from SELECTED SHORTER POEMS by James Reaney, reprinted by permission of the author and Press Porcépic Ltd., Victoria/Toronto.
Let No Charitable Hope by Elinore Wylie. Copyright 1932 by Alfred A. Knopf, Inc. and renewed 1960 by Edwina C. Rubenstein. Reprinted from COLLECTED POEMS OF ELINOR WYLIE, by permission of Alfred A. Knopf, Inc.
The Lifeguard by James Dickey. Copyright © 1960, 1961 by James Dickey. Reprinted from DROWNING WITH OTHERS by permission of Wesleyan University Press. "The Lifeguard" first appeared in THE NEW YORKER.
like an eddy by Earle Birney. From RAG AND BONESHOP by Earle Birney. Used by permission of The Canadian Publishers, McClelland and Stewart Limited, Toronto.
Like Two Slant Trees by Fred Cogswell. From NINETY SEASONS edited by Robert Cockburn and Robert Gibbs. Used by permission of The Canadian Publishers, McClelland and Stewart Limited, Toronto.
The Listeners by Walter de la Mare. The Literary Trustees of Walter de la Mare and The Society of Authors as their representative.
Little Miss Muffet by Paul Dehn. Reprinted by permission of Simon & Schuster, Inc. Copyright 1958, 1961 by Paul Dehn.
The Logical Song by Roger

Hodgson and Rick Davies. Copyright © 1979 ALMO MUSIC CORP. and DELICATE MUSIC (ASCAP). All Rights Administered by ALMO MUSIC CORP. (ASCAP). This arrangement Copyright © 1979 ALMO MUSIC CORP. and DELICATE MUSIC (ASCAP). International Copyright Secured. Made in U.S.A. All Rights Reserved.

The Lonely Land by A.J.M. Smith. From POEMS: NEW AND COLLECTED by A.J.M. Smith. Used by permission of The Canadian Publishers, McClelland and Stewart Limited, Toronto.

love is more thicker than forget by e.e. cummings. Copyright 1939 by e.e. cummings; Reprinted from COMPLETE POEMS 1913-1962 by e.e. cummings by permission of Harcourt Brace Jovanovich, Inc.

Lynx in Winnipeg by W.D. Valgardson. Reprinted by permission of Turnstone Press Ltd. from IN THE GUTTING SHED.

The Man Who Finds that His Son Has Become a Thief is reprinted from COLLECTED POEMS OF RAYMOND SOUSTER by permission of Oberon Press.

The Mary Ellen Carter written by Stan Rogers PROC, © 1979 Fogarty's Cove Musical Inc.

The Memory of a Poem by Michael Bullock: from A SAVAGE DARKNESS. Reprinted with the permission of Sono Nis Press.

Mending Wall by Robert Frost. From THE POETRY OF ROBERT FROST edited by Edward Connery Lathem. Copyright 1916, 1930, © 1969 by Holt, Rinehart and Winston. Copyright 1944, © 1958 by Robert Frost. Copyright © 1967 by Lesley Frost Ballantine. Reprinted by permission of Holt, Rinehart and Winston, Publishers.

Minotaur Poems from DREAMING BACKWARDS by Eli Mandel. Reprinted by permission of the author and General Publishing Co. Limited, Toronto, Canada.

Museum Piece by R. Glenn Martin. By permission of the author.

A narrow fellow in the grass by Emily Dickinson. Reprinted by permission of the publishers and the Trustees of Amherst College from THE POEMS OF EMILY DICKINSON, edited by Thomas H. Johnson, Cambridge, Mass.: The Belknap Press of Harvard University Press, Copyright 1951, © 1955, 1979, 1983 by the President and Fellows of Harvard College.

Neighbors by David Allen Evans. Copyright 1971 by Washington and Lee University, reprinted from SHENANDOAH: THE WASHINGTON AND LEE UNIVERSITY REVIEW with the permission of the Editor.

Newfoundland by Earle Birney. From RAG AND BONE SHOP by Earle Birney. Used by permission of The Canadian Publishers, McClelland and Stewart Limited, Toronto.

New Year's Day, 1978 by Elizabeth Brewster is reprinted from THE WAY HOME by permission of Oberon Press.

A note on the public transportation system from I'M A STRANGER HERE MYSELF by Alden Nowlan - 1974. Used by permission of Irwin Publishing, Inc.

Oh No by Robert Creeley. Department of English, State University of New York.

On Mona's Smile by Winona Baker. From WOMANSONG. Sandstone Publishing Ltd., Calgary.

On the Move by Thom Gunn. Reprinted by permission of Faber and Faber Ltd. from THE SENSE OF MOVEMENT by Thom Gunn.

"Out, Out—" by Robert Frost. From THE POETRY OF ROBERT FROST edited by Edward Connery Lathem. Copyright 1916, 1923, © 1969 by Holt, Rinehart and Winston. Copyright 1944, 1951 by Robert Frost. Reprinted by permission of Holt, Rinehart and Winston, Publishers.

Overheard at a Taxpayers' Meeting by Francis Sparshott. From Francis Sparshott, THE HANGING GARDENS OF ETOBICOKE, Toronto, Childe Thursday, 1983; copyright © 1983 by Francis Sparshott.

Paper Matches by Paulette Jiles. New Oxford.

The Pardoner by Geoffrey Chaucer. From THE CANTERBURY TALES BY GEOFFREY CHAUCER edited by A. Kent Hieatt & Constance Hieatt. Copyright © 1964 by Bantam Books, Inc. By permission of Bantam Books, Inc. All rights reserved.

The Parson by Geoffrey Chaucer. From THE CANTERBURY TALES BY GEOFFREY CHAUCER edited by A. Kent Hieatt & Constance Hieatt. Copyright © 1964 by Bantam Books, Inc. By permission of Bantam Books, Inc. All rights reserved.

The Piano by Frank Davey. Reprinted by permission of the author.

Picketing Supermarkets by Tom Wayman. From WAITING FOR WAYMAN by Tom Wayman. Used by permission of The Canadian Publishers, McClelland and Stewart Limited, Toronto.

Pinball Wizard, by Peter Townshend, COPYRIGHT © 1969 FABULOUS MUSIC LIMITED. All rights in the United States, its territories and possessions, Canada, Mexico and The Philippines are controlled by Towser Tunes, Inc. All Rights Reserved. International Copyright Secured. Reproduced by kind permission of Peter Townshend, Fabulous Music Limited, and Towser Tunes, Inc.

Pioneer by Dorothy Livesay. From COLLECTED POEMS: THE TWO SEASONS by Dorothy Livesay. Reprinted by kind permission of McGraw-Hill Ryerson Limited.

Copyright © 1976 by J.R. Colombo. Reproduced with permission from COLOMBO'S LITTLE BOOK (Hurtig, 1976).

Poetry by Marianne Moore. Reprinted with permission of Macmillan Publishing Company from COLLECTED POEMS by Marianne Moore. Copyright 1935 by Marianne Moore, renewed 1963 by Marianne Moore and T.S. Eliot.

Poetry for Intellectuals by Louis Dudek. From: LAUGHING STALKS © 1958 Louis Dudek.

Portrait by Anne Marriott. By permission of the author, and Mosaic Press of Oakville, Ontario, publishers of THE CIRCULAR COAST from which the poem is taken.

Preludes by T.S. Eliot. Reprinted by permission of Faber and Faber Ltd. from COLLECTED POEMS 1909-1962 by T.S. Eliot.

The Prize Cat by E.J. Pratt. Reprinted by permission of University of Toronto Press.

Pullman Porter by Robert Service. From: COLLECTED POEMS OF ROBERT SERVICE. Used by permission of the Estate of Robert Service.

Rain Song by Roo Borson. From A SAD DEVICE by Roo Borson. By permission of Quadrant Editions, English Department, Concordia University.

Reading the Brothers Grimm to Jenny reprinted by permission of Louisiana State University Press from THE PRIVATE LIFE by Lisel Mueller, copyright © 1976. Originally published in THE NEW YORKER, Vol. 1583, November 1, 1967.

The Red Wheelbarrow by William Carlos Williams. From COLLECTED EARLIER POEMS OF WILLIAM CARLOS WILLIAMS. Copyright 1938 by New Directions Publishing Corporation.

Return by Lou Lipsitz. Copyright © 1965 by Lou Lipsitz. Reprinted from COLD WATER by permission of Wesleyan University Press.

The Road Not Taken by Robert Frost. From THE POETRY OF ROBERT FROST edited by Edward Connery Lathem. Copyright 1916, 1930, © 1969 by Holt, Rinehart and Winston. Copyright 1944, © 1958 by Robert Frost. Copyright © 1967 by Lesley Frost Ballantine. Reprinted by permission of Holt, Rinehart and Winston, Publishers.

Sampler by Robert Finch. For permission to reprint "Sampler", from POEMS, copyright Canada, 1946, and published by The Oxford University Press, Canada, thanks are due to Robert Finch, author, & Sybil Hutchinson, literary agent.

Saturday, August 27 by Carl Fernbach-Flarsheim. From CONCRETE POETRY: A WORLD

VIEW, ed. Mary Ellen Solt.
Saturday Matinee by Florence McNeil. Reprinted by permission, Florence McNeil.
Sea Fever by John Masefield. Reprinted with permission of Macmillan Publishing Company from POEMS by John Masefield (New York: Macmillan, 1953).
The Second Coming by William Butler Yeats. From COLLECTED POEMS OF WILLIAM BUTLER YEATS. Reprinted by permission of Michael Yeats and Macmillan London Limited
Seven Natural Songs by May Swenson, copyright © 1958 by May Swenson in A CAGE OF SPINES, is used by permission of the author.
She'd Say by Frank Davey. Reprinted by permission of the author.
She Remembers by Shari Ulrich. Reprinted by permission of Sloth Music.
She's Always a Woman to Me by Billy Joel. © 1977, 1978 Impulsive Music and April Music Inc. Administered by April Music Inc., New York. International Copyright Secured. All Rights Reserved. Used by Permission.
Sign (found poem) from SIGNS AGAINST AN EMPTY SKY by Stephen Hume, reprinted by permission of Stephen Hume.
Silences by E.J. Pratt. Reprinted by permission of University of Toronto Press.
Silver Wheels by Bruce Cockburn. Words and music by Bruce Cockburn © 1976 Golden Mountain Music Corp. Taken from The True North album IN THE FALLING DARK.
since feeling is first by e.e. cummings. Reprinted from IS 5 POEMS BY e.e. cummings, by permission of Liveright Publishing Corporation. Copyright 1926 by Horace Liveright. Copyright renewed 1953 by e.e. cummings.
The Skater by Charles G.D. Roberts. Reprinted by permission of Joan (Lady) Roberts.
A Small Room by Melodie Corrigall. Permission to reproduce by Melodie Corrigall.
Snake by D.H. Lawrence. Reprinted by permission of Laurence Pollinger Ltd. and the Estate of Mrs. Frieda Lawrence Ravagli.
Song by Adrienne Rich. Reprinted from DIVING INTO THE WRECK, Poems 1971-1972, by Adrienne Rich, by permission of W. W. Norton & Company, Inc. Copyright © 1973 by W. W. Norton & Company, Inc.
Sound by Jim Harrison. By permission of the author.
Specimen 2001, Probably 21c by Jeni Couzyn. Reprinted by permission of Douglas & McIntyre Ltd., publishers.
The Spell of the Yukon by Robert Service. From: SONGS

OF A SOURDOUGH by Robert Service. Used by permission: Estate of Robert Service.

The Stickhandler by David Solway. Reprinted by permission of the author.

Stopping by Woods on a Snowy Evening by Robert Frost. From THE POETRY OF ROBERT FROST edited by Edward Connery Lathem. Copyright 1916, 1923, © 1969 by Holt, Rinehart and Winston. Copyright 1944, 1951 by Robert Frost. Reprinted by permission of Holt, Rinehart and Winston, Publishers.

Stout Hearted Men. Used by permission of Kerry Cameron.

Such is the power of the lover's sonnet from SIGNS AGAINST AN EMPTY SKY by Stephen Hume, reprinted by permission of Stephen Hume.

T-Bar by P.K. Page. From THE METAL AND THE FLOWER by P.K. Page. Used by permission of The Canadian Publishers, McClelland and Stewart Limited, Toronto.

Terry reprinted from NORTHBOUND by Leona Gom with permission of the publisher, Thistledown Press Ltd., 668 East Place, Saskatoon, Sask., S7J 2Z5.

Thaw by Margaret Avison. From WINTER SUN AND OTHER POEMS by Margaret Avison. Used by permission of The Canadian Publishers, McClelland and Stewart Limited, Toronto.

Then by Robert Hilles. Reprinted by permission of Turnstone Press Ltd. from LOOK THE LOVELY ANIMAL SPEAKS.

there are delicacies by Earle Birney. From WHAT'S SO BIG ABOUT GREEN by Earle Birney. Used by permission of The Canadian Publishers, McClelland and Stewart Limited, Toronto.

There was a young man from Perth by John Robert Colombo. Copyright © 1976 by J.R. Colombo. Reproduced with permission from COLOMBO'S LITTLE BOOK (Hurtig, 1976).

There was a young man of South Bay by John Robert Colombo. Copyright © 1976 by J.R. Colombo. Reproduced with permission from COLOMBO'S LITTLE BOOK (Hurtig, 1976).

There Will Come Soft Rains by Sara Teasdale from COLLECTED POEMS (Copyright 1920 by Macmillan Publishing Co., Inc. renewed 1948 by Mamie T. Wheless).

This is a Photograph of Me © Margaret Atwood 1966, from THE CIRCLE GAME (Toronto: House of Anansi Press).

This Is Just to Say by William Carlos Williams. From COLLECTED EARLIER POEMS OF WILLIAM CARLOS WILLIAMS. Copyright 1938 by New Directions Publishing Corporation.

This Poem Leaves No Survivors by Robert Hilles. Reprinted by permission of Turnstone

Press Ltd. from LOOK THE LOVELY ANIMAL SPEAKS.

Three Bears by Sid Marty. From HEADWATERS by Sid Marty. Used by permission of The Canadian Publishers, McClelland and Stewart Limited, Toronto.

The Three Fates by Rosemary Dobson. Copyright Rosemary Dobson c/o Curtis Brown (Aust) Pty Ltd. Sydney.

To an Athlete Dying Young by A.E. Housman. Used by permission of the Society of Authors as the literary representative of the Estate of A.E. Housman, and Jonathan Cape Ltd., publishers of A.E. Housman's COLLECTED POEMS.

To Kate, Skating Better Than Her Date by David Daiches; © 1957 THE NEW YORKER MAGAZINE, Inc.

Toronto The Golden-Vaulted City by Miriam Waddington. From DRIVING HOME by Miriam Waddington © Oxford University Press Canada.

A Tough Life by Robert Currie is reprinted from YARROW by permission of Oberon Press.

Treasures on earth by Alden Nowlan. From I MIGHT NOT TELL EVERYBODY THIS by Alden Nowlan © 1983 by Clarke, Irwin & Company Limited. Used by permission of Clarke Irwin (1983) Inc.

Variations on a Theme by William Carlos Williams by Kenneth Koch. Copyright © Kenneth Koch 1962.

View of a Pig from NEW SELECTED POEMS by Ted Hughes. Copyright © 1960 by Ted Hughes. Reprinted by permission of Harper & Row, Publishers, Inc.

War on the Periphery by George Johnston. © 1951, 1979 THE NEW YORKER MAGAZINE, Inc. Reprinted by permission.

Water Picture by May Swenson. Copyright © 1956 by May Swenson. First appeared in THE NEW YORKER.

We Are Two Flowers by Gyl Raby. WOMANSONG. Sandstone Publishing Ltd., Calgary.

Weasel by Patrick Lane. Oxford University Press.

The Weather by Anne Szumigalski. By permission of the author and Turnstone Press, first appeared NO 1 NORTHERN published by Coteau Books.

What Do I Remember of the Evacuation? by Joy Kogawa. From A CHOICE OF DREAMS by Joy Kogawa.

The White Buffalo by Susan Landell. Reprinted by permission of Douglas & McIntyre Ltd., publishers.

Wired for Sound by Alan Tarney & B.A. Robertson. © Copyright 1981 ATV Music Limited/Bar Music Limited. All rights reserved. Used by permission.

With Age Wisdom by Archibald MacLeish. From NEW AND

COLLECTED POEMS by Archibald MacLeish. Copyright © 1976 by Archibald MacLeish. Reprinted by permission of Houghton Mifflin Company.

W.L.M.K. by F.R. Scott. From COLLECTED POEMS. Used by permission of The Canadian Publishers, McClelland and Stewart Limited, Toronto.

Wondering Where the Lions Are by Bruce Cockburn. © 1979 Golden Mountain Music Corp. Taken from the True North album DANCING IN THE DRAGON'S JAWS.

The World is a Beautiful Place to Be Born Into by Lawrence Ferlinghetti. From A CONEY ISLAND OF THE MIND. Copyright © 1958 by Lawrence Ferlinghetti.

You Held Out the Light by Gwendolyn MacEwen. From MAGIC ANIMALS: Selected Poetry of Gwendolyn MacEwen. Reprinted by permission of the author and General Publishing Co. Limited, Toronto, Canada.

You Take My Hand by Margaret Atwood. From POWER POLITICS (Toronto: House of Anansi Press, 1971).

The photographs on the following pages are used by permission of Miller Services Limited: 2-ASP; 9-Lambert 13; 19-Drive; 23; 38-Kalmins; 55; 75; 94; 103; 110; 135; 140-Mokveld; 161; 182-Bill Ivy; 209-McCullagh Studio; 231; 245-Bochsler/Phototeque; 259; 276.

Bear, page 177, was reproduced from an original screen print design by Reg Davidson. Distributed by Potlatch Arts Ltd., Vancouver.

Photograph on page 229 is from Trinity College, Dublin.